LIVING IN INTEGRITY

D1065627

Studies in Social, Political, and Legal Philosophy
General Editor: James P. Sterba, University of Notre Dame

This series analyzes and evaluates critically the major political, social, and legal ideals, institutions, and practices of our time. The analysis may be historical or problem-centered; the evaluation may focus on theoretical underpinnings or practical implications. Among the recent titles in the series are:

Faces of Environmental Racism: Confronting Issues of Global Justice
    edited by Laura Westra, University of Windsor, and Peter S. Wenz, Sangamon State University
Plato Rediscovered: Human Value and Social Order
    by T. K. Seung, University of Texas at Austin
Liberty for the Twenty-First Century: Contemporary Libertarian Thought
    edited by Tibor R. Machan, Auburn University, and Douglas B. Rasmussen, St. John's University
In the Company of Others: Perspectives on Community, Family, and Culture
    edited by Nancy E. Snow, Marquette University
Perfect Equality: John Stuart Mill on Well-Constituted Communities
    by Maria H. Morales, Florida State University
Citizenship in a Fragile World
    by Bernard P. Dauenhauer, University of Georgia
Critical Moral Liberalism: Theory and Practice
    by Jeffrey Reiman, American University
Nature as Subject: Human Obligation and Natural Community
    by Eric Katz, New Jersey Institute of Technology
Can Ethics Provide Answers? And Other Essays in Moral Philosophy
    by James Rachels, University of Alabama at Birmingham
Character and Culture
    by Lester H. Hunt, University of Wisconsin–Madison
Same Sex: Debating the Ethics, Science, and Culture of Homosexuality
    edited by John Corvino, University of Texas at Austin
Living in Integrity: A Global Ethic to Restore a Fragmented Earth
    by Laura Westra

BELL LIBRARY - TAMUCC

LIVING IN INTEGRITY

A Global Ethic to Restore a Fragmented Earth

Laura Westra

ROWMAN & LITTLEFIELD PUBLISHERS, INC.
Lanham • Boulder • New York • Oxford

ROWMAN & LITTLEFIELD PUBLISHERS, INC.

Published in the United States of America
by Rowman & Littlefield Publishers, Inc.
4720 Boston Way, Lanham, Maryland 20706

12 Hid's Copse Road
Cummor Hill, Oxford OX2 9JJ, England

Copyright © 1998 by Rowman & Littlefield Publishers, Inc.

All rights reserved. No part of this publication may be reproduced,
stored in a retrieval system, or transmitted in any form or by any means,
electronic, mechanical, photocopying, recording, or otherwise,
without the prior permission of the publisher.

British Library Cataloguing in Publication Information Available

Library of Congress Cataloging-in-Publication Data

Westra, Laura.
    Living in integrity : a global ethic to restore a fragmented earth
/ Laura Westra.
      p. cm. — (Studies in social, political, and legal
philosophy)
    Includes bibliographical references and index.
    ISBN 0-8476-8926-3 (cloth : alk. paper). — ISBN 0-8476-8927-1
(pbk. : alk. paper)
    1. Environmental ethics.   2. Ecological integrity.
3. Environmental policy.   4. Environmental risk assessment.
I. Title.   II. Series.
GE42.W53   1998
179'.1—dc21   97-37219
                                                CIP

ISBN 0-8476-8926-3 (cloth : alk. paper)
ISBN 0-8476-8927-1 (pbk. : alk. paper)

Printed in the United States of America

♾ ™ The paper used in this publication meets the minimum requirements of
American National Standard for Information Sciences—Permanence of Paper
for Printed Library Materials, ANSI Z39.48–1984.

*To Jim Karr, Reed Noss, and Bob Ulanowicz,
who taught me the meaning of integrity*

Contents

Acknowledgments

This work was completed under the auspices of the "Global Integrity Project," with the support of SSHRC Canada Strategic Grant No. 86000. I am very grateful particularly to all the philosophers, scientists, co-investigators, and collaborators in our project for their help. Many thanks to those who read and critiqued one or more of this book's chapters: William Aiken, Ernest Partridge, Mark Sagoff, Alan Holland, Ralph Johnson, Jim Karr, Jim Sterba, Robert Ulanowicz, John Rist, Kenneth Schmitz, Eugene Hargrove, Christopher Gray, Don Brown, Kristin Shrader-Frechette, and some anonymous referees for chapters 3, 4, 5, and 6 that are forthcoming, in press, or published in different forms. Their encouragement as well as their critical input made all the difference, although I did not always take their excellent advice. I also owe a great debt to Lucia Brown and Diane Dupuis for their unfailingly cheerful and competent technical support.

The author and publisher wish to thank the following publishers for permission to reprint these previously published chapters: Chapter 3 was published in Lewis Pojman, ed., *Environmental Ethics*, 2d ed. (Belmont, CA: Wadsworth Publishing Co., 1997). An edited version of chapter 4 was published as "Why Norton's Approach is Insufficient for Environmental Ethics," *Environmental Ethics* 19:3 (Fall 1997), pp. 279–297. Chapter 5 was published in *Environmentalism: Race, Gender, and Class Issues* (Special Edition, December 1997).

Foreword

Alan Holland

Kant's notion, in *Perpetual Peace,* that "a violation of rights in one place is felt throughout the world," although written long before the environment as such became an issue, could scarcely be better chosen to express the theme of Laura Westra's new book. *Living in Integrity* is a major statement of the principles guiding an important research project funded by SSHRC Grant (Canada), for which Professor Westra is Principal Investigator. The project involves an international team of scientists, social scientists, lawyers, and philosophers whose main aim is to demonstrate the practical feasibility of an ethic governed by a "principle of integrity."

After featuring in Leopold's well-known injunction that "a thing is right when it tends to preserve the integrity, stability, and beauty of the biotic community," "integrity" was first used in a policy context in defining the goal of the United States Water Pollution Control Act Amendments of 1972, which was "to restore and maintain the chemical, physical and biological integrity of the Nation's waters." Until now, even though it can boast a longer history in the context of environmental policy than either "sustainability" or "health," the concept of "integrity" has undergone remarkably little scrutiny. But thanks to the work of Westra and her colleagues, that is all set to change.

The principle of integrity is essentially the injunction to respect the integrity of ecological and biological processes (save for the purpose of self-defense). In earlier work, most notably her *An Environmental Proposal for Ethics: The Principle of Integrity,* Westra had advanced such a primary "principle of integrity" and had begun to investigate "what it would mean to acknowledge and institutionalize this primacy." In the present work, she moves to a consideration of the second order principles that convert the general injunction into practical guidance for public policy

and personal morality—a move she characterizes in terms of the step
from living *with* to living *in* integrity. While couched in the modern language of complexity, uncertainty, sustainability, and the like, it is no
accident that these second order principles are the unmistakable expres-
sions of older virtues such as prudence, self-control and moderation.
For philosophical sustenance, Westra has passed over individualistic ethics of the contractarian or utilitarian kind and turned to the likes of
Plato, Aristotle, and Kant, all of whom had a lively grasp of the significance of the context in which human life is lived and, as she puts it,
"help us to recover an ethical position where optimum human capacities and the optimum capacities of natural systems support one another."

Like happiness and justice, ecological integrity is acknowledged to be
a contestable concept, but at the same time it is viewed as a real and
identifiable state of the natural world. Hence, far from being a "mysti-
cal"—and therefore unusable—notion, as some have claimed, ecological integrity as contended here is both observable and measurable, and
eminently suited, therefore, for service as an instrument of policy. Indeed, James Karr and others have succeeded in producing a (scientific)
"index of biological integrity". The "marks" of integrity are health—
understood in a functional sense, natural resilience, optimum potentiality, and freedom from human modification. In challenging for a place
at the heart of environmental decision-making, integrity has to contend
with other likely candidates such as health and sustainability. Westra is
in no doubt that, of the three concepts, integrity is fundamental. Reduced to its simplest, integrity is wildness. Health and sustainability, on
the other hand, are construed as compatible with varying degrees of
human intervention. For Westra, a natural system which manifests integrity will automatically manifest health and sustainability. Furthermore
natural integrity still has to be the benchmark for the health or sustainability of any system in which integrity is lacking. At the purely physical
level, the existence and integrity of natural systems is held to be a necessary condition of the long-term health and sustainability of anthropogenic systems. Inasuch as human fortunes are bound up with
anthropogenic systems, therefore, human well-being and the well-being
of natural systems are inextricably linked. Indeed, her view is that "at a
basic, survival level" human concerns and biocentric concerns coincide.
She adds, for good measure, the point that since overtly human-cen-
tered approaches tend to frame the scope of problems narrowly, and in
ways that do not permit their solution, it is equally if not more advantageous, in policy contexts, to appeal to biocentric concerns, and to the
value that natural systems have in their own right.

Besides facing the charge that it is inoperable, the principle of integrity also faces the charge that it is too demanding. Westra has little patience with such a charge. Her focus on integrity is fueled by a conviction that *only* a full-blooded commitment to integrity will enable us to cope with the environmental threats which we now face. Her stance rests on a compelling analysis of our current predicament. The situation we face is characterized by radical uncertainty and indeterminacy. We live in a world in which even innocent and justifiable actions can conspire to produce devastating consequences—where consequences are slow to materialize, are cumulative in their effects, and combine in unpredictable ways. There is a battery of scientific evidence that indicates an unmistakably rising trajectory of threats to both human and nonhuman well-being, in many cases emanating from modern technological and industrial processes. But increasingly, we face situations in which there are no specific assignable harms, and no specific assignable agents of harm, and where the size, gravity, extent, and likelihood of harms resist the attempt to predict or estimate them. We had thought, following Parfit, that the problem of indeterminate harms was a "future generations" problem. But to our consternation we find that "the future is now."

At the same time, and while surrounded by the twin challenges of inordinate complexity and irreducible uncertainty, science is called upon to play an increasingly complex social role. Political leaders and policy-makers, ensnared in matching webs of uncertainty, look to science for guidance and authority; political judgment is contracted out to scientists and social scientists. The scientists try to oblige and in turn lose the confidence and trust of the public. The public is pronounced ignorant and irrational, and "chairs" are established in "the public understanding of science," when it might be more to the point to establish "chairs" dedicated to improving the scientists' understanding of the public.

The social institutions available to cope with this sorry state of affairs are woefully inadequate. The legal systems in place tend to require clear proof of harm, when none is available. Various piecemeal ad hoc and post hoc restraints are applied, and there are exercises in environmental impact assessment. Accounting mechanisms are established that manage to demonstrate that the area around Prince William Sound is prospering in the wake of the *Exxon Valdez* disaster because of the massive cleanup operation and the level of economic activity that it engenders, and manage also to demonstrate that the optimal site for the third London airport is in the middle of Hyde Park. The decisions of national governments, albeit democratic ones, are waylaid by competing national land international interests. At the back of it all there lies what Dale

Jamieson has rightly called the "conceit" of supposing that the future
can be "managed."

At this point Westra enters her simple message that system-wide problems require system-wide consideration and that we can do worse than
act "on principle"—and are unlikely to be able to do any better. The
principle in question would be, above all, the principle of integrity and
its several subsidiary principles, of which the precautionary principle
would be one. Thus, she urges the need to develop a new "design"
for living, for which the principle of integrity would be a determining
factor—one that allows us to hope, and that brings sanity and justice to
human affairs. But it needs thoroughly to infect our habits, practices,
institutional structures, and political ideology if it is to take root. There
cannot be such a design without a *substantive* conception of the human
good, necessarily connected with a conception of human flourishing
which acknowledges the mutual resonance of individual, specific, and
systemic capabilities. Her analysis brings into sharp relief the havoc that
is wrought when human aspiration and capacity is impeded by environmental "blight," and when conceptions of the human good are reduced
to the rubble of preferences (or "the democracy of choice").

In addition she reminds us, again citing Kant, how the aspiration to
contribute to public policy has a respectable philosophical pedigree; rulers, he said, "should not suffer the class of philosophers to disappear or
be silent, but should let them speak openly. This is indispensable to the
business of government." It is sad to see this aspiration so neglected,
and even denigrated, in some academic circles. Westra, on the other
hand, practices with a whole heart what Kant preaches. The literature
of environmental philosophy is replete with "calls" for a "new" ethic,
or with "calls" for human beings at least to behave or comport themselves in accordance with the canons of the old ethics. But, to be blunt,
one can "call" until the cows come home, but to little effect. "It is no
longer sufficient (although it remains necessary) to preach from the
pulpit," says Westra; new laws and regulations must be "aggressively holistic."

While some of the stands taken in this work are uncompromising,
careful reading will reveal clear water between the positions argued for
here and any paternalistic or even "fascistic" designs that overheated
imaginations have claimed to detect in some environmental writings.
For one particularly significant elaboration of the concept of integrity
developed here concerns its application to individuals, and to the consideration of both present and future capacities—an application that
demonstrates both the reach of the concept and its depth. Thus, the
principle of integrity does not merely serve to protect environmental
"wholes" but serves equally to protect vulnerable individuals. Hence,

Westra advocates some tough remedies, such as coercive restraint, on those who expose others to environmental risks and harms, on the analogy of someone with a contagious disease who might "recklessly endanger" the lives of others. This is not a matter of environmental coercion, however, but a matter of redressing a state of affairs in which basic human freedoms are increasingly and stealthily being eroded—poignantly summed up in Saro-Wiwa's simple complaint: "The environment is man's first right. We should not allow it to suffer blight." Respect for capacities (*potential*)—of both individuals and systems—is more demanding, therefore, than a principle of respect for persons, present and future. But it is also more appropriate to our times. A further advantage, as Westra is quick to realize, is that it begins to make sense of concerns around genetic engineering—which consistently elude the grasp of prevailing ethical theories—for the threats both to integrity and to individual capacity which such technology brings in its wake. Hence Westra is quite clear that "from the standpoint of integrity, any genetically altered organism is at least prima facie undesirable."

Westra's discussion leaves room for fruitful disagreement in a number of areas. One might question, for example, whether (natural) integrity is so wholly incompatible with human modification as she maintains. At least there may be grounds for distinguishing between different kinds of modification. The behavior and life-style of the urban fox is considerably modified by the human presence—but in ways that permit the fox to respond for itself and therefore perhaps to retain its integrity. Again, one might question, for example, whether the link between human well-being and the integrity of natural systems is quite as tightly coupled as Westra suggests. It is certain that respect for integrity would outlaw many practices, such as reliance on chemicals, which we know to be harmful to human health, and practices, such as large-scale destruction of forests and release of greenhouse gases, which affect human health indirectly, for example through climate change. But I must own up to harboring the heresy that certain requirements for human health might actually depend on the *suppression* of elements of natural integrity.

Westra is well aware that her work remains unfinished. Not least is the problem of how to develop the institutions for implementing the practical guidelines for individual and collective activity that she has charted. There remains also the problem of how to accommodate human reproductive capacity—one aspect, after all, of individual integrity—and the thorny issue of overpopulation, which is capable of turning the spade of even the most dedicated laborer. But in displaying so graphically the social, political, and institutional dimensions of the problems which lie beneath the "environmental" label, Laura Westra performs a signal service. She presses home some uncomfortable questions and offers challenging and honest answers. She debates an impressive range of issues in a manner at once vigorous and resourceful. Her judgments are forthright and unclouded. This is an enriching and rewarding book to read.

PART I

1

Living with Integrity:
The Problems and the Promise

We live in a complex world that is going to require innovative approaches to deal with the problems technology has created.[1]

This sentence in the prologue to *Our Stolen Future* highlights the need
for yet another book on environmental ethics. We live in a world whose
complexity we cannot hope to master fully, although a growing understanding of several issues has led to a demand for a radical alteration
not only of interpersonal ethics but, even more urgently, of social institutions and public policy. It is not technology that has single-handedly
created the problems we face with regard to our natural environment,
but our belief that the choices and preferences of the majority in democratic, affluent countries are and should be viewed as absolute, beyond
discussion.

To be fair, some restraints on these activities exist, from the institutionalized acceptance of cost/benefit analyses and risk assessments of
various industrial and technological projects, to purely environment/
species-oriented legislation such as the Endangered Species Act. But
problems remain, because these acts and assessments do not consider
the natural environment to have intrinsic value, and, therefore, they are
ultimately insufficient to protect all life—including ours, as I will argue
later. Other regulations are at times put in place on an ad hoc basis,
created, at best, either when public outcry seems to demand it or when
the proof of harm caused by a product or process is accepted as clear
and overwhelming.

In either case, we face end-of-pipe solutions, as well as regulations that
are finally implemented only after years of human health problems or
environmental damage, or both. An example of a successful global regulation might be the Montreal Protocol set in place to counteract years
of chlorofluorocarbon (CFC) emissions, the effects of which were never

fully tested *before* they were put on the market. Hence, it will be 2000, at best, before we benefit from such regulations and protocols which come too late to prevent negative health effects on animals, plants, and humans.

However, just as one industry's damaging practices are recognized and regulated, others continue unabated to pose threats that are both uncertain and unpredictable.[2] It seems as though our experience with the tobacco industry has not taught us much. Through its activities, millions became addicted to toxic substances and vulnerable to fatal diseases, while powerful interests concealed information about the dangers of tobacco, and the industry subsidized a veritable army of researchers, lawyers, and public relation firms. Their mandate? To stave off regulations, and to support and maintain the status quo.[3]

Hazardous Chemicals, Mad Cows, and Technological Impact

The present institutional structure and political ideology supports enough market freedom to produce this sort of abuse of the public trust repeatedly, and it is particularly serious when the natural environment is affected, as the damage may last for generations. One example is the beef industry. In the fall and winter of 1995, we saw the result of a series of corporate decisions, supported by our collective preference for a meat-based diet "freely " pursued. The result of a series of ecologically and biologically wrong choices was a strange calamity: outbreak of the "mad cow disease." Contributing factors were not only what Jeremy Rifkin termed "the Cattle Culture,"[4] but also Monsanto's biotechnological "advances," that is, the production and manufacture of a genetically engineered hormone designed to increase milk production in cows (bovine growth hormone, or BGH).

Eating beef is one of the most ecologically damaging practices on the globe. The "commercial cattle complex" has significantly altered the land, destroying its topsoil and rendering it unusable for anything but grazing, and caused countless trees to be felled to free more grazing lands. The cattle industry also is a significant factor in the emission of three of the four global warming gases (methane, carbon dioxide, and nitrous oxides), and has destroyed the environment through related agricultural practices, particularly in the United States, where the grain production is based on fossil fuel energy. Rifkin points out that the equivalent of a gallon of gasoline is needed to produce a pound of grain-fed beef in the United States. The industry has also decimated wildlife, from insects to large carnivores, through desertification (in Africa) and ecosystem disruption.[5]

Besides the direct environmental benefits of abandoning our present addiction to the cattle culture, there are substantial individual and collective health benefits to be derived from a decision to eat lower on the planet's food chain.[6] Further, although adults in the Northwest, with access to a varied diet, do not have a particular need to increase their milk, butter, and cheese consumption, a market has been artificially provided, bolstered by advertising campaigns urging increased milk and milk products consumption. The main beneficiaries of these campaigns are not, for the most part, the consumers, but the corporations that manufacture milk-production enhancers like BGH, which spurs and sustains an unnecessary overproduction of milk. The farmers do benefit as well, to some extent, at least in the short term.

The environmental questions of methane gas production and soil depletion aside, the main problem here is that the cows whose diet includes BGH need additional protein in their diet.[7] This need prompts the search for cheap and readily available sources of protein; the farmers find this in the form of other ground-up animals (such as sheep carcasses) as addition to cattle feed, hence the transmission of sheep disease to cows and eventually to humans (in the latter, Creutzfeld-Jakob disease, or CJD), and the recent prominence of mad cow disease, with its long incubation period and unpredictable course and prognosis.

The question is when and how this history of inappropriate products and practices might have been halted. Monsanto, one of the major producers of BGH, is required only to produce evidence of in-house tests (without any external monitoring, or independent testing) before being granted a patent for a specific biotechnology, and the company refuses to label its genetically altered products to allow consumers an informed choice.[8]

When some complain about the violation of their rights to freedom of choice and consent, predictable rhetoric is trotted out in lieu of answers. Monsanto and others call the public ignorant, uninformed, and hysterical, while the difference between *chosen* risks (such as voluntary participation in hazardous sports, or other routine behaviors such as driving) and undisclosed and therefore imposed risks is conveniently forgotten.[9] Our preferences, whether in food or other consumer goods, are manipulated by advertising campaigns, financed by public relations, and other firms whose aim it is to control our very existence.[10] In fact, there seems to be little if anything left of our "preferences" or of "us" as individuals or even as community or national groups that is either distinctive or truly autonomous, while we change from multidimensional, rational individuals into mere "consumers."

In a chapter appropriately titled "Buying Out Democracy," David Korten relates how corporations, not content with their marketing clout, also seek to create a citizenry prepared to accept corporate values as their own. He explains that after the 1970s, "Corporations began to create their own 'citizen organizations' with names and images that were carefully constructed to mask their corporate sponsorship, and their true purpose."[11] "Corporate front groups" work through the media and directly with politicians for the sole purpose of convincing "the public that the corporate interest *is* the public interest." Monsanto and other corporate giants such as Dow Chemical, Exxon, Philip Morris, and DuPont are the mainstay of a growth industry, that of public relations firms and other "business-sponsored policy institutes," who work to produce "facts, opinion pieces, expert analyses, opinion polls, and direct-mail and telephone solicitations to create 'citizen' advocacy . . . campaigns on demand." Korten adds: "William Greider calls it 'democracy for hire' and adds that, given that 'forty percent of the news content in a typical U.S. newspaper originates from public-relations press releases,' we can conclude that 'The distinction between advertising space and news space grows less distinct with each passing day.' "[12]

In contrast, the full disclosure required to make truly informed choices is lacking, not only obscured by the machinations of multinational corporations intent on capturing the global consumer, but also protected by trade secrecy legislation. Hence consumer "consent" is not real consent, nor can marketing success be equated with voting with our dollar, as—for the most part—we have no clear comprehension of what we are voting for. Of course, the other undemocratic aspect of these choices can be found in the contrast with real democracy, whereby each person is entitled to one vote. In contrast, the person who "votes" by buying in effect commands as many votes as she has dollars.[13]

The ethics reevaluation that is needed is based on an in-depth analysis and critique of the status quo, and a step-by-step review should reconsider our rights, our political regimes, and most of our Western assumptions. To this aim, I have proposed an environmental ethic based on the "principle of integrity," one that *starts* with the fundamental need for ecological and biological integrity and raises questions about what it would mean to acknowledge and institutionalize this primacy. *An Environmental Proposal for Ethics: The Principle of Integrity* (1994) essentially proposed a definition of integrity and defended the principle that follows upon it and the biocentric, holistic approach in general.

Although in that work I attempted to sketch some of the consequences of adopting the complete revision (and reversal) of previously accepted primacies and ethical approaches, the time has come, I believe, to move to second-order principles. We need to explore what it means to live *with* integrity, taking seriously the concept and its place in moral theory and in public policy. One might say that it is time to face the problems and the promise of living *in* integrity.

Living with Integrity: The Problems and the Promise

Since I proposed ecological or ecosystem integrity as a foundational value for ethics and as the basis for the principle of integrity, I have had occasion to reexamine some of the claims I made, particularly in light of several reviews of the book that appeared after its publication in 1994, as well as the verbal discussions that occurred at meetings and conferences. I have also started to work toward fulfilling what I perceived to be the promise of that first work, that is, to start moving toward applying the principle of integrity (PI) to actual problems and situations in order to test its usefulness.

In *The Principle of Integrity* I made two general commitments; the first, to be prepared to reopen the discussion and revise the definition of integrity as required in dialogue with philosophy and with science; the second, to be prepared to design second-order principles to supplement the admitted limitations of the first principle, and of the categorical imperatives that followed upon it. Implicit in the second part of this plan was the effort to seek out the most appropriate interhuman ethical doctrines in the sense of discovering which theory might be most compatible with the PI, and with the aim of spelling out this compatibility in some detail.

In my previous work, *The Principle of Integrity,* I developed an argument in support of ecosystem integrity as an ultimate value and as a first principle of moral action.[14] After noting that "integrity" (undefined) was and still is a fundamental part of global regulations, legislative acts, and countless environmental protection acts and mission and vision statements, the second chapter of my earlier work proposed a collaborative definition of the concept of integrity; it was coauthored by five scientists representing the disciplines of ecology, biology, complex systems theory, and physics, united by a common belief in the merits of the ecosystem approach in ecology. Our definition of ecosystem integrity included four major points:

1. Ecosystem health and its present well-being (defined, for our purpose, below). This condition may apply to even nonpristine or somewhat degraded ecosystems, provided they function successfully as they presently are. Some examples might be (a) an organically cultivated farm or a low-input operation but also (b) a lake that, having lost its larger species because of anthropogenic stress,

now functions with a larger number of smaller, different species. Hence, ecosystems that are merely healthy may encompass both desirable and undesirable possibilities and may be more or less *limited* in their capacities (or have become artificially constrained by humans).

2. The ecosystem must retain the ability to deal with outside interference and, if necessary, regenerate itself. This clause refers to the capacity to withstand stress. But nonanthropogenic stress is part of billions of years of systemic development. Anthropogenic stress, on the other hand, may be severely disruptive to the system in that it may contain realities that are radically new to the natural components of the system, or it may operate at intensities that are unprecedented in evolutionary history. Hence, the system may not have ways to correct or compensate for such stress.

3. Integrity obtains when at point *C*, the system's *optimum capacity* for the greatest possible ongoing development options within its time and location remains undiminished. The greatest possible potentiality for options is also fostered by the greatest possible biodiversity (dependent on contextual natural constraints), as the latter is a necessary but not sufficient component of *C*. Biodiversity contributes to integrity in at least two ways:

    a. Through genetic potential, based on the size and diversity of populations and their respective gene pools (hence supporting and enhancing both structure and function of these populations);

    b. Through biodiversity's dimensions as purveyor and locus of both relational information and communication, of which existing populations and ecosystems manifest and embody only a small proportion. We can only theorize about the immense capacities for diverse qualitative interactions among individuals and species that are not *presently* existing or knowable.

4. The system will possess integrity if it retains its ability to continue its ongoing change and development, unconstrained by human interruptions past or present.[15]

In addition, integrity was examined in several aspects, in view of achieving a better understanding of the role it might play in public policy. The aspects examined were viewed from both the scientific and philosophical standpoints, as we believed (and still believe) that integrity's heuristic and prescriptive power is firmly based on its meaning as an ecologically definable concept.[16] This point is worth emphasizing, because only if integrity is scientifically definable, quantifiable, and as predictive (in a limited sense) as other scientific concepts are can it be practically useful in guiding public policy. This could not be the case if it were to be taken as merely stipulative, as mainstream science might have it.[17]

Integrity is also philosophically meaningful, heuristic, and applicable to ethics and useful in decision making precisely because of its scientific characteristics. Its force in moral theory and in public policy analysis exists only if it is an objective state, applicable to real natural systems, and if it signifies a specifiable set of circumstances. The states we normally contrast with it—pollution, degradation, and the like—are not equally disputed, although logic would demand that they should be, if integrity's scientific import is questioned. If degraded ecosystems are merely stipulative, simply because there might be some disagreement about their state in mainstream science, then any law or regulation dealing with cases of pollution or degraded land would be addressing only philosophical debate rather than actual circumstances. Even in the context of "post-normal science" (see chapter 2), where values play a strong role in public decision making, these decisions must consider actual circumstances, not concepts viewed as purely stipulative.[18]

I have also argued for a similarity between integrity and other foundational concepts such as "happiness" or "justice," as they appear in public policy. If we take a very basic component of law and public policy, for instance, the appeal to happiness or to justice, we encounter a similar situation. These concepts are also, to some extent, stipulative. Happiness for Plato, for Aristotle, for Jeremy Bentham, for John Stuart Mill, and for the person in the street may have quite different meanings. Similarly, Plato, Aristotle, Marx, Dworkin, Rawls, and others may well propose different definitions of justice. Both justice and happiness are taken to be foundational in ethics. Integrity is, arguably, an even more foundational concept, as it precedes the other two temporally and conceptually. One must be alive in order to be happy or to be treated justly. As thriving or having one's needs met could be considered the equivalent of happiness for humans, we can also speak of extending justice considerations or fairness to nonhumans and even wholes (as James Sterba does, for instance).[19]

Moreover, there is no quantitative or qualitative research or empirical data to help distinguish one "stipulative" definition of either *happiness* or *justice* from another, nor to assist us in ranking them from the standpoint of "reality." Yet the history of moral theory shows that these concepts have been defined and used by many great philosophers, all of whom took their ethical principles and prescription to be theories based on something quite real. In addition, almost all countries' constitutions and major documents have also included "happiness" or "justice" in their national visions and their citizens' rights. Based upon these foundational documents, the corresponding laws may be either upheld or disregarded. Nevertheless, such concepts as "the pursuit of happiness" or "justice for all," although they may be variously understood by past and present rulers and political theorists, are always taken to be *real.*

In order to be a *real* scientific term, the thing to which the term or concept refers must be materially contingent. The definition of integrity we propose is quantifiable, hence it lends itself to be used in practice: investigators can and do go out and measure the integrity of a given habitat. Thus integrity can be observed, compared to the condition of other habitats; it represents a phenomenological *reality,* and it is not mainly a metaphysical construct.[20] By contrast, I have suggested that the definition should remain open to an ongoing dialogue, consonant with the demands of "post-normal science," that is, with the elimination of deterministic expectations and the quest for absolute scientific answers, while accepting the "challenge of complexity" instead.[21]

As long as we remain philosophically (and scientifically) alert to the various nuances embedded in the terms we use and to the history of their usage, and as long as we are prepared to evaluate critically all possible definitions and senses of each concept in dialogue with others, I believe that the ultimate reality of the concept (as definable, quantifiable, and applicable), and hence its validity in both law and morality need not be questioned.

The "promise" of integrity alluded to in this section's title lies primarily in the openness to debate and discussion and the transdisciplinary dialogue implicit in its definition and analysis. Further, the way integrity was analyzed and defined supports equally the input from stakeholders, without however reducing the concept to a construct relative to social or cultural preferences. This dialogue and the resulting analysis is necessary, I argue, as a corrective to our facile reliance on either scientific expertise and present governmental standards (often understated and unfair), or democratically supported preferences.

I wish that I could say that in the intervening years, as I considered real issues and problems, I found some reasons to qualify my position, to make it less rigid. The contrary is true instead. The more I delved into real issues, perhaps fisheries or global trade, asking myself what, if anything, would the PI suggest about those problems, the more I saw the need for uncompromising holism instead. Readers will be able to judge for themselves, as I will address that question head-on in the next chapters. When some of the issues made environmental news in the last year or so, a recurring theme that emerged was that there was no apparent way to mitigate grave environmental impacts before they happened and thus to prevent, rather than simply attempt to redress, some of the worst consequences for humans and natural systems. At best, most problems are considered from either an individualistic point of view or from a position of "weak anthropocentrism," that is, a point of view that considers "enlightened" or environmentally aware preferences to be primary.[22] Neither approach can encompass the holistic position I believe is necessary for solutions that provide more than temporary mitigation.

After defining and discussing integrity, I proposed a first principle intended to prescribe categorically actions (and omissions) based upon integrity as an ultimate value and now rephrased as follows:

1. The first moral principle is that nothing can be moral that is in conflict with the physical realities of our existence or cannot be seen to fit within the natural laws of our environment in order to support the primacy of integrity.

also

1a. Act so that your action will fit (first and minimally) within universal natural laws.

and

1b. Act so that you manifest respect for and understanding acceptance of all natural processes and laws (although self-defense is acceptable).[23]

The question may be asked whether this first principle and probably its two corollary principles were intended as a first consideration meant to guide public policy and decisions about individual and group activities, or as a first step toward (and as a limitation on) other traditional ethics.[24] The question is not posed well: it is not either one *or* the other position that is correct. The PI and its corollaries are envisioned both as a first-order principle *and* as a constraint on interhuman, or normal, ethical priorities.

A parallel might be found in the moral doctrines of Plato and Aristotle, who viewed the educational system of Athens as both primary and basic to the possibility of teaching and practicing virtue; according to the Greeks, no argument and thus no final defense of a doctrine could even start without a prior agreement and a common understanding through which all citizens were equally capable of knowing right from wrong. They all knew what was right without knowing, initially, the reasons some acts fell into either the category of right or that of wrong.

This analogy between the Greek moral philosophy's role of education and my principle's role, however, is not complete. My principle was not proposed as a starting point, much less as an intuition upon which to eventually mount arguments and derive conclusions. Unlike the doctrines of the Greeks, the Kantian influence that permeates my principle and the imperatives that follow upon it are intended to be universal in reach. Accordingly I cannot expect to be preaching to a limited number of converts, who already accept in principle what I say and simply need to understand *why* the argument they accept is a valid one.

In contrast, the starting point for the PI was based on arguments for the ultimate value of integrity. Aside from this obvious difference, the role of education in the polis is both limiting *and* primary, just as I have argued that the principle of integrity is. Hence, the PI is uncompromising because, in Kantian fashion, it ascribes an infinite, nonnegotiable value to life. As such, it also permits no prima facie "compromise" or "trade-off" on the acceptance of conditions that might impose harm either on others within the biotic community or on ourselves. This position renders the principle even more radical than previously expected. It is radical because liberal democratic emphasis on individual choices precludes a possible quest for "the good," even if this good represents the defense of our own life and health; hence, some other factor must play a role in public policy. I believe that the *precautionary principle* (PP) may be the required factor. In the next section I shall discuss an accepted part of public policy, that is, the precautionary principle, and its connection with the ethics of integrity. If integrity is an ultimate value and if the principle of morality based upon it is not open to trade-offs or negotiations because of its fundamental connection to life and life support, then we need to design second-order principles following upon it, so that we can use the principle of integrity in personal morality and in public policy. It is primarily to fill this need that this book was written.

After arguing for the principle of integrity in chapter 3 of my earlier book, I responded in chapter 4 to the critiques often levied against holistic theories and argued in chapter 5 in support of the principle against the background of social and political philosophy, and the problems posed by ecofeminism, and social problems in general.[25] Finally, chapter 6 addressed particular issues, such as animal ethics considerations, agricultural practices, and democratic institutions, from the standpoint of the primacy of integrity.[26] In order to ensure the presence of the ethics of integrity in public policy, the last chapter proposed turning to the zoning requirements found in the Wildlands Project,[27] because for us, as for other animals, a healthy, supportive habitat is an absolute requirement, not a luxury. Based on this position, the implementation of global "core" and "buffer" zones was proposed.

It is clear that the all-important second-order principles necessary to render operational a principle with radical requirements like the principle of integrity cannot emerge from the limited general discussion in the last chapter of that earlier work. Principles that are intended to govern personal morality as well as public policy require explicit articulation followed by detailed analysis, defense, and discussion. Beyond the philosophical arguments, however, it is equally important to continue here the "reality checks" initiated in the previous volume. That is, it is important to see what new environmental rules and regulations might have come to prominence in the past three years and whether any of these may be compatible with the principle of integrity and the recommendations it supports.

Although the Earth Summit took place in June 1992, Article XV of *Agenda 21* (The Rio Declaration on Environment and Development), that is, the precautionary principle, already had a long history.[28] Despite its historical place in public policy, the PP has been brought to the forefront of our awareness, and has been widely cited and increasingly invoked in the years after the publication of *Agenda 21*.

Because of the prominence of the precautionary principle it is important to understand it, examine its reach, and ensure that policy recommendations are compatible with the best it has to offer. In the next section I will argue that the only environmental ethic (and the only moral position) that explicitly supports the requirements of the PP is the principle of integrity. Moreover, the PI also serves to pinpoint the problems still remaining in the PP as presently articulated. Hence, although the PP is necessary for public policy, it not sufficient; the principle of integrity is required in addition, in order to ensure that all policies affecting the environment and all life through it will be supported by a solid theoretical and scientific basis.

The Precautionary Principle: A Necessary Part of Public Policy

Arguably, one of the best things to come from the 1992 Earth Summit and *Agenda 21* is Article XV, the precautionary principle:

> In order to protect the environment, the precautionary approach shall be widely practiced by the States according to their capabilities. Where there are threats of serious or irreversible damage, lack of full scientific uncertainty shall not be used as a reason for postponing cost-effective measures to prevent environmental damage.[29]

This principle clearly indicates that, because of the gravity and the urgency of many of the environmental problems and crises that face us, it is sufficient to be aware of the threats, even before scientific certainty might be available, to indicate priority action on the part of public policy makers.

The principle is introduced as an agent of change in order to counter the arguments of those who would appeal to scientific uncertainty, or to disagreement among experts, as a delaying tactic and as a reason to postpone actions and decisions. Although the precautionary principle represents a significant advance and a good move toward ethics in public policy, it remains grounded in a scientific paradigm many believe should have been transcended long ago. In other words, the PP *assumes* that although science may not be able to give us answers today, at least in principle (hence, at some future date) such answers are both possible and, in fact, almost assured.

Given the complexity and uncertainty of the present scientific reality, the most appropriate response of public policy makers to environmental hazards is to accept the mandates of the PP while retaining an awareness of a changed scientific paradigm. In affluent northwestern countries, even the "cost-effectiveness" clause should be relegated to a secondary role; in developing southeastern countries, the cost factor should be automatically considered a sufficient reason for northwestern aid, because a delayed global disaster in the making is at issue, albeit not a present, local one. What is at stake is not simply the possibility of adding environmental degradation or faulty conservation practices to those already present on earth, but the addition of yet another straw that may be *the one* to break the camel's back of life-support systems.

Brian Wynne and Sue Mayer put it well when they characterize "green activists" as a "pro-science group" for demanding that the complexity and the uncertainties underlined by post-normal science be clearly acknowledged by industry and scientific institutions. They add,

> this was in marked contrast to the pro-dumping lobby which, for political reasons, subordinated essential aspects of good science—such as acknowledgment of uncertainty and openness to criticism.[30]

It is unfortunate that, despite the extensive evidence of environmental hazards almost everywhere, "the onus is still on the environmentalists to prove that a threat exists." Somehow the hazards to which we are exposed are often taken to be the "other side" of the benefits we crave and the products and services we believe we are entitled to have.[31]

There seems to be little if any analysis of the relation between human rights and the imposition of risks, and between the deployment of various technologies causing the hazards and the consent we are perceived to be giving to the side effects of corporate modernity.[32] The specifics of risk assessment and risk imposition have been well analyzed in the literature from the point of view of both scientific methodology and ethics.[33] But the underlying questions go beyond specifics: the questions that must be raised are whether the present technological lifestyle and the corporate culture that fosters its uncontrollable growth are not foundationally inimical to the public good of human and nonhuman life, and whether there is any possible benefit that might offset the severe risks to which we are exposed, most of which are "uncompensable."

For instance, philosophers like Judith Jarvis Thomson *reject* the "risk thesis" and claim that, while we have the right not to be harmed, we do not have the right not to be exposed to *risks* of harm, as the notion itself, its evidence, and the identity of those who might be harmed are all too imprecise to require moral consideration.[34] Although some argue that our primary motivation is economic,[35] in order to justify the "business as usual" scenario in which exposure to hazards is seen as acceptable, there are more important values, noneconomic ones, for human groups and nations, and these ought to be more relevant to public policy.[36]

Such environmental problems as global change, for instance, when viewed against the background of unmanageable complexity and scientific unpredictability, appear to demand the approach of the PP. Dale Jamieson addresses the question of management in this context:

> What I have been arguing is that the idea of managing global climate change is a dangerous conceit. The tools of economic evaluation are not up to the task. However, the most fundamental reason why the management approaches are doomed to failure is that the questions they can answer are not the ones that are most important and profound.[37]

What is at stake is the radical alteration of our moral considerations, because the linear causality between unethical behavior on the part of some agent and unintended and (to some extent) unanticipated harm can no longer be traced: "Apparently innocent acts [that] can have devastating consequences, causes and harms may be remote in space and time."[38] Hence, the appeals to precise, "mainstream" science, invoked to legally establish the presence of specific harms and therefore guilt on the part of specific agents, are no longer sufficient. In contrast, there are not many acts left that can be termed truly innocent, in Jamieson's sense. Enough is known to condemn overconsumption, resource exploitation, and an "expansionist worldview"[39] out of hand. But the previously expected precise requirements for legal proof are no longer applicable in the face of multiple threats and uncertain and unpredictable consequences.

Diffuse problems such as global change,[40] and biodiversity losses,[41] as well as the impact on human health owing to the present "planetary overload,"[42] demand the employment of the precautionary principle and, as I argued earlier, the switch to a holistic environmental ethic such as the position supported by the principle of integrity. The risks encountered through these environmental threats are incalculable and irreversible. Norman Myers asks, "How many species can we afford to lose biologically and ecologically?" In addition, "What is *legitimate scientific caution* in the face of uncertainty, as concerns the true extinction rate?"[43]

In both science and morality, there has been an increasing emphasis on analytic precision. Mainstream science is essentially mathematical and deterministic; moral theory is normally taken to forbid imposing harms; but not only are these understood to be immediate and, in some sense, visible, but also the imposers of these harms can only be blamed when the harm is clearly identifiable and can be traced causally to some agent. This approach must be abandoned in favor of a holistic position: the ethics of integrity in conjunction with the precautionary principle may provide our only hope of halting and even reversing the global attacks on life we witness today.

Alan Thein Durning has recently argued that the resource exploitation practiced in the American and Canadian Northwest may be compared to the six floods. Like the historical and mythical floods of old, six waves of ruthless exploitation—the fur trade, mining, fishing, agriculture, damming, and logging—have systematically devastated fertile, productive lands to the point where almost all the natural resources are beyond recovery, at least without drastic alterations of our lifestyles, public policy, and ethics. Speaking of old forests, Durning concludes:

> Their biological wealth had been converted into shareholders' dividends, tax revenues and pay checks. And then, like the fur trade, the mining boom, the fishing industry, the farm surge, and the dam extravaganza, the lumber industry slid toward the periphery of the regional job market.[44]

As I have argued,[45] even the presence of democratic institutions and due process is insufficient to save the ecological base on which all life and all human choices depend. Regional and national preferences and the public policies they support do not protect either present or future generations, despite the fact that both are viewed as a present obligation in all national and international regulations (see chapter 4 for a detailed discussion). Further, philosophers and political theorists also argue for future generations' rights.[46] And if neither regional nor national preferences support the ecological reality on which we depend, then the use of the precautionary principle ought to be both mandatory and enforced in public policy, supported as it is both by scientific imprecisions, factual and methodological, and by the ethics of integrity.

I believe that problems arise when integrity is excluded a priori from the realm of science. Its strong presence in legislation and other public policy documents does not guarantee its scientific credibility but does indicate its general acceptance as more than a purely philosophical concept. Integrity is named as the first priority in the principles of the "Warning to Humantity" by the Union of Concerned Scientists, for instance, and also named as an absolute requirement in the new *Earth Charter*,[47] to mention but two documents. The concept is not used here the way a purely stipulative concept might be used by scientists and policymakers. As long as integrity is recognized as a scientific albeit debated concept, it can be useful in the ways these documents imply. This means that scientists in turn ought to join in the debate and discuss its definition. Because integrity is already present in laws and public policy, it is neither useful nor accurate to treat it as though it did not belong in the scientific assessment of the problems that confront us.[48] Far better to debate it, examine it, and help to reach a collective understanding of its meaning.

Integrity refers to a real condition, despite the debates that surround it, and it is quantified while, increasingly, indices are designed to measure its presence. Perhaps precise definitions have not been agreed upon, but this is not sufficient to dismiss it as a real if imprecise end point (see chapter 9 for additional discussion). The major step I advocate is to pursue an understanding of integrity and enter the ongoing debate about it: scientists ought not to stand apart from a notion that is so relevant to our survival and to the public decision making that is required. An analogy might be found in the state of Israel. Once its existence has been acknowledged as a reality, what remains is the debate about its borders, its precise shape and limits. Perhaps this approach might be followed for ecological integrity as well.

Although many definitions of such concepts as happiness or justice have evolved through the years, some core components persist in their respective definitions, and on that basis, dialogue remains possible and debates may flourish. Perhaps we might understand integrity in a similar way: even as we are pursuing our dialogue with science to reach a more satisfactory definition, we may agree with our opponents that some key components may be found in all definitions of integrity.

The Outline of This Work

In order to show the need for a radical change aimed at supporting such a good for all life, including ours, chapter 2 starts by showing the link between integrity and life and health for both humans and nonhumans. In this chapter I also sketch six second-order principles that will follow upon the PI. These are used as a framework for understanding the examples and cases that will follow in the next chapters. After this initial presentation, however, the second-order principles are not fully discussed until chapter 9, which addresses the meaning of living in integrity.

Chapter 3 argues for a new way to define, identify, and treat environmental risks based primarily on Kantian doctrine, using examples taken from bioethics—another discipline to which life and health are central—and supports the "risk thesis," against J. J. Thomson.[49]

Chapter 4 shows why we need a holistic environmental ethics approach, not only when dealing with issues and problems in the nonhuman environment but also when our primary concern is human life and health and our right to both. In this chapter, nonanthropocentric holism is thus defended from both a practical and a theoretical point of view against the "weak anthropocentrism" proposed by Bryan Norton.[50]

In chapters 5 and 6, the points made in chapter 4 are also supported through two other detailed examples, one an examination of biotechnology and aquaculture and their impact on macro- and microintegrity, and the other a case study involving the consumerist northwestern lifestyle in relation to environmental racism and genocide in Nigeria, where oil interests and human rights came into conflict, with tragic consequences. Chapter 7 raises a general question about our interhuman ethics. It seems clear that we do need a new ethic and a new approach to public policy, both of which should emphasize the primacy of integrity. I find that virtue ethics in Plato, Aristotle, and Kant include several components of what it is to be a human being and what is our good and that of human society. This renders them compatible with the environmental aspects of the ethics of integrity. Hence, ancient Greek virtue ethics and Kantian ethics, with their inclusion of duties to oneself, and the nonnegotiable role of duty and right action are shown to fit best with the ethics of integrity.

Chapter 8 raises questions about our "ecological footprint" and argues that a holistic biocentric ethic position will entail a radical change. If our northwestern lifestyle and our "footprint" are unsustainable *now,* the just demands for economic changes in less-developed countries will aggravate the present ecological impasse. I shall argue that present national laws and regulations are insufficient to redress the many wrongs perpetrated upon us through the environment, and that even a move to render many other nations democratic is insufficient to prevent violent upheavals. In contrast, the proposed new *Earth Charter* provides a compatible international mandate.

Chapter 9 returns to the second-order principles proposed in chapter 2 and discusses them in greater detail, in order to clarify what is involved in going from a position that accepts the primacy of integrity, and an approach that can be characterized as living with integrity, to a fully committed position that accepts the necessity of a completely altered approach and can thus be described as "living in integrity." To this end, questions of *micro*integrity are also discussed and additional second-order principles proposed. Chapter 10 supports the need for a new "design" to restore a fragmented earth and proposes answers to some possible objections to the second-order principles outlined in chapter 9.

Notes

1. Theo Colborn, Dianne Dumanoski, and John Peterson Myers, *Our Stolen Future* (New York: Dutton, 1996).
2. K. Shrader-Frechette, *Risk and Rationality* (Berkeley: University of California Press, 1991), see especially chapter 9, pp. 131–32.
3. Jon Cohen, "*Tobacco Money Lights Up a Debate*," *Science* 272 (April 26, 1996): 488–94.
4. Jeremy Rifkin, "The Cattle Culture," in *People, Penguins and Plastic Trees*, ed. C. Pierce and D. VanDeVeer (Belmont, CA: Wadsworth, 1995), pp. 445–51. First published in J. Rifkin, *Beyond Beef* (New York: Penguin Books, 1992).
5. Rifkin, "The Cattle Culture."
6. Robert Goodland, "Environmental Sustainability: Eat Better and Kill Less," in *The Business of Consumption: Environmental Ethics and the Global Economy*, ed. L. Westra and P. Werhane (Lanham, MD: Rowman & Littlefield, in press).
7. *The Gene Exchange* 4, 2 (August 1993). "A Connection between BGH and Bovine Encephalopathy" (published by *The Union of Concerned Scientists*), p. 8.
8. J. Rissler and M. Mellon, *Perils Amidst the Promise: Ecological Risks of Transgenic Crops in a Global Market* (Cambridge, MA: Union of Concerned Scientists, 1993); L. Westra, "A Transgenic Dinner? Ethical and Social Issues in Biotechnology and Agriculture," *Journal of Social Philosophy* 24, 3 (Winter 1993): 215–32; L. Westra, "Biotechnology and Transgenics in Agriculture and Aquaculture: The Perspective from Ecosystem Integrity," in *Environmental Values* (Lancaster, England: White Horse Press, in press; see chapter 6 of this volume).
9. Schrader-Frechette, *Risk and Rationality*, pp. 14–26.
10. David Korten, *When Corporations Rule the World* (West Hartford, CT: Kumarian Press, 1995).
11. Korten, *When Corporations Rule the World*, p. 143.
12. Korten, *When Corporations Rule the World*, p. 146.
13. Korten, *When Corporations Rule the World*, pp. 149–53.
14. L. Westra, *An Environmental Proposal for Ethics: The Principle of Integrity* (Lanham, MD: Rowman & Littlefield, 1994), especially chapters 2 and 3.
15. Westra, *An Environmental Proposal*, pp. 24–27.
16. James R. Karr, "Landscapes and Management for Ecological Integrity," in *Biodiversity and Landscape: A Paradox of Humanity* (New York: Cambridge University Press, 1994), pp. 227–49; James Karr and Ellen Chu, "Ecological Integrity: Reclaiming Lost Connections," in *Perspectives on Ecological Integrity*, ed. L. Westra and J. Lemons (Dordrecht, The Netherlands: Kluwer, 1995), pp. 34–48; James R. Karr, "Ecological Integrity and Ecological Health Are Not the Same,"

in *Engineering within Ecological Constraints* (Washington, DC: National Academy Press, 1996), pp. 100–113; James J. Kay and E. Schneider, "The Challenge of the Ecosystem Approach," *Alternatives* 20, 3 (1994): 1–6, reprinted in *Perspectives on Ecological Integrity*, ed. L. Westra, and J. Lemons, pp. 49–59; R. Ulanowicz, *Ecology, The Ascendent Perspective* (New York: Columbia University Press, in press).

17. In a recent review of my book *An Environmental Proposal for Ethics: The Principle of Integrity*, Kristin Shrader-Frechette argues that "mainstream science" cannot agree on a definition of integrity, and this disagreement renders the concept difficult to use either in regulations and public policy or in the courts. Nevertheless, integrity is not simply a "construct," any more than "degraded" or "polluted" ecosystems are. Further, the concept of energy presents an important parallel, as it is a concept that is regularly used in scientific discourse:

Where does the concept of conservation of energy come from? Can it be proved? These are frequent questions, the answers for which lie in the concept of energy. We want to be able to predict nature, and so we conceive of energy. In a very real sense, energy is an invention of humans, not of nature. Rather than being "that which makes things go," perhaps we should view it as something that we use to predict and explain how things go. Whenever conservation of energy is apparently violated, the physicist "discovers" a new form of energy. That is, a new form of energy is defined in order to keep the principle of conservation energy unviolated . . . practically all scientific and engineering analysis involves energy conservations. [William Craig Reynolds, *Engineering Thermodynamics* (New York: McGraw-Hill, 1977, p. 34)]

18. Despite the fact that some argue against the soundness of the ecosystem approach, for instance, others argue that ecosystems may function in a unitary manner; perhaps selections occur at the feedback loop. That is, some argue in support of congeneric homeotaxis, that is, they show that in some cases group selection occurs when certain populations take over the function formerly filled by a presently extinct species. The function played by the substitute population is a systemic one. The systems where these substitutions occur are not agents, nor are they "live" in the same sense that a human or other organism might be, but it can be said that the system, in that case, acts as a unity; hence it is meaningful to speak of its integrity, as the structural foundation of its functions. I am indebted to Robert Ulanowicz for this information.

19. James Sterba, "Biocentrism and Ecological Integrity," in *Ecological Sustainability and Integrity: Concepts and Approaches*, ed. John Lemons, Laura Westra, and Robert Goodland (Dordrecht, The Netherlands: Kluwer, 1997).

20. Kristin Shrader-Frechette, review of *An Environmental Proposal for Ethics: The Principle of Integrity*, by L. Westra, *Environmental Ethics* 17, 4 (Winter 1995).

21. Kay and Schneider, "The Challenge of the Ecosystem Approach." See also S. Funtowicz and Jerome Ravetz, "Science for the Post-Normal Age," in *Perspectives on Ecological Integrity*, pp. 146–61; Ulanowicz, *Ecology, The Ascendent Perspective*.

22. Bryan Norton, "Why I Am Not a Nonanthropocentrist: Callicott and the

Failure of Monistic Inherentism," *Environmental Ethics* 17, 4 (Winter 1995): 341–58; see chapter 4 for a detailed discussion.

23. Westra, *An Environmental Proposal*, pp. 92–93, 97.

24. Westra, *An Environmental Proposal*, pp. 161–70.

25. Westra, *An Environmental Proposal*, pp. 170–80.

26. Westra, *An Environmental Proposal*, chapter 6.

27. Reed F. Noss, "The Wildlands Project: Land Conservation Strategy," *Wild Earth*, Special Issue (1992): 10–25; see also Reed F. Noss, "Wilderness Recovery: Thinking Big in Restoration Ecology," *The Environmental Professional* 13 (1991): 225–34; and Reed F. Noss, "Sustainability and Wilderness," *Conservation Biology*, 1 (March 1991).

28. Don Brown, "The Role of Law in Sustainable Development and Environmental Protection Decision-Making," in *Sustainable Development: Science, Ethics and Public Policy* (Dordrecht, The Netherlands: Kluwer, 1995), pp. 64–76; see also S. P. Johnson, ed., *The Earth Summit. The United Nations Conference on Environment and Development* (UNCED), (London: Graham and Trottman/Martinus Nijhoff, 1993).

29. Brown, "The Role of Law in Sustainable Development, p. 67.

30. Brian Wynne and Sue Mayer, "How Science Fails the Environment," *New Scientist* 5 (June 1993): 33–35.

31. Wynne and Mayer, "How Science Fails the Environment."

32. See Shrader-Frechette, *Risk and Rationality*, chapter 10, for a discussion of this belief in the context of technology transfers to less-developed countries, especially pp. 148–53; see also chapter 4 of this volume.

33. K. Shrader-Frechette and E. D. McCoy, *Method in Ecology* (New York: Cambridge University Press, 1993); see also Shrader-Frechette, *Risk and Rationality*; K. Shrader-Frechette, *Burying Uncertainty* (Berkeley: University of California Press, 1993).

34. J. J. Thomson, *The Realm of Rights* (Cambridge, MA: Harvard University Press, 1990), chapter 3.

35. N. Myers, "Biological Diversity and Global Security," in *Ecology, Economics and Ethics* (New Haven: Yale University Press, 1993), pp. 11–25.

36. M. Sagoff, *The Economy of the Earth: Philosophy, Law and the Environment* (Cambridge, England: Cambridge University Press, 1988), pp. x, 271.

37. Dale Jamieson, "Ethics, Public Policy and Global Warming," *Science, Technology and Human Values* 17 (1992): 139–53.

38. Jamieson, "Ethics, Public Policy and Global Warming."

39. W. E. Rees and M. Wackernagel, *Our Ecological Footprint* (Gabriola Island, BC: New Society Publishers, 1996).

40. Dale Jamieson, "Managing the Future: Public Policy, Scientific Uncertainty, and Global Warming," in *Upstream/Downstream*, ed. D. Scherer (Philadelphia: Temple University Press, 1990), pp. 67–89; see also Jamieson, "Ethics, Public Policy and Global Warming," pp. 139–53.

41. Myers, "Biological Diversity and Global Security."

42. Anthony J. McMichael, *Planetary Overload* (Cambridge, England: Cambridge University Press, 1995).

43. Myers, "Biological Diversity and Global Security."

44. Alan Thein Durning, "The Six Floods," *World Watch* 9, 4: 41.

45. Westra, *An Environmental Proposal*; L. Westra, "Ecosystem Integrity and Sustainability: The Foundational Value of the Wild," in *Perspectives on Ecological Integrity*, pp. 12–33.

46. E. Partridge, "On the Rights of Future Generations," in *Upstream/Downstream*, pp. 40–66; see also Derek Parfit, *Reasons and Persons* (Oxford, England: Oxford University Press, 1984); E. Partridge, ed., *Responsibilities to Future Generations* (Buffalo, NY: Prometheus Books, 1981).

47. Steven C. Rockefeller, "Earth Charter," *Principles of Environmental Conservation Summary and Survey*, April 1996 (unpublished). In this work I refer to the April 1996 version of the "Earth Charter"; but the Earth Charter is presently evolving and is changing its format through discussion and interaction with NGO representatives. This is not its final version, but its thrust and basic principles remain constant, even as the format undergoes modifications.

48. Shrader-Frechette, review of *An Environmental Proposal for Ethics*.

49. Thomson, *The Realm of Rights*.

50. Norton, "Why I Am Not a Nonanthropocentrist."

2

The Link between Ecological Integrity and Human Health in the Present and the Future: Second-Order Principles

> Once you start destabilizing large-scale natural systems, you are actually tinkering with the very foundations of life support.
>
> Anthony J. McMichael,
> epidemiologist, London School of
> Hygiene and Tropical Medicine

Ecocentric environmentalists have often been accused of caring so much for wild animals and wild areas that they leave human concerns out of the equation. A fortiori, the interests of disadvantaged groups and minority communities appear to be totally left out of their concerns. As group leader and activist Whitlynn Battle put it, "If it does not swim upstream or hoot in the night, environmentalists don't care about it."[1] To some extent, this critique is well founded. Groups like the World Wildlife Fund and the Sierra Club concentrate their efforts on the conservation and preservation of species and habitats in the wild. Perhaps they believe that other groups or initiatives exist to deal with the plight of humans and that their primary mission is to speak for those who cannot. This may well be true of activists and scientist-advocates, who must concentrate their efforts and focus their expertise on a specific issue rather than diffuse their work over a broad range of interests.

In contrast, I believe, the philosopher is in an altogether more advantageous position: whatever her particular concern or expertise, her argument must fit within a logically coherent whole. Hence, if her position in regard to the environment is holistic, she should ensure that her beliefs do not conflict with her interspecies moral beliefs, for instance with Kantian doctrines in this case, but that the two are compatible and mutually enhancing. But some of the problems that beset scientists affect philosophers. There are often strong disciplinary boundaries that are

23

not easy to cross, and professional respect is gained through specialized expertise.

Despite these difficulties, this work is unapologetically interdisciplinary, as it reaches across several domains, such as ethics, political philosophy, ecology, biology, and epidemiology.

Environmental Holism and the Implications of the Principle of Integrity: Six Second-Order Principles

Environmental holism demands the recognition of the commonality among all that exists, so that no artificially constructed argument is necessary to link the two areas of concern, that is, human society and non-human individuals, species and wholes. The argument I have proposed in the principle of integrity (PI) reconciles the two areas, but only at the most basic level, that of life and life support. The principle of integrity in the revised form given in chapter 1 states:

1. The first moral principle is that nothing can be moral that is in conflict with the physical realities of our existence or cannot be seen to fit within the natural laws of our environment in order to support the primacy of integrity.

This principle in turn gives rise to two corollaries, proposed as "categorical imperatives":

1a. Act so that your action will fit (first and minimally) within universal natural laws.

and

1b. Act so that you manifest respect and understanding acceptance of all natural processes and laws (although self-defense is acceptable).[2]

At this level, the PI demands respect for the primacy of life, but it is too general to give specific guidance. It needs discussion and explanations to help formulate second-order principles to provide practical directives. The second-order principles that can be shown to support the principle of integrity, because they add clarity and specificity for cases and issues taken together, define the ethics of integrity. In other words, once we accept the ultimate value of integrity and we understand the role it must play in life support, or to provide "nature's services"[3] to all life, to use Gretchen Daily's terms, we can seek to outline principles and directives to provide the bridge from the PI to actual conflicts and problems demanding resolution.

It is important to note that the second-order principles I propose are not derived deductively from the principle of integrity. In contrast, extensive research and collaborative, interdisciplinary dialogue over the past two years yielded some specific indication about what must be done, in order to respect and protect the integrity of natural systems. The focus of my previous work was the meaning and the role of integrity and the reasons I chose that concept as foundational for ethics in my argument. This work takes a different path, as it argues for the principles required in order to respect integrity in practical cases, so that the goal of integrity can become more than a catchphrase or a political vision as it is integrated into public policy.

Nobel Laureate Henry Kendall heads the Union of Concerned Scientists. That group's Declaration is a document in which integrity occupies a prominent place, as it is listed in its very first principle. At a meeting in June 1997 in Toronto, Kendall expressed his fear that the massive "environmental movement" to which many other speakers had alluded was not the positive step forward many had praised. He listed what he considered the most catastrophic environmental problems facing us, such as agricultural failures due to climate changes. But he argued convincingly that the threat of "delayed injuries" was not a powerful enough motive to unite the most powerful Western nations in seeking environmental change.

This lack of a strongly supported environmental movement has been the major reason to support a categorical imperative of integrity, rather than rely on grassroots movements and democratic forces alone. Each of the problems Kendall and others cite requires the acceptance of certain specific activities as well as certain specific omissions. The principles I propose in this chapter are intended to indicate the scientific, methodological, and practical guidelines that ought to govern our activities from the perspective of the primacy of integrity. They stand out from my own and others' recent work, as necessary conditions for living in integrity.

Of course I make no claim that the principles I propose are the only ones necessary, but merely that they are sufficient for our purpose. I simply propose some second-order principles that seem the most appropriate to accomplish the task we have set out, while remaining open to the possibility that further research and dialogue may not only disclose possible modifications to the present principles but also reveal additional useful principles for our consideration. The frame of reference remains the principle of integrity and the goal of protecting and, where feasible, restoring integrity in spaces sufficient to support life. My ap-

proach, in itself, is inspired and "sanctioned" by second-order principles (SOPs) 1 and 2, that is, by recognizing and embracing complexity
and by accepting the tenets of post-normal science.

The second-order principles I propose apply to both individual actions and public policy. The first six principles may be divided as follows:
SOPs 1, 2, and 3 provide suggestions that are methodological and cognitive, whereas SOPs 4 and 5 may be termed the sustainability principles.
SOP 6 directs us specifically in how to "live in integrity."

The first of these principles (1) prescribes that, in order to protect
and defend ecological integrity, we must start by "embracing complexity."[4] This is in itself a complex suggestion that involves changing and
reducing our expectations about science's precision and its predictive
capacities; it requires understanding that we cannot hope for simple,
linear relations between causes and effects. Therefore, it forces us to
accept that the limits to our activities must be set far more conservatively
than in times when we expected science to tell us precisely how far we
could safely go. Complexity also includes acknowledging the general
role of the synergistic and cumulative effects of various substances, even
when this role is not precisely defined, and including these uncertainties
in our public policies. Embracing complexity also means recognizing
that not all natural systems can and should be managed, as the side
effects of our management and control often give rise to unmanageable,
long-term problems.

The next second-order principle (2) therefore requires that we engage in no activity that is clearly potentially harmful to natural systems
and to life in general. It seems self-contradictory to base any principle
on knowledge, which the previous principle defined as, at best, imprecise. That is why the next two principles of action I suggest render explicit the precautionary aspects that this principle demands. In the face
of uncertainty, the dimensions of what can be expected of science are
constantly changing, as discussed, for instance, in the recent work on
postnormal science. Post-normal science "fosters a new methodology,"
as it relies on "interactive dialogue" rather than on "formalized deduc-
tion."[5] This approach can be contrasted with the demand for precision
and definitions that characterizes much of today's scientific work.[6] Kristin Shrader-Frechette, for instance, has suggested that the ecosystem approach and the ethics of integrity are based on "soft ecology." But post-
normal science shows that "the traditional domination of 'hard facts'
over 'soft values' has been inverted."[7] In this case, any science can be
characterized as soft, in the factual and theoretical senses, and Shrader-
Frechette herself shows in detail the role of values not only in public
discourse, but also in scientific methodology.[8] Thus, it is no longer a
problem specific to a "lesser" science, nor is it a question of a faulty

approach. The thoughtful, concerned, and open dialogue envisioned. by post-normal science is tempered by a healthy recognition of our own limits and ignorance, so that extreme caution must be our guiding rule. The interactive dialogue indicated by the incapacity of science to present us with "hard facts" about environmental issues must then represent our third second-order principle.[9]

On that basis, and in order to support the caution recommended by SOP 2, we must also accept constraints on our "expansionist worldview" (4); thus we must ensure that our "dialogue" produces a clear reduction of our "ecological footprint."[10] We cannot continue to produce and consume at present levels, not only for ecological reasons—that is, because neither sources nor sinks are infinite on a finite earth—but also for reasons of justice. Finite sources and sinks must be equally available to all humans; hence if we are sincere about the right of less-developed countries to develop, we must be prepared to reduce our overdevelopment and overconsumption accordingly.

This in turn means also accepting the elimination of many of our practices and choices, including our uncritical desire for "technical maximality" (5), or the belief that newer and bigger is better and that somehow persons, communities, and even countries can be judged better or worse entirely on the basis of the large and complex technologies they own, operate, or command.[11]

The sixth second-order principle mandates that not only the quality of our activities (as outlined in SOPs 3, 4, and 5) must be changed and strictly monitored by the stakeholders, but also the quantity or scale of such activities must be subjected to scrutiny. Zoning is necessary: the true integrity of wild, core areas, that is, of the most naturally evolving systems left on earth, must be carefully guarded and protected so that all our activities are viewed as falling into a "buffer zone."[12] This is no longer to be viewed as a specialized concern for the conservation biologist or other scientist: the ethic of integrity means *essentially* living as in a buffer zone, and this prescription becomes everyone's concern and obligation. The second-order principles will be discussed in detail in chapter 9. The first six principles described here are:

SOP 1   In order to protect and defend ecological integrity, we must start by designing policies that embrace complexity.[13]

SOP 2   We should not engage in activities that are potentially harmful to natural systems and to life in general. Judgments about potential harms should be based on the approach of "postnormal" science.[14]

SOP 3   Human activities ought to be limited by the requirements of the precautionary principle.

SOP 4   We must accept an "ecological worldview," and thus reject
        our present "expansionist worldview" and reduce our eco-
        logical footprint.[15]

SOP 5   It is imperative to eliminate many of our present practices
        and choices as well as the current emphasis on "technical
        maximality" and on environmentally hazardous or wasteful
        individual rights.[16]

SOP 6   It is necessary for humanity to learn to live as in a "buffer."
        Zoning restraints are necessary to impose limits both on the
        quality of our activities, but also on their quantity. Two corol-
        lary principles follow: a) we must respect and protect "core"/
        wild areas;[17] b) we must view all activities as taking place
        within a "buffer" zone. *This is the essential meaning of the ethics
        of integrity.*

Having set out the first six second-order principles as a starting point
to understanding the ethics of integrity, we now focus on respect and
protection for the elements of the systemic whole defended by the PI.
In addition, we will show how integrity ought to be considered a foundational value, even by those whose main concern is human individuals
and even human rights, although the latter will be the main topic of the
next chapter. After an explanation of the link between integrity and
health, the next section addresses one aspect of the problems engendered by disintegrity, specifically by one of its results, climate change.
The following sections address the value of integrity now and in the
future. The concluding section addresses microintegrity, or the concept
of integrity in the individual, as well as its importance for the whole.
This will support two additional second-order principles.

Ecological Integrity and Health: The Necessary Link

In the previous section I argued for six second-order principles following from the ecocentric ethics of integrity. Any traditional moral theory
makes the principle of harm primary: for various reasons, physical and
other harm ought not to be inflicted on our fellow humans. For now,
leaving aside the needs of nonhuman animals and the protection of
systems *for themselves*, I want to argue that my approach is necessary even
if we limit ourselves purely to a consideration of human health, surely
an easy goal to defend. What is the relation between ecological integrity
and human health? Literature exists about the necessity to establish,
respect, or restore wild areas (core areas) in order to reestablish within
them the large fauna originally native to each habitat (to the best of our

knowledge) and at the same time ensure that all the biota necessary to the functioning of each ecosystem are present on each site.[18] In essence, then, our first concern based on respect for others, ourselves, and all life should be the resilience of the ecosystems on which human activity depends, and of these system's ability to continue to provide valued ecological services to all biota. To achieve this, not only does the *quality* of ecosystems in the wild need protection, but also their quantity (the size of the core areas required). A holistic approach is needed so that the separate channeling of legislation affecting pollution, agricultural practices, fisheries, or forestry can all be viewed through a perspective that starts from the necessary centrality of integrity, and only then moves on to particularities. Just as it is not possible to save animal species and communities without a primary concern for their habitat, so also should concern for individuals and communities of humans start with respect for the habitat we share with the rest of the biota.

It might be useful to define *integrity* once again at this point. An ecosystem can be said to possess integrity when it is wild, that is, as free as possible from human intervention. It is an "unmanaged" ecosystem, although not necessarily a pristine one. This aspect of integrity is the most significant one as it differentiates integrity from ecosystem health, which is compatible with support or manipulation, for example, the use of careful agricultural or agroforestry practices.[19]

Ecosystem integrity is further defined through the characteristics of health it exhibits, the capacity to withstand anthropogenic stress, but primarily the system's undiminished optimum capacity for the greatest possible ongoing developmental options within its time and location. The latter is fostered by the greatest possible biodiversity (dependent on contextual natural constraints) in its dual role as basis for genetic potential and as locus of relational information and communication, both actual and potential; thus, the system in a state of integrity will retain its ability to continue its ongoing change and development, and will therefore retain its excellence (ergon/function). Ecosystem integrity represents the necessary condition for the support of areas of ecosystem health and for areas in less "natural" settings, that is, areas of human culture. It represents both goal and benchmark of restored or restorable ecosystems, and as such it is absolutely required for areas covering at least one-third of the global landscape. Lack of concern for what is or should be in a specific landscape, as well as for the role each component must play to ensure the appropriate function of each ecosystem, leads to anthropogenic stress. Unlike "natural" stress, anthropogenic stress often interferes with a system's evolutionary development. But the causal effect of inappropriate human activities does more than affect something "out there," external to those humans. As Aldo Leopold and others have shown, our human position as part of the ecosystem's biota renders each imposition of inappropriate stress a reciprocal one: in an "upstream/downstream" world,[20] everything we do comes back to affect us in some way.

The difficulty is that disrupting natural processes in large areas not only disrupts the life and health of their biota, it also affects *ours*: cutting down forests, for instance, reduces the "services" the trees perform for all air, hence for all forms of life that need to breathe. Introducing toxic substances into waterways and oceans affects not only all the wildlife that depends on clean water for its life, but also all humans in various ways: our own food supplies are affected not only in the water but also through evaporation, which distributes the toxins on whatever is grown for food.

We are familiar by now with the almost automatic association between chemicals and their carcinogenic and mutagenic properties. Additional recent research shows no less ominous but different effects of "herbicides, fungicides, insecticides, nematocides" and most other "industrial chemicals." Theo Colborn recently sketched a "toxic chemical profile" of these substances and their effects: she shows that they

a) mimic natural hormones;
b) antagonize hormone effects by blocking binding sites;
c) react directly or indirectly with natural hormones;
d) alter natural patterns of hormone synthesis, metabolism, and excretion;
e) alter hormone receptors' levels.[21]

These effects are supported by solid research involving wildlife, controlled laboratory toxicology tests, and tests on human epidemiological exposure.[22] Although these substances affect gene expression, they are "organizational, activational, not mutational, as they do not affect the integrity of the DNA."[23] What we do see is an almost endless series of sexual and reproductive effects, engendered by very low doses of most of these substances; the loss of structural integrity of male and female reproductive apparatus is followed by the loss of functional (reproductive) capacity, and often by the loss of natural gender orientation and parenting abilities.[24]

Many of these effects of low-dose exposure may be found in birds, fish, and mammals, including humans. The increasing frequency of these abnormalities is due to the worldwide exposure to chemicals we are experiencing. Colborn traces the first "wide-scale exposure to manmade chemicals" to the 1940s (after World War II), so that in the 1940s and 1950s a first generation was exposed. In the next twenty years (1950s to

1970s), worldwide exposure in the womb occurred, for the first time. By the 1990s this generation itself reached reproductive age, continuing the pattern of exposure.[25]

But not all the results of these low-dose exposures are clear, observable, or sexually related or represent examples of recognizable diseases. Some are far more subtle: they are not visible. For example, hyperactivity, reduced head circumference, auditory and verbal deficits, poorer reflex functions, stress intolerance, and reduced average intelligence are just some of the problems increasingly found in populations in the Great Lakes area, for example.[26] Colborn points out that even some economists are beginning to be concerned about the possibility of whole populations "whose intelligence, capacities and reactions are abnormal."

We must become aware of the urgent and grave threats to our health, the health and survival of our children, and indeed the survival of our species and all other species on earth. The effects of these chemicals ought to emphasize the "imperative of responsibility" to the very idea of humankind[27] and, as the principle of integrity proposes, to all life on earth.[28] Those who do not recognize their responsibility and continue to pursue their own agendas without considering the side effects of their activities, if found to be guilty, should be charged with reckless endangerment and assault causing bodily harm and punished accordingly. (See chapter 3.) These harms are perpetrated directly by corporate and industrial enterprises for the most part, not by individuals, although they are aided and abetted by consumers everywhere who uncritically accept the goods these enterprises provide and market. In addition, and beyond the direct harms discussed, there are various complex effects engendered by global warming and other changes, as these too affect health worldwide.

Some may question the connection between ecological integrity and human health. For instance, William Aiken asks whether it can be proven that a certain quantity of wild space is necessary to preserve human health and, if so, why.[29] The answer is that at this moment there is no research showing specifically what size of wild landscape is absolutely required to support human life and health, as there is for nonhuman species. In contrast, when the protection of integrity is not the primary concern of policy, then many activities are routinely permitted, with serious consequences for human life and health.

We do know that rich, biodiverse systems provide "nature's services" reliably and for the long term. Even healthy agricultural and agroforestry systems do not perform the same services. As James Karr puts it, "a place has integrity if the biota present is the product of evolutionary and biogeographical processes at that place, with relatively little or no

influence from human society."[30] This condition makes a vital difference, because in that case, "the biological complex is able to sustain
itself through time . . . in the face of the standard environmental disturbances of that region." Complex-systems theorists may characterize the
element of self-maintenance, or self-organizing behavior, as follows:

> A system with integrity is characterized by two properties:
> 1. Self-organizing behavior;
> 2. Rich diversity (that is, a system that is diverse beyond the minimum
>   required to behave in a self-organizing fashion).
>
> Self-organization is characterized by the following attributes:
> a. The system exerts some degree of selection upon its own
>   makeup;
> b. The system exhibits centripetal behavior; that is, it actively at-
>   tracts matter and energy itself,
> c. The ensemble has a preferred direction in which it develops;
> d. The life span of the system structure exceeds that of its compo-
>   nent elements;
> e. Perhaps most important, the system is autonomous to a degree
>   of its component parts.[31]

The aspect of integrity that is listed here as (c), however, is not accepted
by many ecologists, including Karr.

Despite possible differences of interpretation and perspective, indicated by the two positions cited, a basic, core understanding of integrity
emerges, to render it alone an optimal condition to sustain life and
health through the services the system provides.

In addition, unrestrained economic activities have effects well beyond
specific pollution or species depletion, and current institutional and
regulatory conventions do not help toward global protection of natural
services. Most often competing preferences, not ecological realities, govern public policy decisions, and activities are limited on the basis of legal
proof of present and immediate harms to humans. The sheer proliferation of industrial/urban complexes that house and support these activities is a hazardous development in itself. Since 1986 the Institute for
Environment and Public Health of the Netherlands has termed the
"fragmentation of nature" a form of pollution and documented its impact on human health. Piecemeal legislation based on current laws
about burden of proof in cases of harm might be sufficient to halt some
of the grossest abuses (for example, the proliferation of toxins and
chemicals in the air, water, and land, to some extent), but it will only
provide end-of-pipe regulations at best.

My claim is that only regulations about the earth as a whole will acknowledge our common habitat and help halt and reverse the present disastrous trends and that the ethics of integrity, or the totality of the second-order principles I propose, should serve as a guideline to achieve our common good in this basic sense.

Global Warming, Climate Change, and Human Health

Recently the Intergovernmental Panel on Climate Change published a report of its working group.[32] Its work also emphasizes the public health impacts of the changes it discusses on "whole communities and populations." The origin of all disturbances is acknowledged to be climate change. The report also notes that:

> Populations with different levels of natural, technical and social resources would differ in their vulnerability to climate-induced health impacts. Such vulnerability due to crowding, food insecurity, local environmental degradation and perturbed ecosystems already exists in many communities in developing countries.

As noted earlier, not only populations in developing countries but also disadvantaged populations in affluent northwestern countries are disproportionately affected by the consequences of our lifestyles. The latter, unfortunately, are both supported and manipulated by large economic interests and their allies in the governments and political systems of our large democracies. These powerful connections and cooperations form the "iron triangle," a conjunction of indefeasible strengths that Shrader-Frechette describes, for instance, in connection with the storage of radioactive waste despite strong popular protests.[33]

Aside from distributive problems and lack of global equity, in general, the link between climate changes/global warming and the imperative of maintaining and protecting ecosystem integrity is present in two separate senses. First, deforestation of large, biodiverse areas would be prohibited from the standpoint of integrity, and the role of forests in regard to global climate would be preserved. These landscapes would be largely protected as "core" areas, and they would be kept in their wild state, in sizes large enough to ensure safety (according to the prudential principle). Second, the major contributors to the problem—the "global warming brought about by the injection of greenhouse gasses (i.e., carbon dioxide, methane, nitrous oxides and chlorofluorocarbons) into the atmosphere"[34]—would not have been freely permitted even in areas beyond the wild, such as buffers or "culture"/urban areas. No "risky business" would have been allowed to operate if it could be reasonably anticipated that it would have an adverse impact on wild/core areas, buffers, or areas of "culture" themselves.[35]

This, however, has not been the case: although ecosystem integrity is the goal of many regulatory acts, the consequences of these mandates are neither well understood nor accepted and implemented in public policy. Public recognition and support for the foundational role of ecosystem integrity and, in general, for the ecosystem approach is now gaining momentum. In Canada, especially in the Great Lakes region, much work has been done to clarify the notion of integrity and the implications of the ecosystem approach because of the original mandates of the Great Lakes Water Quality Agreement (1978), which is a binational act.

We have noted the increase of skin cancers as one effect of the ozone layer's depletion. It might be possible to take measures to protect ourselves from harmful UVB and UVA rays by avoiding the sun, using special blocking lotions, and wearing protective clothing outdoors. But there are other direct threats to human health (such as "killer" heat waves in major cities worldwide) that cannot be avoided, and there is not enough scientific evidence and knowledge to give us confidence in our capacity to withstand these threats. For instance, it has been hypothesized that "El Niño may have helped promote a deadly cholera outbreak in 1991." The basis of this hypothesis, which is now gaining solid support through the work of such scientists as Rita Colwell, is that climate changes fostered by ecological disintegrity due to anthropogenic stress produce ocean warming. This in turn fosters the proliferation of plankton in the oceans; the abundant plankton harbors the E. coli bacterium and thus supports the spread of cholera pandemics from continent to continent.[36]

Therefore, it seems reasonable to suppose not only that we may face physical havoc such as rising sea levels, flooding in low-lying areas, and violent storms, but also that we might have to prepare ourselves for dramatic increases in the spread of infectious diseases. Mosquitoes, flies, and snails will "respond to subtle changes in temperature." Some have said that even the recent U.S. outbreak of hantavirus (27 deaths in 1993) may have been related to El Niño. Perhaps the increased temperature led to an explosion in the deer mouse population, due to the increased food supply. It is plausible that higher temperatures may give rise to increases in both insects and bacteria: hence, the subsequent increase in bacteria-borne diseases may be the result of environmental causes arising from human interventions.[37]

The 1992 climate treaty called for global research by epidemiologists: environmental monitoring is mandatory for "the atmosphere, the oceans and terrestrial ecosystems." It is for this reason that an imperative of integrity was proposed imposing limits on human activities, in

order to protect and restore natural life-support systems in certain proportions, as well as limits on certain kinds of human activities, even if
these occur outside wild areas, to minimize the catastrophic risks noted
above.

Further, both the general call to restore and protect ecosystem integrity and the specific emphasis on strict zoning are foundational for sustainability in food production in several senses. First as David Pimentel
states, "soil erosion is a major environmental threat to the sustainability
and productivity capacity of agriculture," and further, "the loss of soil
degrades arable land and eventually renders it unproductive."[38] Moreover, large amounts of fertilizer, pesticides, and irrigation are used to
help offset erosion problems. But the trade-off is the creation of "pollution and health problems, the destruction of natural habitats while
boosting energy consumption and rendering agricultural systems unsustainable."[39]

The same intensive petrochemical agricultural practices, coupled with
the use of high-impact mechanical equipment, also combines with the
effects of climate changes to further aggravate the latter's adverse effects. Whether floods are indeed the product of global warming, one
thing is indisputable. Soil does not always have the capacity to properly
absorb the floodwaters because of the intensive agricultural practices to
which it has been subjected and because the chemicals used to boost
crop yields eliminate most of the biomass that maintains the ecosystems'
functions, seriously affecting food production. Thus a vicious cycle de-
velops. Soil erosion lowers productivity as soil depth is lost, and it takes
hundreds of years to replace a single centimeter of lost topsoil. Intensive
agropractices may temporarily alleviate the food production problems,
but in the long run they aggravate the very problem they are intended
to correct. As further use decimates soil biota, the soil's water-holding
capacity and its productivity decline. Moreover, the vicious circle has
strong negative effects on the environment as a whole. Some of the damage includes "eutrophication of waterways, siltation of harbors and
channels . . . loss of wildlife habitat and disruption of stream ecology,"
as well as "damage to public health."[40]

Oceans and fisheries are similarly damaged. The alternative is to turn
to aquaculture instead, but "aquaculture is the aquatic counterpart of
agriculture,"[41] and probably because of the problems of natural fisheries
over the past twenty years it has increased exponentially, and it now
accounts for 17 percent of the world's fisheries. Aquaculture has potentially deleterious effects on the environment and on human health. It is
not a natural process, and it affects biodiversity in several ways: through
the consumption of resources; through the transformation process itself; and through the production of wastes. Its effects on biodiversity are

both direct and indirect. Releasing "exotic genetic material into the environment" has a direct impact that in turn effects changes "to the biotic components of an ecosystem," causing possible loss of habitats or alterations in systems' function.[42]

We can now review the effects of these practices on human health. The need for food is basic, but the practices employed to secure it are often hazardous. When epidemiologists and other scientists seek clear causal links between some substance and human health, they do not turn their attention to other events and processes in which causation is neither obvious nor direct. If environmental epidemiologists were to consider the problems from a holistic environmental perspective, with a starting point in ecosystem integrity, human health considerations would be enriched.

Instead, the practice of considering environmental problems and human health problems separately leads to misunderstanding and incomplete knowledge. For instance, a dialogue appears to be necessary with agricultural scientists and others whose realm of expertise is related to food production. Complex-systems theorists can also provide a vitally different perspective.

This discussion has not addressed the question of the increasing global population in relation to food supplies, because I have treated this question in detail elsewhere.[43] In brief, there are desirable consequences for world hunger from the approach suggested here, despite population increases. First, the wild's role as benchmark and reserve will help in cases of crop blights and failures; second, the requirement of nontoxic buffers will lead to sustainable agriculture, so that the problems arising from chemically treated soils will be avoided. Finally, the respect for ecosystem integrity will discourage the present wasteful northwestern diet and suggest vegetarianism instead. David Pimentel and Paul Ehrlich both support the change, although they disagree somewhat on the numbers that could be fed as a consequence of changes in dietary habits. Pimentel thinks about 300 million more could be fed globally. Ehrlich places that figure at closer to 700 million.[44] Incidentally, practicing some sort of vegetarianism is not only environmentally better but also far superior from the standpoint of human health.[45]

For now, numerous possible health effects have been related to forms of environmental degradation and the lack of an overarching holistic perspective in laws and regulations as well as morality. Climate changes and global warming have given rise to increased skin cancers in humans. Ozone depletion also affects plants and animals, hence humans indirectly. Other issues include the proliferation of insects and bacteria, with corresponding increases in the infectious diseases they might carry; the possibility of killer heat waves with resulting triple and quadruple rates of heat-related summer deaths in large cities worldwide; and physical problems connected with the geography of many locations, such as flooding of seas and inland water bodies, with corresponding human health problems and deaths. The latter will be more acute in less-developed countries, which do not enjoy well-organized medical and social services.

The Role of Integrity: The Present Link

Scientific research and literature have recently emphasized much of the material discussed in the previous two sections. Yet there is one trend that has not received as much recent attention: the growing impact of ecological disintegrity, although I have convened meetings involving the scholars and scientists who are working in that area and published the results.[46] In contrast, much has been written about "ecosystem health."[47] The metaphor of ecosystem health is useful to focus public attention on environmental problems and to interject an evaluative component into scientific discourse, as health is generally taken to be a desirable state of affairs.

In contrast, the opening sentence of the executive summary of the intergovernmental document cited earlier states: "The sustained health of human populations requires the continued *integrity* of Earth's natural systems." Even in a health context, the required condition for human health is described as the earth's integrity, not the "health" of its ecosystems. One might question this seeming anomaly, particularly in a document devoted to health itself. It might simply be a case of appealing to the language of most regulatory and legislative documents.[48] But perhaps the use of *integrity* here is intended simply as a public relations ploy to evoke warm positive feelings without demanding any change in the status quo. Any such intention, I am happy to say, appears to have backfired.

Much of the material available on ecosystem health deals, as Baird Callicott justly suggests, with the areas of the world where humankind is actually living and actively engaged in pursuing its goals.[49] In order to survive, we need to manage and manipulate large areas of the world, and in that sense the goals of ecosystem health in managed areas appear to be appropriate. What is less appropriate is the fact that all the material on ecosystem health tends to ignore the *foundation* of the health it advocates; that is, it ignores ecosystem integrity.

Ecosystem health may thus be a useful metaphor, but only if its basis and the necessary condition for its existence are acknowledged and supported. On the other hand, if the emphasis remains exclusively on ecosystem health, we ultimately support the status quo with possible "green" modifications of various degrees, or as I have put it in another context, we remain wolves in "green" sheep's clothing.[50] In this sense, the metaphor is not useful but misleading, as it draws public attention away from the conditions and the background for health.

Moreover, ecosystem health suffers from conceptual and philosophical problems of its own, not only as a metaphoric goal of public policy, but also as a practical goal. I have argued that as a goal of management, it explicitly excludes the very landscapes that support life through their services, and therefore that it cannot support "health" in a meaningful sense, but only, at best, the sustainability of certain specific production goals.[51] Dale Jamieson also shows several problems with the concept: a "weakness about the supposed objectivity of human health"; the lack of motive when the metaphor is applied to ecosystems rather than to humans and other creatures; and the instability of "our preferences with respect to ecosystems" and their composition.[52] Other problems are discussed by Shrader-Frechette and by Hammond and Holland to name but a few other critics.[53]

From our point of view, the major difficulty is that aside from its conceptual problem, the emphasis on ecosystem health as the goal of public policy is particularly hazardous to our health. Given our previous record in dealing with the environment and the production goals of our management, it is clear that to preserve, respect, and restore are not our main aims. The lesson has not been learned yet, despite our present precarious environmental situation: we need to stop believing that all on earth can be managed, and start to manage our own selves and society instead.[54] Whatever is "managed" for production may be plentiful, even sustainable in itself. But if it involves any management "tools" such as chemicals, toxic substances, or intensive practices of any sort, not only is the productive area eventually affected, but also the "fragmented nature"[55] that is left; and this is not conducive to our own health, as we have seen. Further, the technological optimism that governs these management goals also excludes zoning, controls for harmful activities, and the possibility of serious restraints. The human health paradigm provides examples. Why do we need to seriously restructure our lifestyles, consider our diet, and avoid excesses when we can "manage" our so-called health through chemical and technical means—say, liposuction if we are obese, heart bypass operations if our arteries are clogged, and other medical interventions? A plethora of medical interventions exists not only for the diseases caused by our natural deterioration but also for those we actively court through our inappropriate lifestyles. There are many ways of managing our health.

In contrast, as the Intergovernmental Report on Climate Changes and

Human Health clearly states, the *integrity* of a largely unmanaged earth is necessary for our health, and therefore our managing expertise must be exercised where it is most needed: in ourselves and our activities. Understanding the role of integrity in the prevention of harm to all life ensures that the goal is recognized as more than a prudent, desirable choice, something in our interest. It also becomes a moral imperative.[56]

Integrity, Health, and Obligations to the Future: The Future Link

When we embrace the primacy of integrity, we take a holistic stance not only in the sense of including the synchronic aspects of our lives, but also in the sense of considering the diachronic aspects of our lives, extending globally into the future. Does the integrity approach suggest a different perspective on future generations' problems? I shall argue that it does, precisely by virtue of its holistic thrust. The argument is that the ethics of integrity and the principle of integrity (PI) I have defended[57] can provide a stronger basis for duties to future generations than traditional moral theories can.

From the perspective of integrity, future generations are to be understood as encompassing both human and nonhuman species. Therefore, they can be viewed as more than a collection of individuals; they can be considered to be wholes. "Future generations" considerations are also as much a part of present regulations and legislation as are the concept of integrity and the ecosystem approach, of which the latter is the goal. For this reason it is particularly important to trace the connection between these two emphases, as they ought to be viewed as complementary.

Documents that refer to "the integrity of the earth" and to "the rights of future generations" do not connect these explicitly, and this is urgently needed. Some philosophers even contrast the appeal to "future generation rights" with ecocentric ethics, appealing to the intrinsic value of natural wholes.[58] The truth of the matter is that all appeals to future generations and their rights require the holistic thrust I have proposed. The arguments that show why we need to consider future generations in morality and public policy are based on the right of the future world to a global environment that is substantially similar to or perhaps better than ours. Those who defend future generations' rights argue that, whatever their possible choices, preferences, and even needs will be, certain requirements will remain constant: clean air and water and a safe earth to inhabit. Their rights and even their very lives depend on the natural life-support systems they will inherit from our generation.

Because we cannot specify precisely which resources, places, and life-

styles will best fit future preferences, a coherent defense of future generations' rights will have to focus on the most basic requirements for
health and life, as PI does, in its first principle in support of the role of
ecological integrity.[59] It can be argued, therefore, that an appeal to future generations' rights *must* be both holistic and ecocentric: it must be
based on ensuring to the best of our ability that harm is not caused to
future generations, in the sense of not interfering with their future life-
support systems and their physical health and reproductive capacities.[60]

Whatever choices, preferences, and desires future people may have,
their safe physical existence is the most basic requirement, and the foundation of all other choices. It is therefore incorrect to contrast ecocentrism based on the intrinsic value of natural systems with the rights of
future generations, as Bryan Norton, for instance, does.[61] As we have
seen, the arguments in defense of the two positions make it easier to
refute specious arguments about (1) our lack of information about the
specific needs and preferences of future people and (2) our lack of
knowledge about those whose rights we are attempting to protect. A
holistic position is all-encompassing by its nature and requires no details
about what, precisely, is part of the systems it is intended to respect and
protect, now and in the future. The main goal of the ethics of integrity
centers on the *capacity*, the *functioning*, and the natural *evolutionary trajectory* of these systems, without time constraints or limits (see chapter 9).

The commonality between these ethical concerns is found more
clearly when all future generations, human and nonhuman, are considered. For those who are not prepared to accept that position, I have
argued that holistic concerns do not trivialize, much less exclude, the
humans who are part of these systems' biota.[62] Biocentric holism, as a
philosophical position, finds additional support in the work of Aristotle,
although it owes a great deal to ecology and complex-systems theory,
particularly in relation to the value of integrity itself. The holistic defense of moral concern for future generations can also be viewed from
an Aristotelian perspective.

Aristotle In Support of Biocentrism: Being and Eternity

> . . . being [is better] than non-being and living than non-living—for
> these reasons there is a generation of animals. For since the nature
> of such a kind cannot be eternal, that which comes into being is
> eternal in the way that is possible for it.
>
> Aristotle, *De Generatione Animalium* (Bk. III, ch. 1,731b30–33)

Two premises are made explicit in this passage, but both are often
taken as implicit by moral philosophers today: (1) that being, generally,

is better than its opposite and (2) that living is superior to or more desirable than not living. Aside from arguments about "quality of life" issues in biomedical ethics, it is only in the literature regarding future generations that these questions are even raised. On the topic of future generations, they represent the focus of the disagreement between different positions. I briefly discuss some of these positions in the next section. Here I review Aristotle's doctrine of life as an ultimate value and a good beyond discussion. I have argued that its position is primary because it represents the basis for all other goods and ends. As it is unique in that sense, it provides the best first value uniting humans and nonhumans, individuals and wholes, as a firm basis for a moral principle.

Aristotle takes the ultimate value of life to be obvious, and he uses it as a first principle rather than as a conclusion for which he needs to argue. Given our instinctive as well as our reasoned responses to life questions in general, and the fact that most regulations and laws also take life for granted and enunciate it as a starting point for all other human rights, Aristotle might be generally correct in his starting point. In the *Generation of Animals* Aristotle speaks of eternity and the limits of what is possible for that which comes into being:

> For since the nature of such a kind cannot be eternal, that which comes into being is eternal in the way that is possible for it. Now it is not possible in number (for the being of existing things is in the particular and if this were such, it would be an eternal) but it is possible in form. That is why there is always a kind of men and animals and plants. (Bk. II, ch. 1, 731b32–732a)

Of course what Aristotle believes is that all that happens in nature is "for the sake of something," and the telic, eternal unfolding of the universe is also not in question for him. Generation and corruption, growth and decay are all part of this orderly unfolding, which supports life and guarantees the eternity of universal kinds, in the face of the limits of particularity. Yet his effort is not to escape, much less to disdain, particularity itself. Martha Nussbaum says:

> In the *Parts of Animals* (1.5), he addresses some students who had evidently protested against the study of animals, and their form and matter, asking for something more sublime. He tells them that this reluctance is actually a form of self-contempt: for they are, after all, creatures of flesh and blood themselves. (654a27–31)[63]

Thus, long before Aldo Leopold's "land ethic," we find a clear, unequivocal statement of our own kinship to all life, in clear rejection of much of Platonism and, later, Cartesianism. Nussbaum adds: "We could generalize Aristotle's point by saying that the opponent of the return to appearances is likely to be a person not at peace with his humanity."[64] Hence it is a normal part of human life to want to understand the laws and the functioning of the universe. But it is also part of our humanity to accept our commonality with the rest of life, aside from our position as external observers, as scientists.

Yet many argue that the ancient Greeks, including Aristotle, perpetuate the split between humankind and the rest of nature because of their emphasis on rationality as the element that separates us from other animals. However, to say that we are rational *animals*, as we have seen, is not to deny our commonality with the rest of nonhuman creatures. Aristotle sees the eternal waxing and waning of natural processes, natural entities and wholes, as part of a desirable, even divine plan for the universe, without for a moment ascribing intentionality to either individuals or processes.

We can therefore say that living is better than its opposite, and that all of nature unfolds "for the sake" of the continuance of life through eternity. Because actual individuals are particulars, and therefore mortal, the true "divine" aim is for eternity through forms and their universality. Further, for Aristotle, "we should always act for the sake of happiness," which includes a number of goods; hence, the pursuit of other "intrinsic goods" beyond mere virtue will be necessary, as these too are components of happiness, the pursuit of which is our obligation.[65] These goods will include health (including a healthy habitat), reproductive success, and children whose lives will also include these conditions.

Hence it is not only a naturally unfolding physical "is" that represents nature's end or goal; the continuance of life is both a precondition and a component of our moral commitment to virtue and happiness. Both of these values are, of their very nature, intrinsically good and temporally unlimited.

The advantages of this approach are clear: unfolding not only in the present but also in the future, they are part of the universal telos. Rather than adding posterity and the future to a temporally and locally limited moral theory, Aristole's theory *includes* these from the start. These intrinsic goods, however, do not appear to include individual entities; rather, they apply to wholes so that their correspondent parts gain value and can be considered equally parts of that intrinsically good whole, by virtue of their participation in its functions.[66]

Another connection between the "integrity" approach and Aristotle is particularly constructive from the standpoint of providing a better basis for obligations to future generations: it can be found in Aristotle's theory of potentiality in relation to actuality. In an earlier discussion of integrity's meaning and role, I indicated that it was wrong to identify an ecosystem in a state of integrity with one that is flourishing or a "climax" system. I suggested instead that the evolutionary processes' unconstrained, natural unfolding depended absolutely on the nonimposition of strong anthropogenic stresses, so that unstressed, unmanipulated natural systems would be closest to a state of true integrity and hence possess the utmost capacity (c) for sustaining and continuing the full range of potential evolutionary paths for a specific system at its specific time and location. Only this "optimum capacity" could denote the presence of ecosystem integrity, particularly as no landscape on earth today can be termed pristine or has entirely escaped anthropogenic alteration.[67]

Aside from his emphasis on the telic nature of all single physical processes and the universe as a whole, Aristotle was the first philosopher to clearly articulate the connection between potency and actuality. In fact, all "matter" is potency, awaiting actualization in various forms. Hence we need not have any specific information about the future actuality evolving from matter's potency, in order to acknowledge its value as intrinsically good. For example, we need not know that Michelangelo will use it to sculpt his *David* in order to attach intrinsic value to a slab of Carrara marble and to understand it to be worthy of respect *now* without any present assurance about its fate. The same could be said about presently uncultivated land or untouched forest or the embryo of a horse or human. Nor is intrinsic value in this sense separable, except in thought, from the instrumental value of what we consider. All things have a range of capacities, which in turn limit their possible function. But function, for Aristotle, is a "movement," hence it requires life in natural entities. Flesh, for instance, is not really "flesh," unless it is that of a live animal; a dead man's eye is not an "eye" in the sense of possessing the *capacity* to function, in the manner appropriate to it.

In conclusion, I defended elsewhere the relation between parts and wholes as fundamental to the intrinsic value of integrity; I also proposed the telic thrust of natural processes in relation to that value.[68] In this section, the relation between potency and actuality, and the foundational value of life, appears to be additional constructive aspects of Aristotelian thought. All these Aristotelian arguments are valuable in support of a holistic environmental ethic and also for the obligation to future generations. In essence, the ultimate telos lies in the functioning of all matter, not only because it is the basis of all that exists, but also because it encompasses the capacity to exist and to develop into all it can be. Both are then, in a sense, final causes and goods that escape all time constraints.

The Future-Generations Argument and Parfit's Theory X

The previous two sections showed a new parameter within which a theory of obligation to future generations could be based. Derek Parfit deals at some length with future generations in *Reasons and Persons*, and he encounters serious problems in the attempt, as many others have done. But he starts, it is important to note, with "persons," individuals; hence, he is heir to all the problems that arise through that approach. After proposing, discussing, and ultimately rejecting several theories, he says:

> I am searching for theory X, the new theory about beneficence that both solves the Non-Identity Problem and avoids the Repugnant Conclusion. More generally, theory X would be the best theory about beneficence. It would have acceptable implications when applied to all the choices that we even make including those that affect both the identities and the number of future people.[69]

In contrast, the approach I propose requires no special consideration of either identities or numbers of future people. It proposes that future generations should be viewed not as an aggregate of individuals but as wholes. This seems appropriate because, particularly from the point of view of environmental considerations, usually coupled with future-generations issues, the future includes the natural systems, with all their biotic and abiotic components; that is, it must refer to wholes, not just to aggregates or communities of individuals considered singly and apart from their natural habitats.

Concern for the future hinges on the quantity and quality of safe air, water, and land that will be left for all. This clearly includes the continuation of the processes and functions appropriate to the specific landscapes and the changing climates of various futures. And if future generations can be viewed as wholes—that is, not as numbers of individuals or as separate though indeterminate communities of humans—then most of the problems arising from attempting to put faces and numbers on future generations are no longer as damaging to the argument in their support. Future generations must instead be considered as wholes, connected and interdependent with all other future forms of life and with natural processes at future stages of evolution, which cannot be clearly defined but must continue to have the undiminished capacity to support life. From this perspective, we no longer need to concern ourselves with improbable calculations about their probable "happiness" or "wretchedness," their future wants or preferences. From the integrity perspective, we are concerned with only one major aspect of the problem: the interface between future generations and the natural life-support systems that we leave them. Arguments about how much oil or other resources it would be appropriate for us to use in light of future generations' needs,[70] or about whether "future people are different, in morally relevant ways from present people,"[71] or about the importance of "the temporal location of future people or ignorance of them, and the contingence of their existence"[72] lose much of their significance.

Our primary moral responsibility is to the optimum capacity of natural life-support systems. Our present respect and protection is intended precisely to preserve their future evolutionary paths and trajectories, including whatever changes in communities, populations, and interactions these might entail.[73] Not only is the lack of precision and predictability about the future not a particularly serious problem about "futurity," it is also necessarily accepted as part of "embracing complexity" and of the "ecosystem approach."[74] Its central focus remains the "causal necessity of integrity."[75]

The integrity perspective precludes attempting to predict whether the unmanipulated, evolutionary development of wild areas will lead in specific directions. We do know that these areas, and an attitude toward the earth that does not conflict with the needs of such areas, are central to our present concerns about human and nonhuman life and health. It is the capacity of these systems to retain an optimum number of choices, based on their temporal and geographical locations, as well as on the information available through the biological diversity appropriate to each system, that is the primary good.

Moreover, we are not expected, in this scenario, to be "ideal observers" and either arrange or calculate any future human chance at happiness: our obligation is to preserve our/their life-support systems in perpetuity. This appears to be a less stringent demand than those advocated through other arguments in support of future generations. In contrast, this position demands a much tougher stance *now* and is ultimately more respectful of all possible future developments and choices. By rigorously forbidding actions that would diminish natural systems' capacities, in essence it does preserve maximum human choice without paternalistic attempts at defining or limiting those choices. As the respect is aimed at all life, this position is neither speciesist nor racist or gender biased: its primary focus is the respect for life in the most general form, yet its mandates are far more restrictive than mandates attempting to "balance" present preferences alone.

As Aristotle indicated, the respect for life as a whole entails respect for nature's *telos* and the preservation of the "eternity" of being in the way that is "possible for it."[76] From the integrity perspective, the obligation to protect the capacity of natural ecosystems is necessarily future oriented: it is their present optimum capacity for their future evolutionary trajectories that is at issue. From this perspective, environmental ethics is holistic and future-oriented for all generations, human and nonhuman. The defense of naturally evolving systems and the respect for the wild in various quantities and across geographical and temporal scales is equally as valid for holistic environmental biocentrism as it is for duties to the future, and this conclusion will be reflected in two additional second-order principles (numbers 7 and 8) that are provisionally listed below and will be discussed in chapter 9.

SOP 7   We must respect the individual integrity of single organisms (or micro-integrity) in order to be consistent in our respect for integrity and also to respect and protect individual functions and their contribution to the systemic whole.

SOP 8   Given the uncertainties embedded in SOPs 1, 2, and 3, the "Risk Thesis" must be accepted for uncertainties referring to the near future. We must also accept the "Potency Thesis" for the protection of individuals and wholes in the long term.

The Individual Dimensions of Health and Integrity

These last two second-order principles show clearly the connection between the health of individual organisms and their integrity. Most moral theories support a "harm" principle or demand respect for individuals and take the position that individuals ought not to be harmed or to have pain inflicted upon them, and that all are equally deserving of respect. Aristotle's scientific writings tie together the development of individual entities, actualizing their potential over time, the part they play the universal whole, and the eternal persistence of life. Through their actualization and through their role in the natural systems in which they exist, single perishable individuals partake of the "eternity of being" according to their capacities.

But they cannot function as they are intended to do, if their natural capacities are altered so drastically that their reproductive and parenting abilities are no longer present. But that is precisely what has been happening through the increasing disintegrity to which we are all exposed in various ways. Colborn and others have shown in great detail and with the support of extensive research that the chemicals and toxic substances we use indiscriminately may be either carcinogenic or mutagenic for humans and nonhumans exposed to large doses. But in addition, Colborn has shown that even minute doses of a number of chemicals act as hormone mimics and endocrine disrupters, creating precisely the reproductive failures and parenting inabilities that will preclude an entity's participation in what Aristotle terms the eternity of being.[78]

In all these cases, a being's individual integrity has been breached and grievous harm has been done, not only to the individual but also to the species to which the individual belongs and to the habitat or systemic whole. Hence to show that microintegrity is as fundamentally important as macrointegrity is also to argue that we must broaden the basis on which we decide that something presents an immoral and unacceptable harm. The tiny doses of endocrine disrupters do not necessarily result either in clearly visible harms that can be shown in a court of law or in harms to the exposed individuals. *Harm* is normally taken to mean either fatality or morbidity, and *risk* is defined primarily as the probability of harms. Hence neither is sufficient to represent all consequences of actions and practices that are unacceptable from either the moral or the practical point of view.

We need to include yet another form of risk in order to have an inclusive moral principle and a comprehensive public policy truly able to protect the public interest. We need to include *potential* harms, that is, harm that may affect not only present but also future individuals. A harm to someone's future choices or an imposed limit to someone's future capacities, or a harm to someone who will exist only in the future, cannot meet legal standards of proof and obtain redress in a court of law. But health is about function, and impaired function equals diminished health. In this sense, impaired individual health/function, whether human or nonhuman, can be protected only through the protection of biological and ecological integrity and the ethics of integrity (and second-order principles) proposed in this chapter.

These examples and Aristotle's scientific theories support the arguments proposed by the ethics of integrity: (1) the necessary connection between the role and function of individuals and wholes and therefore (2) the primacy of the integrity of both individuals and wholes from both a practical scientific and a theoretical point of view. Aristotle shows in principle how both points must be accepted if we are prepared to accept also the primary importance of the persistence of life over time (or, as he puts it, the "eternity of being"). In addition, the research of modern biologists and epidemiologists like Colborn show the actual, practical connection between attacks on natural individual capacities and species survival on one hand, and the sustainability of "nature's services" on the other. Hence, the practical necessity of respecting both micro- and macrointegrity is based on their intimate relation and the need for both in order to preserve life. The next chapter discusses the reasons for incorporating possible harms and future health effects in our argument as well as the problems arising from present Western institutions and laws.

Notes

1. L. Westra and P. Wenz, introduction to *Faces of Environmental Racism* (Lanham, MD: Rowman & Littlefield, 1995), p. xvii.

2. L. Westra, *An Environmental Proposal for Ethics: The Principle of Integrity* (Lanham, MD: Rowman & Littlefield, 1994), pp. 92–93, 97.

3. J. P. Myers and Joshua S. Reichert, *Perspectives on Nature's Services* (Washington, DC: Island Press, 1997), pp. xvii, 6.

4. James J. Kay and E. Schneider, "The Challenge of the Ecosystem Approach," *Alternatives* 20, 3 (1994): 1–6, reprinted in *Perspectives on Ecological Integrity*, ed. L. Westra and J. Lemons (Dordrecht, The Netherlands: Kluwer, 1995), pp. 45–59.

5. S. O. Funtowicz and J. R. Ravetz, "Science for the Post-Normal Age," *Futures* (September 1993): 739–55, reprinted in *Perspectives on Ecological Integrity*, ed. L. Westra and J. Lemons, pp. 146–61, 114.

6. K. Shrader-Frechette and E. D. McCoy, *Method in Ecology* (New York: Cambridge University Press, 1993); see also K. Shrader-Frechette, "Hard Ecology, Soft Ecology, and Ecosystem Integrity," in *Perspectives on Ecological Integrity*, ed. L. Westra and J. Lemons, pp. 125–45.

7. Funtowicz and Ravetz, "Science for the Post-Normal Age."

8. K. Shrader-Frechette, *Risk and Rationality* (Berkeley: University of California Press, 1991).

9. D. A. Brown, "The Role of Law in Sustainable Development and Environmental Protection Decision-Making," in *Sustainable Development: Science, Ethics and Public Policy* (Dordrecht, The Netherlands: Kluwer, 1995), pp. 64–76.

10. W. E. Rees and M. Wackernagel, *Our Ecological Footprint* (Gabriola Island, BC: New Society Publishers, 1996).

11. Robert E. McGinn, "Technology, Demography, and the Anachronism of Traditional Rights," *Journal of Applied Philosophy*: 11, 1 (1994), 57–70.

12. Reed F. Noss, "The Wildlands Project: Land Conservation Strategy," *Wild Earth*, Special Issue, (1992): 10–25; see also Reed F. Noss and A. Y. Cooperrider, *Saving Nature's Legacy* (Washington, DC: Island Press, 1994).

13. James J. Kay and E. Schneider, "The Challenge of the Ecosystem Approach," *Alternatives* 20, 3 (1994): 1–6; reprinted in *Perspectives on Ecological Integrity*, ed. L. Westra and J. Lemons, pp. 49–59.

14. Funtowicz and Ravetz, "Science for the Post-Normal Age."

15. Rees and Wackernagel, *Our Ecological Footprint*.

16. McGinn, "Technology, Demography, and the Anachronism of Traditional Rights."

17. Noss, "The Wildlands Project: Land Conservation Strategy"; Noss Cooperrider, *Saving Nature's Legacy*.

18. Reed F. Noss, "Sustainability and Wilderness," *Conservation Biology* 5, 1 (March 1991); Noss, "The Wildlands Project: Land Conservation Strategy"; D. Pimentel, et al., "Conserving Biological Diversity in Agricultural/Forestry Systems" *BioScience* 42, 5 (1992).

19. L. Westra, "Ecosystem Integrity and Sustainability: The Foundational Value of the Wild," in *Perspectives on Ecological Integrity*, ed. L. Westra and J. Lemons (Dordrecht, The Netherlands: Kluwer, 1995); L. Westra, "Integrity, Health and Sustainability: Environmentalism without Racism," in *The Science of the Total Environment*, for the World Health Organization (Oxford, England: Elsevier, 1996).

20. D. Scherer and T. Attig, *Upstream/Downstream* (Philadelphia: Temple University Press, 1990).

21. Theo Colborn, "Plenary Address" to International Association of Great Lakes Researchers, May 27, 1996, Erindale College, Toronto, Ontario.

22. Colborn, "Plenary Address."

23. Theo Colborn, Dianne Dumanoski, and John Peterson Myers, *Our Stolen Future* (New York: Dutton, 1996).

24. Colborn, et al., *Our Stolen Future.*

25. Colborn, "Plenary Address."

26. Colborn, "Plenary Address"; see also Colborn, et al., *Our Stolen Future.*

27. Hans Jonas, *The Imperative of Responsibility* (Chicago: University of Chicago Press, 1984).

28. Westra, *An Environmental Proposal for Ethics.*

29. William Aiken, personal communication, June 1997.

30. James Karr, personal communication, June 1997.

31. Robert Ulanowicz, personal communication, June 1997.

32. Report of the Intergovernmental Panel on Climate Change, Working Group II, Montreal, October 20, 1995.

33. K. Shrader-Frechette, *Burying Uncertainty* (Berkeley: University of California Press, 1993); see also L. Westra, "On Risky Business—Corporate Responsibility and Hazardous Products," *Business Ethics Quarterly* 4, 1 (January, 1994): 97–110; L. Westra, "Integrity, Health and Sustainability: Environmentalism Without Racism."

34. Dale Jamieson, "Managing the Future: Public Policy, Scientific Uncertainty, and Global Warming," in *Upstream/Downstream*, ed. D. Scherer (Philadelphia: Temple University Press, 1990), pp. 67–89.

35. Westra, *An Environmental Proposal for Ethics*; see also Westra, "On Risky Business—Corporate Responsibility and Hazardous Products."

36. Rita Colwell, "Global Climate and Infectious Disease: The Cholera Paradigm," President's Lecture, February 10, 1996, American Association for the Advancement of Science in *Science* 274 (December 20, 1996): 2025–31.

37. A. J. McMichael, *Planetary Overload* (Cambridge, England: Cambridge University Press, 1995); see also A. J. McMichael, "The Health of Persons, Populations, and Planets: Epidemiology Comes Full Circle," in *Epidemiology and Society* (Oxford, England: Epidemiology Resources, 1995).

38. D. Pimentel, C. Harvey, P. Resosudarmo, K. Sinclair, et al., "Environmen-

tal and Economic Costs of Soil Erosion and Conservation Benefits," *Science* (February 24, 1995): 1117–23.

39. D. Pimentel, et al., "Conserving Biological Diversity in Agricultural/Forestry Systems"; see also D. Pimentel, et al., "Environmental and Economic Costs of Soil Erosion and Conservation Benefits."

40. D. Pimentel, et al., "Environmental and Economic Costs of Soil Erosion and Conservation Benefits."

41. M. C. Beveridge, M. Lindsay, G. Ross, and L. A. Kelly, "Aquaculture and Biodiversity," *Ambio* 23, 8 (December 1994): 497–502.

42. Beveridge, et al., "Aquaculture and Biodiversity."

43. L. Westra, "Biodiversity and Food Production: The Perspective of Ecosystem Integrity." Read at the AAAS meeting, February 11, 1994.

44. Paul Ehrlich, personal communication, June 1996.

45. Denis Burkitt, "Putting the Wrong Fuel in the Tank," *Nutrition* 5, 3 (May–June 1989): 189–91; see also Denis Burkitt, "Are Our Commonest Diseases Preventable?" *The Pharos of Alpha Omega Alpha* 54, 1 (Winter 1991): 19–21; see also Robert Goodland, "Environmental Sustainability: Eat Better and Kill Less," in *The Business of Consumption: Environmental Ethics and the Global Economy,* ed. L. Westra and P. Werhane (Lanham, MD: Rowman & Littlefield, in press).

46. Westra and Lemons, *Perspectives on Ecological Integrity.*

47. R. Costanza, B. Norton, and B. Haskell, *Ecosystem Health* (Washington, DC: Island Press, 1993); see also B. G. Norton, "A New Paradigm for Environmental Management," in *Ecosystem Health*; and J. B. Callicott, "The Value of Ecosystem Health," *Environmental Values* 4, 4 (November 1995), special issue on ecosystem health: 345–61.

48. Westra, *An Environmental Proposal for Ethics.*

49. Callicott, "The Value of Ecosystem Health."

50. L. Westra, "A Transgenic Dinner? Ethical and Social Issues in Biotechnology and Agriculture," *Journal of Social Philosophy* 24, 3 (Winter 1993): 215–32.

51. Westra, *An Environmental Proposal for Ethics*; see also *Nature's Services,* ed. Gretchen Daily (Washington, DC: Island Press, 1997), especially chapter 1.

52. Dale Jamieson, "Ecosystem Health: Some Preventive Medicine," *Environmental Values* 4, 4 (November 1995), special issue on ecosystem health: 333–44.

53. K. Shrader-Frechette, "Hard Ecology, Soft Ecology, and Ecosystem Integrity," in *Perspectives on Ecological Integrity,* ed. L. Westra and J. Lemons (Dordrecht, The Netherlands: Kluwer, 1995), pp. 125–45; see also M. Hammond and A. Holland, "Ecosystem Health: Some Prognostications," *Environmental Values,* 4, 4 (November 1995), special issue on ecosystem health: 283–86.

54. Kay and Schneider, "The Challenge of the Ecosystem Approach"; see also Westra, "Ecosystem Integrity and Sustainability: The Foundational Value of the Wild," in *Perspectives on Ecological Integrity.*

55. RIVM, *National Environmental Outlook, 1990–2010* (Bilthoven, The Netherlands: Rijksinstituut voor Volksgezondheit en Milieuhygiene, 1986).

56. Westra, *An Environmental Proposal for Ethics,* chapter 3.

57. Westra, *An Environmental Proposal for Ethics,* especially chapter 3.

58. Bryan Norton, "Why I Am Not a Nonanthropocentrist: Callicott and the

Failure of Monistic Inherentism," *Environmental Ethics* 17, 4 (Winter 1995): 341–58.

59. Westra, *An Environmental Proposal for Ethics.*
60. Colborn "Plenary Address"; see also Colborn, et al., *Our Stolen Future.*
61. Norton, "Why I Am Not a Nonanthropocentrist."
62. Westra, *An Environmental Proposal for Ethics,* especially chapters 1 and 2.
63. Martha C. Nussbaum, *The Fragility of Goodness* (Cambridge, MA: Cambridge University Press, 1986), p. 260.
64. Nussbaum, *The Fragility of Goodness,* p. 260.
65. Richard Kraut, *Aristotle on the Human Good* (Princeton: Princeton University Press, 1989).
66. Westra, *An Environmental Proposal for Ethics,* especially chapter 4.
67. Westra, *An Environmental Proposal for Ethics,* chapter 1.
68. Westra, *An Environmental Proposal for Ethics,* chapter four, pp. 134–41.
69. Derek Parfit, *Reasons and Persons* (Oxford, England: Oxford University Press, 1984), p. 405.
70. R. De George, "The Environment, Rights and Future Generations," in *Responsibilities to Future Generations,* ed. E. Partridge (Buffalo, NY: Prometheus Books, 1981).
71. Gregory Kavka, "The Paradox of Future Individuals," *Philosophy and Public Affairs* 2, 2 (Spring 1982): 92–112.
72. Kavka, "The Paradox of Future Individuals."
73. Kay and Schneider, "The Challenge of the Ecosystem Approach."
74. Kay and Schneider, "The Challenge of the Ecosystem Approach."
75. Robert Ulanowicz, "Ecosystem Integrity: A Causal Necessity," in *Perspectives on Ecological Integrity,* pp. 77–87.
76. Aristotle, *De Generatione Animalium,* BK. III, ch. 1, 731b30–33.
77. J. J. Thomson, *The Realm of Rights* (Cambridge, MA: Harvard University Press, 1990).
78. Colborn, et al., *Our Stolen Future.*

3

Environmental Risks, Rights, and the Failure of Liberal Democracy: Some Possible Remedies

> If you only have procedural democracy in a society that's exhibiting internal environmental stress and already has cleavages, say, ethnic cleavages, then procedural democracy will tend to aggravate these problems and produce societal discord, rather than social concord.
>
> T. Homer-Dixon, 1996[1]

The list of environmental assaults on the physical integrity of ecosystems and, through them, on our own physical integrity and capacities occurs equally in affluent northwestern and in developing southeastern countries. The global distribution of the threats, from remote islands in the Pacific[2] to "pristine" areas in the Arctic,[3] demonstrates that geographical and political boundaries cannot contain or limit environmental degradation and disintegrity. A careful study of the "hot spots" and the locations where the worst hazards persist shows that they are equally global in distribution. Democracies are no different from, say, military regimes or other nondemocratic states in terms of the severity of the environmental threats to which their citizens are exposed, although the threats themselves may be different in different nations and communities.

Democracy Is Not Enough

The "toxic doughnut" area in Chicago is a persistent threat to the life and health of its residents,[4] although it is located in a country that proudly calls itself the land of the free, and whose leaders routinely praise its democratic institutions. Equally hazardous, Royal Dutch Shell Oil's operation in Ogoniland, Nigeria, uses the dictatorship of General

53

Sani Abacha and its military clique to enforce the acceptance of extreme health hazards to its citizens. (See chapter 5 for details of this case.) Of course, those who oppose these hazardous corporate activities in Nigeria are brutally and violently repressed or murdered, while the Chicago residents are not.

The U.S. residents, primarily minorities in most large cities,[5] are not imprisoned or executed, and the army is not sent in to restrain and eliminate their protests. In some sense, their plight is therefore "better": they suffer only the physical harms imposed upon them by others, and their life and health are slowly, insidiously attacked and diminished. They suffer only from "eco-violence"; they are not imprisoned and executed if they protest, as they might be in Nigeria. But in some sense their plight is even worse. Ostensibly possessed of civil rights, basic education, access to information, and various constitutional and political guarantees about freedom of choices and the right to life and the pursuit of happiness, they are in fact manipulated to contribute willingly (but unknowingly) to their own plight. Aggressive advertising and marketing techniques cause the public to regard the products of modern technology as not only extremely desirable but even "necessary." Consumers regard these choices as "free," while corporate sponsors employ "trade secret" and other hard-won rules and regulations to protect themselves and keep citizens in the dark about the consequences of their choices.

At the same time, public relations departments work steadily so that questions about the risks and harms imposed, and whether they are offset by the so-called benefits available, are raised as rarely as possible. Further, as David Korten shows, two other severe problems arise in connection with the pursuit of economic gain through techno-corporate activities. The first is a clear attack on democracy, as independent PR firms are hired at great cost to generate "public movements" and campaigns, with the double aim of selling their ideas and preparing the public to accept and actively pursue certain products and services. The second problem is that businesses seek legislative modifications, regulations, or deregulations favorable to their interests. In some cases, corporations select and buy legislatures through campaign financing.

The result of these activities is that "free democratic choices" are neither truly free nor truly democratic. Korten cites Washington journalist William Greider:

> [the corporations'] tremendous financial resources, the diversity of their interests, the squads of talented professionals—all these assets and some others—are now relentlessly focused on the politics of governing. This new institutional reality is the centerpiece in the breakdown of contemporary democracy. Corporations exist to pursue their own profit maximization, not the collective aspirations of the Society.[6]

The problem is embedded in democracy in two senses. First, corporations, as fictitious legal "persons,"[7] are free to pursue their aims, unless it can be legally proven that citizens are directly harmed by their activities. Further, there is no overarching conception of "the good" for all that can be contrasted with the corporations' perception of the good, which is economic rather than intellectual or spiritual. Moreover, because there is no "good" to guide public policy, aside from aggregate choices and preferences, and because the public can be and in fact often is routinely manipulated and underinformed, the myth of "one person, one vote" remains a vague ideal, not a reality.

The arguments often proposed to justify these negative effects center on the alleged economic advantages provided by multinational corporate giants. But as we saw in the Chicago example, this "economic advantage" is not evenly distributed or fairly apportioned among rich and poor. Moreover, if we shift to the global scene, even economic advances depend on relative rather than absolute income. The Bruntlandt Commission proposed a "3 percent global increase in per capita income." That would translate into a first-year per capita increase (in U.S. dollars) of $633.00 for the United States and, among others, $3.60 for Ethiopia. After ten years, the respective figures would be $7,257.00 for the United States and $41.00 for Ethiopia: a vast advantage for the haves over the have-nots. Korten adds, "This advantage becomes a life-and-death issue in a resource-scarce world in which the rich and the poor are locked in mortal competition for a depleting resource base."[8]

Objections may be raised about such polarized descriptions of corporate activities. For instance, David Crocker believes that "demonizing" corporations as such is philosophically fallacious and practically incorrect, as many corporations do seek to support and implement the common good in their activities.[9] This objection, however, is open to a counterobjection. The main point at issue is not that this or that corporation is "bad" and needs to be stopped, but that Western democracies and their institutions appear to have no mechanism available now to protect the public from hazards and harms, many of which are in part self-inflicted under conditions of public misinformation and manipulation.

In this case, to say that there is no need to institute radical changes or to press criminal charges against the corporations is, as I will argue, like saying that because many of us are generally decent people who do not view physical assault and murder as acceptable actions, there is no need for strong legal sanctions against these crimes. Leaving to the corporate goodwill of individual firms the choice to either engage in harmful activities or not, within the ambit of the present loose regulatory structures and unrealistic legal criteria,[10] is to tacitly support the status quo and condone the crimes perpetrated thereby.

So far, this work has addressed the operation of legitimate business, registered, licensed, and—to some extent—regulated. This sort of business is global in scope, but even licenses and regulations tend to lose their force when they extend beyond national borders. And what about business that is not regulated, licensed, or even *known* as such to any nation or state? The "shadow economy," as Ed Ayres terms it, represents an additional global threat. We used to think of some of those "business" activities or of their concomitant effects as "externalities," and others as "anomalies." Ayres says:

> These are untaxed, unregulated, unsanctioned and—often—unseen. Most of them are things we've heard about but only fleetingly; we think of them as anomalies, rather than as serious or systemic threats to our mainframe institutions. They range from black markets in illicit drugs, cheap weapons, endangered wildlife, toxic waste, or ozone-depleting chemicals, to grey markets in unlisted securities or unapproved treatment for cancer.[11]

Activities that fall under the heading of "shadow economy" include the employment of subsistence agricultural workers and those in other "unregistered occupations"; illegal industries, the work of "unlocated populations" such as migrants and refugees; and "non-located activity" such as that arising from "electronic exchanges." Ayres lists the "three largest industries in the world" as: the military ($800 billion), illicit drugs ($500 billion), and oil ($450 billion). All three either have a "shadow" side or are entirely illegitimate. All three are among the most hazardous activities in the world, because, aside from the individual hazards they involve or represent, they are *in principle* beyond the control of society in various ways: when legitimate, because of the reasons Korten suggests, and when illegitimate, because they are not available for control. Ayres adds that "even the most enlightened public officials can't provide protection for what they can't see."[12]

The solution Ayres proposes might be the right one for all forms of techno-corporate enterprise. Neither national nor international databases carry accurate information about the shadow economy; hence, in the face of global threats, Ayres suggests, the "old geopolitical maps" are obsolete. As borders no longer function as they were intended to, because they have become impotent to contain benign and hazardous activities alike, the present maps should be superimposed with a "new kind of map," that is, with "maps illuminating the kinds of phenomena that now count most: the watersheds, bioregions, climatic zones and migratory routes that are essential to the security of all future economies."[13]

For both the legitimate economy and the shadow economy, it is necessary to understand the essential nature of ecological and climate functions and related global threats. It is equally necessary for all of us to understand the natural functions of natural systems and the effects of the products we buy on these systems.

For these reasons I propose a reexamination of environmental risks and harms from the standpoint of the ethics of integrity.[14] Although I argue in chapter 4 that a proliferation of individual and aggregate rights is undesirable from the environmental point of view (and this has been argued here as well, in support of limits for corporate rights), the right to life, health, and personal physical integrity appears to be primary and worthy of strong support. Moreover, the latter is necessarily embedded in ecosystem integrity, as Holmes Rolston argues.[15]

As noted in the previous chapter, even a primary concern with individual humans leads to the adoption of the ethics of integrity for the support and protection of human life and health. I shall continue to pursue that topic in this chapter, as I believe that our rights are not respected by the present laws, regulations, standards of proof, and the like. As Nobel Laureate Henry Kendall has pointed out, an environmental movement is in serious trouble if all it has to promote its mandates is the future threat of "delayed injuries."[16] Yet, to wait for the actual (albeit delayed) body count would mean dealing with irreversible environmental catastrophes. In other words, even the Montreal Protocol about CFCs and climate change cannot reverse immediately the immense, incalculable damage already done and can only support some relief many years after being put in place. Similarly, global warming and other climate changes affect human and nonhuman life directly and indirectly by affecting not only their health but also their food and water supply. The problem is that we do not see these effects or their real causes as immediate threats.

We must reexamine the import of human rights in this context, and we need to accept that delayed injuries and harms are just as real and grave an attack on our microintegrity—that is, our individual life and functioning—as a clear and obvious present attack. After introducing this problem in the first section, I discuss the right not to be exposed to the risk of harm, and the question of consent, and our legal rights. I then argue that democracy is insufficient to contain or eliminate the repeated threats to which we are exposed, and I propose a reexamination of our right not to be harmed, from a Kantian perspective. In addition, I argue that from a Kantian perspective, it is inadmissible to consent to harms that diminish us as humans in any way. The appeal to Kant here may appear odd in an ethic based on respect for wholes and for *all* individual life, but Kant does argue that life has intrinsic infinite value, at least in the case of human life. His argument has also been extended by animal ethicists. Nevertheless, here I argue only that even respect for human life necessarily requires respect for the systemic wholes from which nature's services are derived. I also argue that the risk of harm may be imposed through environmental means, so that respect for habitats and their functions becomes mandatory, even if human life is the main target of our respect.

Later in this chapter, I turn to biomedical ethics in order to show that the risk of harm is sufficient to restrain risks imposed in the field of health care. That approach may suggest a parallel way of dealing with environmental risks. Finally I argue that the goal of promoting the common good ought to encourage the design of laws and regulations that protect individuals and their habitats from grave threats, without waiting to prove conclusively that the injuries they will suffer are clearly directly related to the risks imposed.

Some might object to the strong regulatory thrust of this argument, on the ground that this leads to grave infringements of personal and group liberties. But even if we believe that liberty represents the highest good, liberty from harm *for all* demands restraint for many, so that justice might prevail.

In the next section I consider some examples of the recent literature on the topic of risks and harms, in order to place the integrity argument in context.

Risks and Harms; Rights and Consent

In her book *Realm of Rights*, Judith Jarvis Thomson[17] argues that "we do not have a claim against *merely being put at risk of harm*," and that we ought to reject what she terms the "risk thesis," that is, the thesis that "we have claims against others that they not impose risks of harm on us." In contrast, Anthony Ellis[18] argues that the risk thesis can be defended despite Thomson's condemnation. I argue that his position is essentially correct and that Thomson's difficulty in drawing the line between risk and harm, for instance, is no sound reason to reject the thesis, particularly in the face of diffuse global threats, which prompted the recent acceptance of a "precautionary principle."[19] I also argue that, although democracy is taken to be the form of government that is the best supporter and defender of human rights, it is precisely the unquestioned acceptance of the primacy of democratic institutions that presents the major obstacle to the prevention of public harms, particularly environmentally induced risks to public health.

Hence the problematic interface between rights, democratic institutions, and health risks needs to be reexamined, as the public interest in this respect may not be best supported by democratic choices without further controls. I propose an argument based on an analogy with bio-medical ethics and the moral and legal status of quarantines, in response to disease-engendered public health threats. If, *pace* Thomson, we have the right not to be "put at risk of harm," then we need to find the best way of reaching public policy decisions that will ensure that our rights will not be infringed. Notwithstanding the close links between civil rights and democracy, on both practical and theoretical grounds democratic practices appear insufficient to protect us from endangerment caused by the reckless practices of individuals and corporate citizens. Throughout this discussion and for the purposes of this work *liberal democracy* and *democracy* will refer to the form of democracy we can observe implemented in North America and in Western European nations. I shall not enter into the debate about the various ideological variants present in the constitutions and institutions of democratic states, because my argument is concerned with the real consequences of democracy as it is practiced in the Northwest, not of democracy in any ideal form. Similarly, I shall neither discuss nor debate the nature of a "military" regime (although I refer to a "military regime" in the case of the Ogoni in Nigeria; see chapter 5).

A further point needs clarification. Environmental risks and environmental harms in this section are compared to harms such as exposure to contagious diseases. The environmental harms considered are those that impose threats of grave physical injury to human health: they are the indirect counterparts, I argue, of the direct harms arising from exposure to contagious diseases. The environmental threats considered are those that seriously affect life-support systems on which we depend in various ways. For example, even a noncatastrophic event like the elimination of earthworms and other biomass in the soils at an agricultural location may be a contributing factor to hazardous floods, particularly in conjunction with climate changes. The latter are also fostered and magnified by environmental degradation, such as ozone layer and deforestation problems. Although at times local environmental hazards may be contained so that the functioning of the system or the human health in the area in which they occur may not be affected, the onus of proving this should be on the would-be polluter. In general, the repeated occurrences of seemingly small, localized threats can lead to system failure and global health threats.

It may seem that precise comparison with health threats may not be possible. But one might argue that a combination of infectious disease, malnutrition, some organ malfunction, and lack of local hygiene may be a lethal threat, when these occur simultaneously to someone in a developing country, even though each problem individually might be curable. Hence, for the environmental threats that pose, singly or jointly, an indirect but severe threat to our health, the analogy with health care issues seems apt from several standpoints: (1) the gravity of the threats; (2) the lack of specific intention to harm on the part of those who endanger us; (3) the lack of intention to inflict harm on specific individuals; (4) the necessity to restrain the freedoms of individual risk imposers, although neither punishment nor retribution may be appropriate conceptual categories to describe the restraints imposed; and (5) the lack of precise proofs of either direct guilt or even specific harm inflicted. These difficulties are common to environmentally induced harms as well as to health endangerments, despite the many differences between the two.

Finally, I argue against the common assumption that consent to certain institutionally approved practices and corporate activities entails the consent to all possible side effects, including consent to be put at risk of harm. Even though we might derive some individual and collective benefits from those activities, it can be argued on moral grounds that consent to be harmed cannot be given (see chapter 7).

Risk, Harm, and Consent

From a moral (Kantian) point of view, we can argue against consent to harm, as long as harm is understood in the physical sense, not simply in the sense of being wronged, or not getting one's due.[20] But the claim that embracing the lifestyle of affluent northwestern countries somehow entails giving "tacit consent" to the bad consequences that accompany that way of life needs to be examined from the standpoint of political theory as well. Tacit consent, in the context of one's political obligation to government institutions, may not be assumed simply because we are silent, or because we do not protest, particularly because tacit consent is almost never informed consent, as neither effort nor expense is spared to ensure that the public is not informed, when this is in the interest of corporate power (one example is the addictive nature of tobacco).

John Simmons argues that although "consent is called tacit when it is given by remaining silent and inactive," it must be expressed "by the failure to do certain things," when a certain response is *required* to signify disagreement. Unless characterized by the sequence described by Simmons, the "tacit consent" may simply represent (1) a failure to grasp the nature of the situation, (2) a lack of understanding of proper procedures, or (3) a misunderstanding about how long one has to decide whether to dissent.[21] Another possibility may be that a simple failure of communication has occurred. Thus the conditions needed to establish the presence of tacit consent eliminate the possibility of simple, nonspecific voting in favor of some political institutions, without the particularity required for explicit consent to the hazardous practices in question. After citing the problems inherent in John Locke's position on this question, Simmons adds that "calling consent 'tacit' on my account, specifies its mode of expression, not its lack of expression."[22]

Locke, Simmons argues, was confused about "acts of enjoyment" in one's country, such as enjoying public highways, police protection, and the like on the one hand, and "signs of consent," on the other. Because of this confusion, Locke believed that one gave "tacit consent" to one's government simply because one used and enjoyed a country's amenities. Similarly, some argue that if the enjoyment of some features of a system implies tacit consent for the system in all its activities, including hazardous ones, then by enjoying certain features of our modern, Western, technological lifestyle we thereby give consent to any and all side effects that ensue. Unfortunately this position is as confused as that of Locke, Simmons argues.[23]

Moreover, there are certain things to which we cannot consent in our social and political lives. Enslavement is a clear example. Humans are created free and only acquire the obligations of a nation's citizen through (explicit) consent. But although consent is a powerful tool in general, its power does not extend to relinquishing one's "inalienable" rights, such as the right to life or to freedom itself; the right to self-defense cannot be abdicated. Thomas Hobbes says, "A man cannot lay down the right of resisting them that assault him by force to take away his life."[24]

Simmons says that Immanuel Kant argues for a similar position as well:

> Kant holds that "no contract could put a man into the class of domestic animals which we use at will for any kind of service"; that is because "every man has inalienable rights which he cannot give up even if he would."[25]

Kant holds human life to have infinite value, and he believes that humans cannot affect (or permit others to affect) their physical integrity for any advantage or any other consideration. Hence it may be argued that the human rights that represent and support these inalienable human goods, such as life, freedom, and physical integrity, cannot be transferred or set aside, even if *explicit* consent were present. In this case there is a solid historical and theoretical basis for the somewhat novel position I am advancing in support of criminalizing those activities that represent an attack on our physical being.

To be sure, it is permissible and not immoral to trade off some of our freedom, in exchange for wages, provided we consent and that respect for our humanity is present in the transaction, or for a great common ideal (say, the defense of our common freedom from enslavement), or to engage in warfare in our own country's defense. Not all cases are so clear-cut that they evidently fall in either one camp (of permissible activities) or the other (of activities that represent an immoral trade-off); indeed, some, or perhaps even all, workplace activities normally entail at least some risk of harm. Even a philosophy professor who must drive her car or walk to her teaching institution exposes herself to some risk of traffic mishaps. If she were to remain at home and teach from her house, those risks would be avoided. But inactivity and a sedentary lifestyle are at least as hazardous to one's health.

In contrast, the public health threats considered here, whether directly posed by environmental conditions or indirectly caused by circumstances due to environmental disintegrity and degradation, are the sort of severe threats epidemiologists document;[26] they are not the occasional or possible chance happenings one may encounter in the circumstances outlined in the previous paragraph. The health threats I have in mind are of three kinds:

1. Health threats that seriously impair our natural capabilities (e.g., changes in our normal reproductive, intellectual, emotional, or immune systems)
2. Health threats that pose an imminent danger of death to individuals or groups
3. Health threats including long-term, delayed, and mutagenic effects; like the reproductive effects in (1), there are threats to our *species*, as well as to the affected individuals

These three types of effects have an undeniably negative impact on our rights, both human and legal, and we will consider these further, in order to understand why the risk thesis should be rejected.

Risks, Harms, and Rights

W. N. Hohfeld describes four forms of legal rights: claim rights, rights as privilege or liberty, rights as power, and rights as immunity.[27] It is primarily the last form that concerns us, although where immunity rights are present, claim rights or liberty rights, for instance, may be present as well.

Hohfeld's discussion is primarily intended to clarify the meaning and scope of various judicial terms in common use and their relation to one another, in order to understand the "deeper unity" present in the law: He says, "In short the deeper the analysis, the greater becomes one's perception of fundamental unity and harmony in the law."[28] When we turn to his discussion of immunities, both the cases and the examples he cites show that the concept may not be the most appropriate for our purpose. In a section on immunities and disabilities, he says:

> A right is one's affirmative claim against another, and a privilege is one's freedom from the right or claim of another. Similarly, a power is one's affirmative "control" over a given legal relation as against another, whereas an *immunity* is one's freedom from the legal power or "control" of another, as regards some legal relation.[29] [Emphasis added]

As an example of immunity, Hohfeld cites "exemption from taxation" as a better and more accurate term than "privilege." Hence, the meaning he proposes appears somewhat different from a concept used to refer to the right to freedom from bodily harm. A better way to introduce the sort of "right" appropriate to our argument may be one of the "personal rights," that is, the "rights of bodily safety and freedom." Hohfeld adds that it is "the duty of all of us not to interfere with our neighbors' lawful freedom." This is one of the "primitive rights"; it may also be termed "the right not to be interfered with."[30]

Thomson accepts the Hohfeldian framework, which includes the correlativity between rights and duties, but she rejects the risk thesis, as stated earlier. She may base her rejection on the problem of "thresholds" and question the limits of both probability and gravity of harms as factors of the risk thesis.[31] As Thomson rightly argues, it is problematic to identify *the* harm in many cases. She offers an example. A log left on a highway may well present a risk of harm to someone, but we have no certainty that harm will befall anyone and no information about the possible gravity of such a harm. We can begin here to note the parallel between the example she offers of a log left on a highway[32] and that of risky environmental exposures or changes. She notes that we cannot be sure of several points, and this affects our acceptance of the risk thesis. These uncertainties are primarily (1) who is likely to be passing by and tripping over the log and (2) the precise harm such person or persons may incur, as these may range from very minor to quite grave, depending on circumstances. We might envision icy road conditions and an elderly pedestrian or, at the other extreme, a clear, empty roadway and an athletic young person, who would quickly get up with little or no harm.

In the case of environmental harms, if we accept the risk thesis, we need not specify or prove that process X producing substance Y has actually harmed someone, before claiming that corporation Z (by engaging in process X) is liable, through Y, for the harm produced. This represents the major current problem for those who are harmed: the required proof of harm is often unavailable or unclear. The problems of environmental harm lie in (1) science's lack of predictive capacities; (2) the synergistic and cumulative effects of other contributory causes to the harm; (3) the lack of sustained research to sufficiently support (2); (4) the accelerated introduction of substances, products, and processes, which further reduces the availability of research, as in (3); (5) the difficulty of establishing clear thresholds, in the face of (1), (2), and (3); and (6) the existence of harms that develop and manifest themselves slowly over time (such as cancers). And this list, lengthy as it is, is only a partial list addressing only presently acknowledged problems.[33]

However, both Ellis and Thomson agree on one issue: if an agreed threshold of harm is reached, then the risk violates a right. The difficulties listed above show clearly how hard it is to distinguish between a risk of harm that is plausible or probable and one that is not. It is equally difficult to separate a minor harm from a significant one. It is also hard to indicate who, specifically, is "put at risk." In fact, from an environmental point of view, the level of harm inflicted may vary. For instance, fetuses, pregnant women, and older people may all encounter a greater risk from exposure to a substance than young adult males. It is equally impossible to specify precisely who may be at risk, as some environmental hazards cause harms far from from where they occurred.

An example of the latter can be found in some of the recent cholera pandemics. Rita Colwell showed the connection between environmental degradation (engendered by such practices as deforestation) global climate changes, ocean warming, the extraordinary growth of plankton in the oceans, and the way this growth fosters the spread of the E. coli bacterium from one continent to the other:

> Cholera offers an excellent example of how greater understanding of environmental factors allows us to understand the disease better, not only its virulence but . . . its transmission and epidemiology.[34]

In this case, it would not be possible to point to one perpetrator, at *a* single location, much less to designate specific persons as victims. In response to Thomson, Ellis argues one aspect of these issues:

> Is it merely that it is indeterminate who is put at risk? If this simply means that it is hard, perhaps impossible, to find out who is put at risk, this is true, but irrelevant. If I illegitimately drop a bomb on a city, and it is impossible to determine whom, exactly, I killed, this does not imply that I did not

violate anyone's rights; I violated the rights of all those I killed, whoever they may have been.[35]

Other conceptual problems may include the following: (1) too many people may have claims against those who impose risks; (2) the risk exposure may not actually cause harm (I dropped a bomb, but many were in an air shelter); and (3) such a thesis may commit us to "absurd consequences," for example, "every time you drive your automobile you violate the rights of all those whom you put at risk, no matter how small the risk." Finally, Ellis adds, we could reject such objections as the last one by saying that "permission, in a democratic society, has been obtained in advance."[36]

From the point of view of environmental hazards, this is the crux of the problem. Does living in a democracy, even in a Western industrialized country with the lifestyle common to our society, mean giving *implicit* consent to risk exposure or to the abandonment of our rights to security from harm? It does not mean giving "tacit consent," as shown earlier. Most of the arguments against tacit consent also show that some rights may not be relinquished, not even to one's legitimate government (except in special cases, such as self-defense on behalf of one's own country, for instance, or perhaps to save another's life through a kidney donation). It is certainly immoral and impermissible to do so for economic advancement, even for one's own economic benefit. Yet this thesis, however implausible, is implicit in Ellis's question, and it is often assumed in business ethics literature[37] by those who take for granted that "hazards" (unspecified) are the price one pays for technological advances and for modern progress in general.[38] Although we consider in some detail the reach and the problems of local, national, and international environmental laws in chapter 8, the difficulties manifested by present democratic institutions are taken up in the next section, in connection with John Rawls's argument about the "law of peoples."

Risks, Rights, and Democracy

Rawls has recently argued that a "law of peoples" can be drawn from his theory of justice and that a "social contract doctrine is universal in its reach." He also argues that both are not only compatible with but even dependent on a doctrine of human rights, as these represent an integral part of a society's "common good conception of justice." The law, in such societies, must "at least uphold such basic rights as the right to life and security, to personal property, and elements of the rule of law."[39] For our purpose, the most important element mentioned here is the "right to life and security." The Canadian Charter of Rights refers to this as "the right to life and the security of persons." According to Rawls, it might seem that both human and civil rights could be supported and in fact identified with the practices and the ideals of democratic institutions. Yet in Western democracies as well as in less-developed countries, it does not appear that environmental hazards and risks have been controlled or eliminated on the basis of general human rights to freedom from harm.

It is important to understand why this is so, and a good place to start is by considering a situation in which democracy, civil rights, and due process are invoked in order to demonstrate the "right" way to deal with the hazards of technology transfers to Third World countries. After listing statistics about deaths related to the chemical industry's operation and marketing, Shrader-Frechette argues that corporations "have an obligation to guarantee equal protection from risk across national boundaries" rather than employ what she terms the "isolationist strategy."[40] Corporations cannot restrict their moral and legal restraints to the activities they practice in their country of origin. Yet Shrader-Frechette admits that "a rational risk response may require political activity that is nothing less than revolutionary."[41] But at this time, both those in developing countries and even those in minority communities in Western democracies are treated in ways that infringe on their rights: both are often "isolated" from moral consideration.[42]

The problem is that there is no proof of intent to harm on the part of corporations or other institutions involved in these practices. In fact, if questioned, they may respond with several arguments in support of their activities. These are (1) the social progress argument; (2) the countervailing benefit argument; (3) the consent argument; and (4) the reasonable-possibility argument. But argument (1) works only if we accept the subordination of individual and group rights to some (unproven) aggregated consequentialist good such as "progress," a doubtful notion as it stands because of the gravity of its side effects. Argument (2) is problematic as well: even benefits ought not to be promoted at any cost. Shrader-Frechette says, "The argument is that a bloody loaf of bread is sometimes better than no loaf at all, that a dangerous job is preferable to no job, and that food riddled with banned pesticides is better than no food at all."[43] This argument is hard to defend even on utilitarian grounds, and it is impossible to support on Kantian grounds and from the standpoint of human rights. The consent argument (3) has been discussed and is discussed in detail in the next section. For now it is sufficient to note that the "free, informed consent" to which corporations appeal in defense of their limited responsibility is seldom if ever available from those who are "financially strapped and poorly educated." Argument (4) suggests that risks and harms imposed are not preventable without "heroic" commitments that cannot, in fairness, be demanded of any corporation. But if there are human rights such as the right to the nonimposition of cancer, then heroism is not required, only the simple adherence to morality.

So far only physical, quantifiable harms have been discussed, without even envisaging the possibility of "social" or "group harms."[44] The implication of this discussion is that it is necessary though not sufficient to introduce democratic procedures and due process globally, in order to attempt to prevent the unjust imposition of harms on the vulnerable and disempowered. As we have seen, Rawls also argues for the extension of the constructivist principles for justice as fairness that apply to "the basic structure of a closed and self-contained democratic society" to an ideal of justice and human rights through a "law of people" in general.[45] His starting point is the democratic, liberal society where he supports the "egalitarian features of the fair value of political liberties, of fair equality of opportunity, and of the difference principle," as argued in his landmark book, *A Theory of Justice.*[46] On the basis of this extension, he indicates the existence of an institutionalized respect for human rights, and views it as a condition for permitting any country to participate in the "law of nations." These are viewed as the bedrock of any conception of justice, extended, as it were, from the starting point of appropriate basic principles within a self-contained democracy to the international arena. I now turn to an examination of the real import of democracy when we consider risks and harms.

Democracy entails that collective decisions be based on open acceptance of certain choices and preferences over others and that these choices be reached through majority votes. But even in the countries where democratic systems are in power, it appears that the system is powerless to prevent the infringement of human rights through the imposition of harms to human life and health, at least through environmental means. Why does this happen? First, it is clear that democracy tends to further "the interests of the majority at the expense of the minority,"[47] despite the existence of safeguards in law (for example, the Bill of Rights in the United States). Second, and even harder to address, is the fact that in the face of global hazards that affect everyone on earth, there are still limits to the reach of democratic powers. For instance, in border issues that often give rise to violent conflicts, democracy is powerless, because citizens on either side of the disputed border can vote only within the limits of their national area.[48] Further, the immensely powerful Western multinational corporations, which represent the source of many of these hazards, are not subject to democratic decision making, either in their country of origin or in their (less-developed) host countries.[49]

Hence self-contained democracies are not sufficient to mitigate these risks, and it seems urgent to establish respect and accept a risk thesis that would serve to link more clearly the existence of hazardous products and practices and the clear duties of all not to infringe on the rights to "life and security of persons," through a "law of peoples."[50] This would help not only those who belong to the same community and are part of the same democratic nation, but also all those who might be affected by these risks anywhere else.

Yet it is unclear just how democratic systems, even if globally implemented, would help to solve the problem. Now it may make sense to say that a minority who lost out on its political choice must, under a democracy's rule, learn to live with its loss, as it occurred through fair means, and a fair opportunity exists to change the situation for the future. But it would be much harder to say that all those whose preference was not on the winning side must be equally stoic in the face of unchosen, unconsented, and uncompensated harms, which a majority chose to impose upon them.[51] As Alan Gewirth would argue, the imposition of grave harms cannot be supported on moral grounds, as it constitutes a gross infringement of human rights.[52]

Thus we can drive a wedge between democratic political systems and the absolute support of human rights through a reconsideration of the imposition of risks and harms. Rex Martin discusses the relation between democracy and rights in *A System of Rights*, and he argues that civil rights should have priority status:

> In sum, the priority of civil rights holds over aggregative considerations insofar as those considerations concern policies for civil rights directly, or concern such rights in relation to other social policy matters.[53]

Martin's argument is that in a system of rights, "external checks over and beyond those afforded by the representative principle are required to keep majority rule from mischief." He admits, "representative democracy has some tendencies to the same abuse [as "class-interested majority rule"], and therefore needs additional controls."[54]

The example we considered—hazardous technology transfers to impoverished, uninformed, and unconsenting Third World people— showed a case where the input of moral theories, utilities, rights, and justice was deemed necessary to redress the injustices perpetrated because of the lack of due process and democratic procedures in those countries. But the question now is not whether the consideration of these moral theories is necessary, but whether the input of democracy is *sufficient* to ensure the presence of those moral considerations, especially the primacy of individual and group rights. The main problems with democracy seem to arise in connection with consent to the risk of harm. Should a majority have the right to consent, through their vote, to practices that might impose the risk of harm on defeated minorities? And even if we should answer this question in the affirmative, does anybody in a democracy, whether in the majority or the minority, have the right to consent even to their own harm? Both these questions need to be discussed.

Speaking of environmental justice, D. Wigley and K. Shrader-Frechette say, "The doctrine of free informed consent, an important part of the traditional American value system, likewise provides a foundation for environmental justice."[55] They proceed to analyze the concept of "informed consent" in the context of biomedical ethics, noting that the concept has not been used in either environmental or technological ethics. The following four criteria are suggested to indicate the presence of informed consent:

> the risk imposers must disclose full information about the threat; potential victims must be competent to evaluate it; they must understand the danger; and they must voluntarily accept it.[56]

In the light of our earlier discussion of democratic choices and the lack of precision in both scientific information about specific harmful effects and the possible geographical spread of risks, several other questions may be raised. One might be, How and from whom should consent be sought? Another problem might be that even if we could circumscribe an area where all inhabitants could be polled on such a question, the provided information may not be sufficient to guarantee that the four criteria are met, as Frank Ingelfinger, for instance, argues in "Informed (But Uneducated) Consent."[57] The doctrine of informed consent in the biomedical setting is intended to be directed at the interaction between a health care provider and a patient or, at most, a group of patients. Hence the consent criteria cannot be readily applied to great numbers of people from whom the risk imposers are separated by location, language, cultural background, and the like.

But in that case, the imposition of wide-ranging environmental risks and harms does not fit the informed consent model, as it is more like experimentation on unconsenting subjects, contrary to the Nuremberg Code. The problem is that often grave environmental hazards are, by their very nature, impossible to contain.

So far I have argued that unless we deal with such specifics as environmental justice at a certain location, for instance, the consent criteria cannot properly be applied. But even this argument assumes that, at least in theory, people can consent to harms if they are free to choose, are fully informed, and understand the full extent of the harm to which they are exposed. But this belief is not beyond critique. For instance, we can object to this assumption on Kantian grounds. Moral action implies universalizability and reversibility, and it precludes the use of any autonomous person as means to anyone's ends, even her own. Therefore, as it would be impermissible, on Kantian grounds, to commit suicide, even for our own "good" (for example, for the cessation of excruciating pain from a terminal condition), so too would it be impermissible to accept a trade-off, such as consenting to cancer, to obtain a hazardous job. Hence it can be argued that

> the Categorical Imperative is formulated in such a way that consent can never be relevant in informing us of what our duties to others are. Thus one is precluded from even entertaining the notion that consent would be a defeasibility condition of the Categorical Imperative.[58]

Although Kant's position on suicide is controversial, it is clearly his position. Kant is somewhat closer to contemporary thought on not using any part of ourselves merely as means, even for a personally desired end. He is quite explicit on this point: we cannot consent to a sale or trade that would turn autonomous humans into slaves, for instance, or that might foster the exchange of bodily parts for money.[59] Thus, we can conclude that "consent" to harms is based on weak arguments both from the standpoint of political theory and from that of Kant's moral doctrine.

Moreover, it can also be claimed that, in general, utilitarian arguments should only be considered *after* human rights and justice principles. In that case, if consent to harm is not possible in principle, or if it is questionable even if obtained, then even the introduction of truly democratic conditions and due process will not be sufficient to mitigate, let alone to justify, the wide-ranging imposition of environmental risks and harms on large numbers of unspecified persons. In sum, I have argued that we should, as Ellis suggests, accept as necessary the risk thesis that Thomson rejects, because it can be argued that although not all rights are primary, the right to life and freedom from harm is primary among them.

In contrast, the usually accepted connection between primary human rights and democracy can be shown to be less strong than it is generally thought to be. In that case, our next problem is: how are we to prevent harms and to restrain those who impose risks when even the "best," most enlightened form of governance (that is, democracy) may not be sufficient to accomplish the goal? To attempt an answer, I return in the final section to biomedical ethics and the moral and legal categories used to remedy the possible spread of infectious diseases.

Risk, Rights, and Consent: A Lesson from the White Death

I have noted that biomedical ethics may not offer the best analogy for questions of consent arising from environmental and technological hazards. We could not ensure that full disclosure would reach everyone who might be at risk and communicate clearly and understandably the extent and gravity of the harm. Moreover, neither risk imposers nor risk assessors could accurately predict the probability and gravity of the harms. Yet uncertainties, endemic to scientific discourse involving a large range of variables, added to the unpredictability about location, gravity of exposure, and other specifics, ought not to force us to reject with Thomson the risk thesis.

And if we hold fast to both (1) the primacy of rights, especially the right to life and to freedom from harm and (2) the risk thesis itself, then we need to seek another avenue to ensure that rights are protected, given the failure of present democratic institutions to guarantee appropriate restraints to risk imposers. The resurgence of many infectious diseases assumed to have been conquered and eliminated, such as tuberculosis, may indicate a possible avenue for public policy. Tuberculosis is making a comeback in North America and other parts of the world; resistant now to most antibiotics, and harder than ever to control because of population density and other modern conditions, it brings with it threat of the "White Death." Tuberculosis is highly contagious and requires very little contact to spread, unlike, for instance, sexually transmitted diseases such as AIDS. It is sufficient to sit next to an infected person or to breathe the same air in order to be infected. Tuberculosis is curable, but it requires a lengthy course of treatment. Many people who want to get well decide to abandon the treatment when the worst symptoms subside, even though they are still highly contagious.[60] If these persons are not prepared to persevere with their treatment and yet want to continue to lead normal lives, interacting with others, they are endangering not only their close associates but also the general public.[61] The question is what to do when the course, treatment, and hazards of the disease are fully explained to contagious persons, and they understand and yet refuse to comply with either treatment or restraints. It appears that some action must be taken in defense of public safety.

As in the case of contagious childhood diseases, what is necessary is the use of quarantines and other forms of involuntary restraints and treatment. The starting point is the realization that tuberculosis is a threat to public health par excellence. As far as I know, however, only New York City has clear-cut legislation in this regard. The following course of action is supported by this new legislation:

> The City Department of Public Health may order a person removed to a hospital or detained for treatment there only if two conditions are met. First, the Department must have found the tuberculosis to be active and without treatment likely to be transmitted to others. . . . Second, the Department must have found the subject of the order unable or unwilling to undergo less restrictive treatment.[62]

These requirements are based on "epidemiological or clinical evidence, X-rays or laboratory tests," and the final decision to commit rests with the courts, as it does with the commitment procedures for the mentally ill.[63] Note that in order to restrain the liberty of risk imposers in this context, it is not necessary to "prove" in a court of law that they have harmed someone: it is sufficient to demonstrate that they and their activities are hazardous and potentially harmful to the public. Depending on the response of the infectious person to requests that he be treated, the interests of public health may be served by civil confinement for treatment, which in turn may be justified as preventing harm to the public through "reckless endangerment."[64] In fact, jail could justifiably be used for anyone who might resist the suggested civil confinement for treatment.

How can this situation help us to conceptualize the problem of imposing restraints on those endangering the public through environmentally hazardous practices? First, we need to note that there are public threats that cannot be controlled through democratic institutions, that is, through *voluntary* public choices. One may counter that even the imposition of forced restraints is embedded in a general system of individual rights and democratic institutions. That is, of course, correct. But it is important to understand that rights to life and health are primary and should be put ahead of other choices. This perspective allows us to view environmental endangerment as something that needs to be controlled directly, and even by coercive means, rather than as something that is simply to be limited only by cost/benefit analyses or by a counting of heads and a weighing of preferences. In order to explain detention in medical cases, M. Davis says, "The alternative to detention is the moral equivalent of letting someone, without adequate justification, walk crowded streets with a large bomb that could go off at any moment."[65]

In the White Death threat, we are not sure of the gravity of the harm imposed; we cannot anticipate with any certainty just who is at risk from the infected person; we cannot be sure of precise numbers of potentially affected persons. We have information about risks and harms, but we cannot present a specific infected person or persons as "proof" to justify placing the risk imposer under criminal restraints. The only reason we can offer for imposing criminal or civil restraints is reckless endangerment, without being able to point to any one person who might have been harmed.

In fact, it is in order *not* to have victims that we are justified in invoking civil and criminal restraints. Contrast this preventive approach with that of corporate bodies who expose persons in the immediate vicinity of their hazardous operations to risks of harm, yet demand not proof of endangerment but clear proof of actual harm before they are even prepared to compensate for, let alone to consider discontinuing, their hazardous activities.

Much more could be said about this topic, and it is fair to say that there are disanalogies as well as analogies between cases in biomedical ethics, allowing justification for restraints in cases of reckless endangerment, and the imposition of environmental risks and harms. Perhaps the most problematic difference is that while the restraint of an individual will affect only her life (and provide a much greater benefit in the process), restraints of corporate activities on a grand scale might have grave repercussions for all stakeholders, not only for the corporation. This question is addressed in some detail in the final chapters, although global economic "advancement" was also discussed earlier in this chapter. Nevertheless, it seems that there are enough parallels to make a reasonable case for considering seriously the approach I suggest, as all others employed so far appear to have met with scant success.

The Good and the Community: Laws Restraining Choice

Eternal vigilance is the Price of liberty.

Thomas Jefferson

The argument I have proposed essentially contrasts individualism with communitarianism. But the latter is viewed as a special case: the case of a community of life, whereby each individual's personal integrity and the ecogical integrity of her habitat are so completely intertwined that no question can be raised about whether the value of integrity in each case is intrinsic or instrumental. Holmes Rolston makes this point eloquently in his philosophical analysis of "biological immunity":

The organismic integrity protected by immunity has to fit into an ecosystemic integrity. An organism without a habitat is soon extinct. The immune system is zealously defending the self, but all the while the ecosystem in which this self lives is the fundamental unit of development and survival. There are no immune organisms, period; there are only immune organisms-in-ecosystems.[66]

From the perspective of immunity, our strong individual rights to life and self-defense can easily be extended to our habitat, in line with Rolston's proposed definition of our organisms as organisms-in-ecosystems. Hence, the invoking of stronger, changed laws appears entirely defensible on grounds of self-defense. These laws must replace laws that place economically driven, unintended harms, slowly unfolding over time, in a separate category, so that only clear, quickly evident, and intended harms are deemed criminal. Attacks on bodily integrity and our genetic capacities are also crimes; they might be defined as attacks on our capacities with a small c, embedded in the capital C, or the capacities of ecological integrity. In my previous work, the collaborative definition of integrity (see chapter 1) used the letter C to represent the undiminished capacities of an ecosystem in its unmanipulated state, "following its natural evolutionary trajectory, free as much as possible, from human interference or stress."

To better understand the sort of crime described in these "attacks," we may invoke the difference between premeditated murder and manslaughter. It seems intuitively true to say that pain and suffering aside, no one has the right to remove someone else's organs for his own purposes, no matter how "good" the perpetrator may perceive his purpose to be. It would seem equally intuitively true to add that it is equally impermissible to intrusively interfere with the natural functions of these organs. When the damage caused is more than damage to one individual and becomes, as in the cases researched by Colborn,[67] damage to reproductive capacities, to the next generations, hence to humanity in general, it may be regarded as attempted genocide, deserving even more than the punishment of the laws of the perpetrators' country: it requires that they be accountable to and punished by a world tribunal.

Surely if there is a good that is not in doubt, it is our right to have our own physical and intellectual capacities undiminished by others. This common good is neither based on the preferences of any one culture nor limited to any relative viewpoint, but instead is compatible with a great variety of cultural goods and ideals. Hence, I propose our undiminished capacities (c) as a basic good that permits with varying degrees of appropriateness a number of societal coercive actions, parallel to those needed to support the ecological integrity (C) required for (c) to thrive. This good may also be compatible with moral theories such as the Kantian respect for autonomously chosen ends and the Rawlsian emphasis on fairness and the difference principle. These possible connections need to be examined in some detail. In chapter 7 I return to the connections between my approach and Kantian doctrine.

What does Rawls say about the good? His understanding may raise problems:

> That we have one conception of the good rather than another is not relevant from a moral standpoint. In acquiring it we are influenced by the same sort of contingencies that leads us to rule out a knowledge of our sex and class.[68]

The defense of life through individual and systemic integrity may not be in conflict with a variety of conceptions of the good. But the wholesale acceptance of the possibility of any and all such conceptions of the good may well conflict with the spirit of the principle of integrity, in the same sense that utilitarianism also does. Michael Sandel examines the "status of the good" in Rawls. He argues:

> For Rawls, utilitarianism goes wrong not in conceiving the good as the satisfaction of arbitrarily given desires, undifferentiated as to worth—for justice as fairness shares in this, but only in being indifferent to the way these consummations are spread across individuals.[69]

Although Rawls, in Sandel's estimation, departs from utilitarianism, the remaining connection with "the satisfaction of arbitrarily given desires" is at best compatible with the primacy of life as the necessary prerequisite to the existence of desires. But it is not compatible with the nonnegotiable status of the principle of integrity (PI). Some may argue, for instance, that the desire to accept a trade-off between diminished health, life span, or genetic capacities and economic advantage, if well understood, is legitimate for a society. Some may also argue that this is precisely what is happening in affluent northwestern democracies today and therefore it is only the *distributive* aspect of this "contract" that should be scrutinized from the standpoint of morality, not its existence.

In contrast, the PI takes a strongly Kantian position in not permitting such trade-offs, whether or not they are fairly distributed across society (see chapter 7). The basis of the principle of integrity is the value of integrity, which encompasses the infinite value of all life, life-support systems, and individual and systemic capacities, now and into the future. This excludes the possibility of legitimate trade-offs and places those concerns at the forefront of both morality and public policy. The primacy of this value explains the emphasis on the need for national laws and for global regulative mechanisms to protect it as an absolute, rather than treating it as one value among many, subject to public choice or majoritarian preferences. The holistic perspective is absolutely vital here: life-support systems cannot be protected in a piecemeal fashion. When hazards travel not only between countries but also between continents, national policies clearly will be insufficient. Global regulations and tight global security will also be required, in order to prevent the present techno-hazard transfer between northwestern countries and southeastern ones, and into economically depressed minority areas in the Northwest.

Therefore, to affirm the urgent need for strict global regulations for the protection of public life, health, and integrity is not to tar all corporations, good and bad, with the same brush. It is intended to recognize the primacy of individual and ecological integrity and to attempt to coordinate and institutionalize principles and ideals that are already, for the most part, present in global regulations and in national and international laws. In essence, it is to recognize the role of a holistic perspective in public decision making.[70]

Public decision making assumes the existence of democratic institutions, thus reinforcing the point made here: democracy is necessary, but it is not sufficient to protect all life from grave environmental threats. The reasons for this claim are found in the social consequences of our corporate and consumerist culture and the impact of both on our "democratic" institutions. The problem then is to be found in the interface between social interaction and issues concerning property. In the history of social philosophy many arguments can be found about property, from Plato and Aristotle to Aquinas, Rousseau, Hobbes, and Locke. C. B. Macpherson, in his study of the political theory of the seventeenth century, argues that "political thought [was] fundamentally flawed."[71] Commenting, Andrew Reeve writes that "Macpherson recommended a new understanding of property to replace the defective conception he identified in the foundation of modern thought."[72]

The fundamental problem lies in the "possessive and individualist assumptions appropriate to an age of rising market society."[73] We see the results of these assumptions in the liberal individualism supported by present-day democracy.

In his work on democratic theory, H. B. Mayo examines the "broad principles characteristic of a democratic political system." They are the result of the application of these principles to popular government or policy makers effectively controlled by the electorate."[74] But unless a further test of the system's legitimacy is applied, the result may be a "democratic system compatible with any conception of the purposes of government or the nature of its policies."[75] As noted in our earlier discussion of Rawls the good is not and cannot be specified a priori within his theory. Mayo's test for the justification of any political system goes beyond its "constituent principles," because, he adds, "its social performance must also be considered. Institutions are always judged by what is accomplished through them."[76]

This problem is also discussed at some length in the work of Paul Gilbert,[77] with regard to the possible legitimacy of uprisings against a regime, or even of terrorism. I have discussed the failures within Western democracies' "accomplishments," and on that basis I have argued that additional regulations and limits must be developed as correctives, given the gravity of our environmental crisis. In chapter 9, the principles that ought to govern these regulations are discussed in detail. In the next chapter, I address the need for a holistic approach to all aspects of the technological/corporate enterprise.

Notes

1. Lynda Hurst, "The Global Guru" (T. Homer-Dixon) in *The Star* (July 20, 1996), p. C1; Thomas Homer-Dixon, "On the Threshold, Environmental Changes as Causes of Acute Conflict," *International Security* 16, 2 (Fall 1991): 76–116; see also Thomas Homer-Dixon, "Environmental Scarcity and Violent Conflict: Evidence from Cases," *International Security* 19, 1 (Summer 1994): 5–40.

2. Theo Colborn, Dianne Dumanoski, and John Peterson Myers, *Our Stolen Future* (New York: Dutton, 1996).

3. Theo Colborn, "Plenary Address" to International Association of Great Lakes Researchers, Erindale College, Toronto, Ontario, May 27, 1966; see also A. Nikiforuk, "Arctic Pollution: Poisons for a Pristine Land," *The Globe and Mail* (July 20, 1996), p. D8.

4. C. Gaylord and E. Bell, "Environmental Justice: A National Priority," in *Faces of Environmental Racism: The Global Equity Issues,* ed. L. Westra and P. Wenz (Lanham, MD: Rowman & Littlefield, 1995), pp. 29–40.

5. Westra and Wenz, *The Faces of Environmental Racism*; see also R. Bullard, *Dumping in Dixie* (Boulder, CO: Westview Press, 1994); R. Bullard, "Environmental Decisionmaking," in *Faces of Environmental Racism*, ed. L. Westra and P. Wenz, pp. 3–28.

6. David Korten, *When Corporations Rule the World* (West Hartford, CT: Kumarian Press, 1995), p. 67.

7. Peter A. French, *Collective and Corporate Responsibility* (New York: Columbia University Press, 1984).

8. David Korten, *When Corporations Rule the World*, p. 48; see also Thomas Homer-Dixon, "Environmental Scarcity and Violent Conflict: Evidence from Cases," *International Security* 19, 1 (Summer 1994): 5–40.

9. David Crocker, personal discussion, August 1996.

10. D. A. Brown, "The Role of Law in Sustainable Development and Environmental Protection Decision Making," in *Sustainable Development: Science, Ethics and Public Policy* (Dordrecht, The Netherlands: Kluwer, 1995), pp. 64–76.

11. E. Ayres, "The Expanding Shadow Economy," *World Watch* (July/August 1996): 11–23.

12. Ayres, "Expanding Shadow Economy."

13. Ayres, "Expanding Shadow Economy."

14. L. Westra, *An Environmental Proposal for Ethics: The Principle of Integrity* (Lanham, MD: Rowman & Littlefield, 1994), especially chapter 3.

15. Holmes Rolston III, "Immunity in Natural History," *Perspectives in Biology and Medicine* 3 (Spring 1996): 353–72; see also L. Westra, "Integrity, Health and Sustainability: Environmentalism without Racism," in *The Science of the Total Environment* (Oxford, England: Elsevier, 1996).

16. Henry Kendall, Meeting of the "Society" for Ecosystem Health, Plenary Address, Toronto, June 5, 1997.

17. J. J. Thomson, *The Realm of Rights* (Cambridge, MA: Harvard University Press, 1990).

18. Anthony Ellis, "Risks and Rights," paper presented at the American Philosophical Association Central Meeting, April 1995, Chicago.

19. Brown, "The Role of Law."

20. A. John Simmons, *Moral Principles and Political Obligations* (Princeton: Princeton University Press, 1979).

21. Simmons, *Moral Principles and Political Obligations*, pp. 80–81.

22. Simmons, *Moral Principles and Political Obligations*, p. 81.

23. Simmons, *Moral Principles and Political Obligations*, pp. 83–95.

24. Thomas Hobbes, *Leviathan* (New York: Bobbs-Merrill, 1958).

25. Simmons, *Moral Principles and Political Obligations*, p. 67; see also Immanuel Kant, *The Metaphysical Elements of Justice* (New York: Bobbs-Merrill, 1965).

26. A. J. McMichael, "The Health of Persons, Populations, and Planets: Epidemiology Comes Full Circle," in *Epidemiology and Society* (Oxford, England: Epidemiology Resources, 1995).

27. W. N. Hohfeld, *Fundamental Legal Conceptions* (New Haven: Yale University Press, 1923), pp. 35–50.

28. Hohfeld, *Fundamental Legal Conceptions*, p. 64.

29. Hohfeld, *Fundamental Legal Conceptions*, p. 60.

30. Hohfeld, *Fundamental Legal Conceptions*, p. 48.

31. J. DeCew, "Rights and Risks," comments on Ellis, "Risks and Rights," paper read at the American Philosophical Association Central Meeting, Chicago, April 1995.

32. J. J. Thomson, *The Realm of Rights*; see also Ellis, "Risks and Rights."

33. K. Shrader-Frechette, *Risk and Rationality* (Berkeley: University of California Press, 1991); see also Colborn, et al., *Our Stolen Future*.

34. Rita Colwell, "Global Climate and Infectious Disease: The Cholera Paradigm," President's Lecture, February 10, 1996, American Association for the Advancement of Science in *Science 274* (December 20, 1996): pp. 2025–31.

35. Ellis, "Risks and Rights."

36. Ellis, "Risks and Rights."

37. Milton Friedman, "The Social Responsibility of Business Is to Increase Its Profits," in *Ethical Issues in Business*, ed. T. Donaldson and P. Werhane (Englewood Cliffs, NJ: Prentice-Hall, 1993), pp. 249–54.

38. Emmanueal G. Mesthene, "The Role of Technology in Society," in *Technology and the Future*, 5th ed., ed. A. Teich (New York: St. Martin's Press, 1990), pp. 77–99.

39. J. Rawls, "The Law of Peoples," in *On Human Rights* (New York: Harper-Collins, 1993), pp. 41–82; see also J. Rawls, "Justice as Fairness: Political not Metaphysical," in *Justice and Economic Distribution*, 2d ed., ed. J. Arthur and W. B. Shaw (Englewood Cliffs, NJ: Prentice-Hall, 1991), pp. 320–39.

40. Shrader-Frechette, *Risk and Rationality*, p. 148.

41. Shrader-Frechette, *Risk and Rationality*, p. 147.

42. Westra, *Faces of Environmental Racism*, pp. 113–34.

43. Shrader-Frechette, *Risk and Rationality*, p. 149.

44. Thomas Simon, "Group Harm," *Journal of Social Philosophy* 26, 3 (Winter 1995): 123–39.

45. Rawls, "The Law of Peoples."

46. J. Rawls, *A Theory of Justice* (Cambridge, MA: Harvard University Press, 1971), pp. 284–93.

47. Paul Gilbert, *Terrorism, Security and Nationality: An Introductory Study in Applied Political Philosophy* (London: Routledge, 1994).

48. Gilbert, *Terrorism, Security and Nationality*; see also Westra, *An Environmental Proposal*.

49. L. Westra, "On Risky Business—Corporate Responsibility and Hazardous Products," *Business Ethics Quarterly* 4, 1 (January 1994): 97–110; see also Korten, *When Corporations Rule the World*; Donaldson and Werhane, "Moral Minimums for Multinationals," in *Ethical Issues in Business*, ed. T. Donaldson and P. Werhane, pp. 58–75.

50. Rawls, "The Law of Peoples."

51. L. Westra, "Integrity, Health and Sustainability: Environmentalism without Racism."

52. Alan Gewirth, "Human Rights and the Prevention of Cancer," in *Human Rights* (Chicago: University of Chicago Press, 1982), pp. 181–217.

53. Rex Martin, *A System of Rights* (New York: Oxford University Press, 1993), p. 175.

54. Martin, *A System of Rights*, pp. 175–77.

55. K. Shrader-Frechette and D. Wigley, "Environmental Racism: A Louisiana Case Study," in *Faces of Environmental Racism* by L. Westra, p. 139.

56. Shrader-Frechette and Wigley, "Environmental Racism."

57. Franz L. Ingelfinger, "Informed (But Uneducated) Consent," in *Biomedical Ethics*, ed. Jane Zembaty and Thomas Mappes (New York: McGraw-Hill, 1991), pp. 220–21.

58. C. Barnes, "Consent Theory: Can One Consent to be Harmed?" unpublished paper presented at the University of Windsor, 1996.

59. Immanuel Kant, *Lectures on Ethics*, tr. Louis Infield (Indianapolis: Hackett, 1997), pp. 116–26; 157–60; see also Immanuel Kant, *The Metaphysical Elements of Justice* (New York: Bobbs-Merrill, 1965).

60. M. Davis, "Arresting the White Death: Involuntary Patients, Public Health, and Medical Ethics," paper presented at the American Philosophical

Association Central Meeting, April 1995; "Arresting the White Death: Preventive Detention, Confinement for Treatment, and Medical Ethics," *APA Newsletters* 94, 2 (Spring 1995).

61. "Reckless endangerment" and "endangerment" are terms used in laws. M. Davis, my authority on these issues, cites the New York City Health Code (3-31-93), ch. 11.47 (RCNY: 103039-10312); the Illinois Criminal Code, ch. 38, secs. 4-6 and 12-5 (in "Reckless Conduct"); N.Y. Penal Law 120.25. In Canada, the strongest legislation on consent is under the heading of "Suicide" (Martin's Criminal Code, 1996; 241s.14): "no person is entitled to have death inflicted upon him, and such consent does not affect the criminal responsibility of any person on whom death may be inflicted." "Criminal negligence" is defined in the same code, Park VIII, 5.219(1), as "wanton or reckless disregard for the lives or safety of other persons." This is also discussed under "Causing Harm by Criminal Negligence" (5221). "Everyone who by criminal negligence causes bodily harm to another person is guilty of an indictable offense." This may cause "culpable homicide," defined in 5.222(1) as "when a person causes the death, indirectly, directly, of another person." Finally, "Murder, Manslaughter and Infanticide" (5.229), under "Liability of Party," refers inter alia to "the perpetrator . . . cause[s] bodily harm of a kind likely to result in death and be reckless whether death ensues or not." The Health Promotion and Protection Act (Ontario Law) permits "confinement" through loosely defined steps, and this includes, for infectious diseases, "known and suspected cases." These might lead to court orders for detention and treatment.

62. Davis, "Involuntary Patients."

63. Davis, "Involuntary Patients."

64. Davis, "Involuntary Patients."

65. Davis, "Involuntary Patients."

66. Rolston, "Immunity in Natural History."

67. Colborn, et al., *Our Stolen Future.*

68. J. Rawls, "From Fairness to Goodness," *Philosophical Review* 84 (October 1975): 537.

69. Michael Sandel, *Liberalism and the Limits of Justice* (New York: Cambridge University Press, 1982), p. 166.

70. Brown, "The Role of Law."

71. C. B. Macpherson, as cited in Andrew Reeve, "The Theory of Property: Beyond Private *versus* Common Property," in *Political Theory Today* (Palo Alto, CA: Stanford University Press, 1971), p. 95.

72. Andrew Reeve, "The Theory of Property."

73. Reeve, "The Theory of Property," p. 95.

74. H. B. Mayo, *An Introduction to Democratic Theory* (New York: Oxford University Press, 1960), p. 213.

75. Mayo, *Introduction to Democratic Theory,* p. 213.

76. Mayo, *Introduction to Democratic Theory,* p. 213.

77. Gilbert, *Terrorism, Security and Nationality.*

PART II

4

Why We Need a Nonanthropocentric Environmental Evaluation of Technology for Public Policy

The Ecological Point of View and the Canadian "Fish Wars"

On March 10, 1995, the story appeared on the front page of Canada's national newspaper, *The Globe and Mail*: "Four warning bursts of machine gun fire across the bow brought the Spanish trawler Estai to a halt after a four-hour chase through the foggy Atlantic." The problem was overfishing beyond the 200-mile limit in the Grand Banks off the coast of Newfoundland. When increased national quotas and the use of complex modern fishing technologies internationally reduced the availability of fish in the North Atlantic,[1] the Spanish fishers pushed their trawlers beyond the legal 200-mile limit, thus coming too close to the already depleted waters surrounding the Canadian mainland. The use of gunpower in defense of fish stocks is almost unprecedented in Canadian history, but Newfoundland's premier, Clyde Wells, explained his action. He argued that the Canadians in many fishing villages have watched their communities slowly die as European vessels fished large amounts of cod and flounder from 1988 to 1993 and caused the disappearance of the cod in 1992; they have also seen Spanish vessels take as much as 50,000 tons of turbot over the last three years, in spite of their own 16,300-ton limit (and the Spaniards' own legal limit of only 3,400 tons).

Is this simply a controversy between two nations, a dispute to be settled through dialogue, diplomacy, and negotiations? This view misses the major point of the controversy, captured in the wording on a placard waved in a Newfoundland fishing village by one of the six thousand demonstrators against Spain: This is a World Fishery, not a Spanish One.[2]

83

The "turbot battle" was eventually settled through an international deal between Canadian Fisheries Minister Brian Tobin and the European Community's representatives. It was clearly a *world* issue in the eyes of the Newfoundland fishers, who had already seen the collapse of the cod stocks and the resulting disappearance of their economy and traditional lifestyles. Canada and all other countries must learn to curb their overall economic goals, and even reduce them from previous years' expectations, if they are not prepared to face the extinction of specific fish as well as traditional lifestyles.

The quest for increased profits based on increased quotas, even if they are sought to support traditional lifestyles, is not necessarily desirable. For instance, although natives in the Amazon claim to be living harmoniously with nature (and they are indeed less disruptive to natural processes than commercially exploitive foreign practices in the area), their goals and those of conservation biology do not necessarily mesh.[3] The problem is that native hunters, for instance, may pursue a species to extinction, then move on to exploit another "resource" beyond its capacity to recover.

From the scientific perspective of the ecosystem approach (and of complex-systems theory), there is no guaranteed "safe," commercial, sustainable catch, but there is also no clear linear causality showing the connection between the overfishing of a resource such as cod and its extinction.[4] Such factors as climate changes, increases in UVB rays because of ozone depletion, increased pollution and dumping in the oceans, and toxic rain are all contributing causes. Hence it is not acceptable to argue that because some practice was not followed in past years, the same guidelines should be followed in the future based on earlier quotas. Continued increases in fishing quotas cannot be supported on the available scientific evidence. New fishing technologies will need to be abandoned—for example, gill nets, which Carl Walters terms "one of the more destructive and wasteful fishing gears ever invented."[5]

Further, neither Canada nor any other country should simply focus on the economic aspects of a natural resource as its only value. The value of natural ecosystems far transcends this narrow view; plants and animals all play important parts in the ecosystems in which they live, fulfilling specific functions that will cease if they become extinct or even if their numbers decrease too significantly. For instance, in a discussion of ecosystems and sustainability in fisheries, M. Hammer et al. state, "Whereas species diversity is a property at the population level, the *functional diversity*, what the organisms do and the variety of responses to environmental changes, especially the diverse space and time scales to which organisms react to each other and the environment, is a *property of the ecosystem*."[6] To limit oneself to dealing with the areas where *our* interest lies (areas of ecosystem health, viewed and treated as instrumentally valuable) is to ignore the larger picture and the life-support and benchmark functions of the wild, in landscapes of appropriate geographical size (biomes). Hence, the primary concern must focus on the wild (core) areas, even when sustainability is the issue. Sustainability is here understood as undiminished function capacity, supported by the undiminished structural systems of wild areas of appropriate size.[7] To put it plainly, sustainable agriculture, forestry, and sustainable fisheries make little sense unless sustainability of wild ecosystems is addressed first, and at least in the long term, anticipated and required by most North American and global regulations and treaties, all of which include future generations in their reach. Some will argue that as we lack a precise reference point or baseline for ecosystem integrity, we do not need anything to which we ought to conform or to return environmentally. But we do not need to know the specific composition or the detailed structure of a landscape in order to know when it no longer functions. Because of all-pervasive pollution and environmental degradation, we cannot be assured that any area is "as it should be," meaning that the changes that have occurred (including biodiversity losses) are purely due to its natural trajectory and to nonanthropogenic stresses. But we do know when a system has collapsed, that is, when it has lost its natural capacity to function appropriately for its scale and geographic location. Reed Noss says:

> Ecosystems remain viable only when their processes—nutrient cycling, energy flow, hydrology, disturbance-recovery regimes, predator-prey dynamics, etc.—continue to operate within their natural range of variability. . . . Furthermore, the integrity of aquatic ecosystems is directly linked to the condition of the landscape around them.[8]

In a general sense, neither specific systemic processes nor predator/prey dynamics can remain unaffected when naturally occurring predators or prey are eliminated from a system. We also know that when whole areas or whole countries are so affected, they no longer function in support of humans.

For example, in the Netherlands, a totally "managed" country, the balance, however precarious, between intensive manipulation of land and water systems and production results of such manipulation has been lost. Too much chemical input may render agricultural production and the land itself impotent,[9] although not every episode of manipulative intervention equals system collapse. But Holland is presently suffering from the consequences of its neglect of the wild and taking steps to correct its mistakes by closing roads and imposing penalties for excessive cattle and pig operations, rather than offering subsidies, and allowing environmental authorities veto power over all projects found to be ecologically unsound.

Where and how do we draw the line? How much information do we need in order to enforce policies that are contrary to present and past economic growth trends? These are hard questions; answering them is not an easy task, and we must rely on imprecise and divided science to perform it. Although answers are earnestly sought, the immediate priority is to discontinue, alter, or mitigate all practices currently "on trial" and abide by strong precautionary principles instead.[10] All available information indicates that most of the practices in our present technological lifestyle are not "innocent," and that both "juries" and "legal counsel teams" that defend and support them have strong financial interests in their continued existence, in direct opposition to the real public good, as shown in the fish wars example.

When sustainability is discussed in the context of techno-consumerist lifestyles, it is intended purely as ecological sustainability (ES). This does not mean, however, that either economic sustainability (ECS) or social sustainability (SS) are ignored or deemed unimportant. The thrust of my argument is that ES, although some may view it as potentially inimical to the other two (ECS and SS), in the long term, is not. Although this can be shown to be true, for the most part it is the short-term economic advantage that policymakers most often seek and deliberately contrast with ecological imperatives. Robert Goodland argues that there are three types of sustainability, and that they are "clearest when kept separate."[11]

Because ecological sustainability must remain primary, I argue that (1) as many others have noted, current evaluations of technology (and of the business enterprises that depend on these technologies) are insufficient for public policy if they are based only on cost/benefit analyses,[12] and that (2) even the necessary introduction of traditional moral theories and of respect for democratic institutions and practices is not sufficient to acknowledge the required ecological component of public policy decisions, as the fish wars indicated, despite the free, informed citizens' choices that prevailed at the time. As the case for the ethics of integrity unfolds, this chapter attacks consumerism, anthropocentrism, and the reliance on often untested and unproven technologies as the major sources of problems in affluent northwestern countries. None of these represents the only problem we need to address, because the population question is also a major problem. That discussion occurs in the last chapter of this work, because at that stage I will also have addressed the question of microintegrity, and I will have attempted to reconcile the respect for the integrity of individual organisms and the reality of overpopulation as a basic environmental threat.

In the next section I examine the limits of economic evaluations based purely on human preferences. I then turn to a major stumbling block one encounters when proposing a biocentric, holistic approach, that is, the belief that nonanthropocentric theories fail when they are used in support of environmental choices. Some people view all holistic theories as lacking from both a philosophical and a practical point of view. I argue instead that they are superior on both theoretical and practical grounds, and therefore we need to go far beyond both economic and even traditional (intrahuman) moral evaluations to achieve sound environmental policy.

The Limits of Economic Evaluation and Anthropocentrism

Although the use of firearms to protect the natural world was new to Canada in March 1995, illegal protests and even violence have occurred elsewhere. For example, in 1994, protesters from Canada and the United States made their way to British Columbia, threatened violence, and chained themselves to trees to subvert corporate activities and prevent the logging of old-growth forests in Clayoquot Sound. In taking this action, protesters were appealing to international law and to regulatory bodies beyond those of the countries of the dispute, as happened in the Newfoundland fish wars. This was an unprecedented tactic, as for instance, protests by native groups, whether in Canada or the United States, have been intended to support the right to certain lifestyles (and the beliefs that support them). I have argued this point in detail elsewhere.[13] In essence, although traditional native lifestyles are far less disruptive to the environment (because they are far less technologically "advanced") than today's affluent northwestern lifestyles, the natives' main concerns are ethnic self-preservation and, at least in Canada, sovereignty. The goals of conservation biology and sustainability are important and form an integral part of the self-understanding of traditional Inuit and native peoples,[14] but they may be viewed as secondary to present individual and group development goals.

One wonders whether an appeal to traditional, anthropocentric moral doctrines is sufficient to prevent such problems from developing in the face of increasing environmental degradation and mounting scarcity of resources as populations increase. Many have addressed the need to ensure that cost/benefit analyses and economic evaluations of technology focus prominently on ethical considerations beyond aggregate utilities and majority preferences.[15] I believe that the anthropocentric/

nonanthropocentric distinction presents a false dichotomy in several senses and that it is no more than a red herring, advanced by those concerned with defending the status quo. Accordingly, they are led to propose a somewhat modified "greened" revamping of the same hazardous, uncritically accepted practices to which all life on earth has been subjected, as I argue in the next section.

Utilities and preferences are normally understood in philosophical and political theory as reflecting the wishes and maybe the (descriptively) perceived good of a society, as do appeals to rights, justice, fairness, and due process. The question, however, is whether ethical considerations based on moral doctrines designed primarily for intraspecific interaction, that is, designed to guide our interpersonal behavior, are in fact sufficient as well as clearly necessary to ensure that our activities conform to an inclusive and enlightened morality. Recent global changes affecting our resource base everywhere prove the inadequacy of calculations that depend solely on economics, so that evaluations founded on moral doctrines and upholding both natural and civil rights appear indeed mandatory. Would that approach have been sufficient in the case of the Newfoundland fishers and the North Atlantic fish stocks? The fishers' earlier arguments, even before the decline of the cod population, could have been supported from the standpoint of human ethics and anthropocentrism. They were concerned with (1) sustainable development (Newfoundland is probably the poorest province in Canada) and increased financial security for themselves and their families; (2) aggregate utility, not for their "preference wants" but for their basic needs; (3) their local/national "visions" specific to the place they inhabited;[16] and (4) their democratic right to free choice.

Although their grounds appeared prima facie to be unimpeachable and could be defensible morally as well as legally in our present worldwide environmental situation, all the four points listed need reexamination in the light of what Don Scherer terms our "upstream/downstream" world.[17] The underlying notion of human rights is also questionable, in view of Robert McGinn's argument about "technological maximality" and the hazards that approach engenders. The combination of (1) "absolute" human rights—that is, human rights viewed as primary even when they support nonessential, nonbasic preferences, (2) greatly increased numbers of such "rights-holders," and (3) the well-entrenched drive to newer, bigger, and more—that is, to "technological maximality"—jointly engenders threats that are not present in any separate individual action. As we saw in the previous section, Goodland argues for the primacy of ecological sustainability; McGinn proposes "contextualized" theories of rights:[18] either of these positions would have helped to respond to the mounting environmental problems that eventually led to the Canadian fish wars by demanding that the scientific information be available to both policymakers and the general public, and that the "rights" of fishers to increasing quotas and the access to more complex fishing technologies be jointly evaluated.[19]

While both these arguments focus primarily on human beings, they are anthropocentric in an enlightened and morally sensitive way. This sort of anthropocentrism (at least on the part of McGinn) may be close to what Bryan Norton terms "weak anthropocentrism."[20] However, Goodland's argument hinges also on the basic role of natural systems' integrity, in regard to general life support (for both humankind and nonhuman nature).[21] McGinn acknowledges the existence of the ecological impasse to which we are brought by present individualism and by preference-based, largely unrestricted choices, but he believes that it might be sufficient to shift the emphasis to *community* concerns, hence to contextualize present theories of rights.[22]

Could the communitarian emphasis have prevented the crash of the fisheries, which led to violence in the normally peaceful fishing industry? It seems that this would not have been enough. Returning for a moment to the arguments to which the fishers might have appealed, we see that at least one of the strongest is already a communitarian one. One of their concerns was the support of communitarian values and traditional lifestyles. Yet in this typical case, even subordinating *individual* rights to aggregate community or national ones was not enough, unless the community that would have been accepted as primary could have been, minimally, the international global community, or—as I argue in the next section—the community of life.

In contrast, neither the Canadian nor the Spanish fishing communities would have raised the question of other international community rights or the need to reexamine or contextualize their own, as McGinn suggests. Even Mark Sagoff's position in *The Economy of the Earth,* if adopted, might have been insufficient to prevent the violent conflict that arose. He would suggest that the Canadian government should have supported its *citizens*' values, incorporating their local beliefs and practices, rather than the consumers' (and producers') values of increased availability of reasonably priced fish and profit maximization. But Newfoundlanders are a proud people who love both their land and their traditional lifestyles. In their case, their continued dependence on successful local fisheries represents far more than either a consumer's or a producer's preference. It is instead the embodiment of a national or specifically place-based vision of what a traditional good life should be. Therefore, one could argue that it was citizens' values, rather than consumers' values, that motivated their continued quest for increased quotas for cod and eventually turbot.

The same argument could be applied to the Spanish fishers and their traditional village values, on the other side of the ocean. Thus, even if the motive of *all* fishers was not purely economic, the problem of the commons, or of the "common pool" as Eric Freyfogle has it, persists. He says, "According to many economists, the solution to the tragedy of the common pool is to divide the common asset and distribute shares or parts to individual users."[23]

Yet while such privatization emphasizes the need to recognize our limits, and might ensure that "we do not exceed our fair share," it also "divides the haves from the have nots."[24] Hence, it would conflict with traditional moral principles by running counter to both human rights and justice considerations. Privatization also would not offer a solution to the problems raised in the fundamental question posed here about the necessity for additional, but primary, environmental value considerations. As a general prescription, it does nothing to help us limit our overconsumption or to find appropriate locations to dispose of the waste generated. For the latter, we must "stop producing the wastes to begin with, or to break them down into harmless component parts," which is not always possible. We tend to view the earth as a giant pool of resources, unchanging and always there, a stable value where the only question is the allotment of its bounty and the most efficient way of extracting it. "Depletion accounting" also normally fosters this illusion, by depreciating buildings, equipment, and machinery, but not land. Yet the land, too, is vulnerable: through "our pollution and land use practices [we] poison the soil and drain its fertility."[25] The same, mutatis mutandis, could be said about the sea and its fisheries. The basic problem remains our unsustainable lifestyle, particularly in the urban Northwest. Conventional economic rationality rejects the notion that "carrying capacity imposes serious constraints on material growth."[26] The position of those who disagree with the necessity for limits is based on the belief that unlimited substitutions will make ecological critiques and appeals to scarcity obsolete.[27] This optimistic, protechnology attitude, however, appears unjustified.

Returning to the fish wars, if we were to continue our present practices without restraints other than a different allocation of the quotas, and all the North Atlantic fish stocks crashed, we might be able to develop some alternative source of protein, but this would do nothing to restore the fishers' communities or lifestyles. Conversely, we might instead turn to aquaculture as a comparable source of food and a socially adequate source of comparable employment. Nevertheless, aquaculture is also environmentally hazardous, as it releases nutrients and wastes into ecosystems, disrupting their natural processes. The introduction of transgenic fish also affects natural populations, thus biodiversity, and often releases antibiotics into the system and into the food chain.[28] Questions may be raised about the reasons for viewing these results as irrevocably bad. What is wrong, it may be asked, with changes in the species presently existing in various locations? William Broad's *New York Times* article "Creatures of the Deep Find Their Way to the Table" cites the examples of the orange roughy, the rattail, the royal red shrimp, and others as newfound delicacies harvested and marketed in substitution of other, more familiar fish species.[29]

But even though we may change our tastes, and so could future persons, the other side of this particular issue is also brought out in the same article, as Broad asks, "eat it first, study it later?" and in essence admits that "nobody knows how harvesting will affect deep-sea fish species." We are now harvesting more than orange roughies; we are living with the results of our exploitive practices in too many areas. Perhaps the uncertainty, and the possibility of additional future species disappearances, will prompt us to rethink and retrench rather than forge ahead with misplaced hubris and optimism.

The basic problem anywhere, not just for Canadian fisheries, is sustainability. William Rees, for instance, proposes adopting an "ecological worldview," in contrast with the prevailing established "expansionist worldview," which represents "the dominant social paradigm."[30] As Aldo Leopold did before him, Rees recognizes that we are not independent of an "environment," but, as we also saw earlier in Goodland's work, ecological sustainability is foundational, so it makes perfectly good sense to abandon our present unsustainable and indefensible worldview. Rees and Wackernagel say, "By contrast, an ecological economic perspective would see the human economy as an inextricably integrated, completely contained, and wholly dependent sub-system of the ecosphere."[31]

This position is supported by Rees's research in the Vancouver–Lower Fraser Valley region of British Columbia, but it can be easily generalized for all urban, affluent northwestern centers. His findings show that "assuming an average Canadian diet and current management practices," the local regional population supports its consumers' lifestyles by importing "the productive capacity of at least 22 times as much land as it occupies." To put this in a more general way, "the ecological footprints of individual regions are much larger than the land areas they physically occupy."[32]

When we continue to import others' carrying capacity, we are "running an unaccounted ecological deficit," and "our populations are appropriating carrying capacity from elsewhere or from future generations."[33] The same can be said about sinks for our wastes: for both resource appropriation and waste disposal, our northwestern approach has been one of neocolonialism in regard to less-developed countries and ruthless exploitation (through environmental racism) toward minorities and the disempowered in our own countries.[34]

Environmental racism is a concern about humans, but for all other concerns and problems mentioned here it is easy to find arguments that might give a spurious legitimacy to the maintenance of the status quo, perhaps with minor "cosmetic" green changes to put public anxiety to rest, but without actually effecting the radical reorganization of our own and our society's priorities, which are warranted by the present environmental situation.[35] In fact, despite its imprecise language and its undercurrent of inconsistencies, the principles of *Agenda 21* (and the Rio declaration following the 1992 Rio de Janeiro Earth Summit) also demand such a radical review of all national and international laws and regulations.[36]

The fish wars example is even more useful in assessing what sorts of principles we need to resolve such potentially volatile situations. It may be possible to use anthropocentric moral doctrines concerned with human issues, at this point in the dispute, in order to adjudicate fairly among the various affected parties. But what of the original practices—that is, technologically enhanced fishing—that led to the fish wars?[37] Over time, these practices, along with nonpoint pollution, the steady rise of toxic wastes in the oceans, anthropogenically induced climate changes, and careless overuse through constantly increasing fishing quotas, led to the crash of the fish stocks. This crisis could have been avoided only through policies and practices consistent with an "ecological worldview," one going beyond competing aggregate preferences of various human groups.

In the next section I discuss what such a worldview might require and argue that the radical change called for by the current emergencies can only be supported through an ecocentric or biocentric viewpoint, whether or not our concern is primarily directed toward human beings.

It follows that in an actual situation, such as the fish wars, the contributing factors leading to the problems in the North Atlantic could all be traced back to the exercise of human and civil rights, not all of which can be indicted as supporting only consumers' preferences. Waste, pollution, and the proliferation of hazardous processes and products can all be identified as the result of fast-spreading, untested (or inadequately tested) technologies. It might be argued that some of these technologies (such as time-saving devices, automobiles, and even all-terrain vehicles in some areas) could be viewed as supporting citizens' values: the individual's right to self-fulfillment and actualization could be supported by household time-saving devices; the so-called right to the freedom of mobility, by all kinds of transportation vehicles. Producers' economic interests in growth, development, and successful competition with other producers are also fostered by the same practices. What about equity and the rights of those who are not benefited but are forced to bear the burdens of these technologies? The question raised earlier returns. It is absolutely necessary to consider and reconsider human rights and equity questions. But these questions raise primarily distributive problems. They are not foundational questions like those raised by biocentric concerns: that is, why is it necessary to have these "advanced" fishing technologies and a lifestyle dependent on them?

We may want to modify the way the corporate/technological enterprise operates from the moral point of view by raising some of the questions suggested above. However, we are still not attempting to alter it in a radical way, and this would be a mistake since a partial imposition of restraints is not sufficient. Kristin Shrader-Frechette recounts the example of a fungicide, ethylene dibromide (EDB), which was proven to be carcinogenic in 1973. The procedures necessary for its regulation required another ten years and during that period, "EDB began showing up in bread, flour and cereal products in such quantities that risk assessors predicted that, based on lifetime consumption, EDB would cause up to 200,000 cases of cancer per year in the United States."[38] Even more chilling is that the substitute the industry eventually used, methyl bromide, is a very close chemical relative of the banned EDB and probably equally carcinogenic. To this day, methyl bromide is still not regulated.

A lesson can be learned from such cases. First, it is absolutely necessary to start by introducing moral considerations into the risk assessment of all technologies; second, it seems that even faster, more ethically sensitive assessments may be insufficient to prevent the perpetration of ecoviolence (that is, violence perpetrated in and through the environment). What is required is a radically changed approach, starting from ecocentrism, and a major shift in burden of proof theories and standards. Robert Ulanowicz argues that even in highly funded, uncontroversial research, such as research into cancer causes, a holistic approach would be far more fruitful than the present reductionist method, with exclusive focus on genes or viruses.[39] Holism can make a large difference in issues concerned with the interface between humans and the environment. In addition, an ecocentric perspective would regard all untried and potentially hazardous substances as guilty until proven innocent beyond a doubt. It would suggest that, even then, given the uncertainties endemic to the scientific method, the precautionary principle still needs to be applied.[40]

The shift in the burden of proof suggested here is already part of the language of the Great Lakes Water Quality Agreement (of 1978, ratified in 1987), through its emphasis on "zero discharge" and on "sunset" and "sunrise" chemical controls.[41] These substances can be viewed minimally as not contributing to the natural evolutionary processes of ecosystems, thus as naturally inimical to the mandated respect for ecosystem integrity. In essence, I have argued that an ecosystem can be said to possess integrity (I_a) when it is an unmanaged ecosystem, although not necessarily a pristine one. This aspect of integrity is the most significant one; it is the aspect that differentiates I_a from ecosystem health (I_b), which is compatible with support/manipulation instead.[42] Hence, exotic, potentially hazardous substances and processes would be judged inappropriate, and their introduction into natural systems would not be permitted. As McGinn argues, meaningful changes in our evaluation of technology cannot occur unless we are willing to question our assumptions about rights and the role of democracy.[43]

Beyond the Anthropocentrism/Nonanthropocentrism Debate

The conclusion reached in the previous section indicates that to ameliorate presently accepted technology-dependent lifestyles or redress present inequities, it would be preferable to change our approach and accept the primacy of ecological integrity, as many national and international laws and regulations already do, at least in their language, rather than expect real change from end-of-pipe solutions. Insofar as ecocentrism is akin to deep ecology's platform, however, such a position is in direct conflict with a position such as Norton's: "As academics, spokespersons for deep ecology have been able to avoid adopting policies on difficult, real world cases such as elk destroying their wolf-free ranges, feral goats destroying indigenous vegetation on fragile lands, or park facilities overwhelmed by human visitors."[44]

On the contrary, a truly holistic position such as the one supporting the primacy of integrity has clear-cut answers for all such questions, though not necessarily popular ones, as can be seen from our approach to the fish wars. In every case, when there is human interference giving rise to problems in the wild, it is not only acceptable but mandatory to interfere again to redress the difficulty, temporarily, and with the clear goal to withdraw when the system's evolutionary path has been restored, according to the best scientific information available and under the guidance of the precautionary principle.[45] The goal in this case is one of restoration, as the area affected is wild. That is to say, although the immediate goal is to restore natural function and systemic health, the ultimate goal is to withdraw all support and manipulation, so that some restored systems can return to a state of integrity or unmanaged evolutionary processes once again; hence the present call for the establishment of marine fisheries reserves.[46]

This does not mean that we must altogether discontinue human practices that utilize nature everywhere. It simply indicates that we must recognize the necessity of (1) leaving appropriately sized areas on both land and seas wild and unmanipulated (the required sizes need to be established in dialogue with conservation biology and aquatic ecosystem science) and (2) limiting our intrusive practices upon the rest of the earth to whatever will not have an adverse impact on core/wild areas.[47] Conservation biology, entomology, ecology, and biology will all contribute to the necessary dialogue to establish the scales appropriate to either one or the other of these approaches in different landscapes, globally. As I have argued elsewhere,[48] the ultimate goal of the principle of integrity is to protect and restore both structural and functional aspects of ecological integrity, and this requires that large areas be kept wild.[49] It also demands that we be prepared to "embrace the challenge of complexity," as James Kay and Earl Schneider argue, and thus to abandon the misconception that all systems can and should be managed.[50] Instead, management and controls should be confined to human individuals and societies, except briefly for restoration purposes in core and buffer areas.

By way of contrast, we noted in the case of Canadian fisheries the dismal failure of the presumption to manage nature. Educated guesses about how far we can push the safety factor with our quotas, particularly when these are manipulated by economic and political interests (both of which are notoriously shortsighted) and supported by uneducated democratic preferences and values, are simply insufficient to protect either the fish species or the local survival needs of affected humans. Norton has argued that "long-sighted anthropocentrists and ecocentrists tend to adopt more and more similar policies as scientific evidence is gathered because both value systems—and several others as well—point toward the common-denominator objective of protecting ecological contexts."[51]

Norton is not alone in this belief. Gary Varner, for instance, appears to concur.[52] But in his effort to continue his ongoing campaign against the supporters of intrinsic natural value, Norton appeals to two concepts that as we shall see, are also problematic, either practically or theoretically. He refers to a rare if not nonexistent ethic—that of the long-sighted anthropocentrist. Where does one find such a position? Not among politicians and policymakers, to be sure: the hard pressure of political correctness with regard to other issues tends to relegate green concerns to the back burner, although some examples can be cited, such as the Endangered Species Act and some policies on radioactive waste disposal, both of which take a longsighted approach. What about large multinational corporations? These are somewhat vulnerable to public opinion, but even more vulnerable to shareholders' displeasure and internal and external competition. It will be hard to find much longsightedness in those boardrooms, beyond public relations campaigns to calm the public's "irrationality" and their fears. And if one were to encounter that rara avis, a longsighted anthropocentrist, how would one distinguish her from her ecocentrist counterpart?

Norton describes her salient characteristics: she would appreciate "scientific evidence," and thus be disposed to share with the ecocentrist the "objective of protecting ecological contexts."[53] But this is only superficially true. That is, she would be willing to follow that path only if she were convinced that no other path would support her interests equally well. Such beliefs and sentiments are indeed shared by politicians, industry giants, and many others; they are easy to voice because they remain vague and unspecific. Serious questions can be raised: for instance, how far would the weak/longsighted anthropocentrist (WLSA) go to protect such systems? Another question is, For what would she understand that protection to be necessary? For the WLSA, continued exploitation, variously defined, might be a convincing candidate. But, given science's imprecision and the "challenge of complexity," and thus the impossibility of finding a guaranteed "safe" degree of pollution/exploitation, particularly in the face of cumulative and synergistic stresses, how easy would it be to convince the WLSA that her interest would be amply served by an ecologically untenable position? Newfoundland's fishers had every interest in the continued thriving of the fish species upon which they depended, in a far more immediate and vital way than any politician, yet they could not make the connection, even in their own interest.

One could object that scientific uncertainty would also work against the ecocentrist's approach. The differences between the two approaches are significant instead, and they can be captured in two main points. First, the ecocentrist would start from the primacy and value of wilderness and thus begin by questioning any intrusive or risky practices, shifting the burden of proof to the would-be risk imposers. Her criteria would become progressively more stringent as the proposed technology and economic activity would be intended for human settlements and cities, or for areas of ecosystem health (sustainable agriculture of forestry areas, for instance). Most technological intrusion would be excluded from wild, core areas as required in order to protect their role and function.[54]

Second, given the primary value of preserving or restoring natural, evolutionary function in certain designated areas, and the necessity of ensuring this function through human activities compatible with this goal, the nonanthropocentric holist would use the precautionary principle to decide on all economic and technological issues. The precautionary principle (Principle 15 of the Rio Declaration on Environment and Development) states:

> In order to protect the environment, the precautionary approach shall be widely applied by States, according to their capabilities. Where there are threats of serious or irreversible damage, lack of full scientific certainty shall not be used as a reason for postponing cost-effective measures to prevent environmental damage.[55]

Finally, how will the WLSA vote and act when environmental protection conflicts with local jobs or other legitimate human aspirations, without relying entirely on the example I have proposed? This, it seems to me, is the litmus test for the convergence of ends Norton envisions between his WLSA and the ecocentrist, despite Norton's assertion that his position "recognizes the crucial role of creative, self-organizing systems in support of economic, recreational, aesthetic and spiritual values."[56] As we saw in the fish wars example, even all this may not be enough.

Yet, in some sense, Norton is right: there is a commonality between the two positions, but this commonality emerges only when we subordinate "human economic, recreational, aesthetic and spiritual values," whatever these might be, to the imperative of survival. This imperative represents the common denominator we share with the rest of life. And when we recognize the primacy of that commonality and the ways in which ecological integrity supports it for all, globally, then we are ecocentrists, or biocentric holists (the term I have chosen), because our anthropocentrism has been so weakened as to be nonexistent, dissolved into the reality of our presence first and foremost, as part of the biota of natural systems.[57]

But, some will argue, perhaps it is sufficient merely to recognize that we are a part of the biota of natural systems and that we share our habitat with the rest of life; in that case, it is not necessary to argue for the intrinsic value of nonhuman animals and other individuals and wholes. Those who support this position will view the WLSA as theoretically and philosophically defensible; all other positions, based on ecocentrism or biocentrism, will not be acceptable. This has certainly been Norton's position through the years.[58] The polarization of the two positions is well documented in the environmental ethics literature.[59] But this polarization remains—to say the least—misguided.

The weaker anthropocentrism becomes, the less defensible it is, as such, that is, as a variant of anthropocentrism. But why should we weaken anthropocentrism in the first place? Norton's answer, if I understand him correctly, is because humankind has more than economic interests. These other interests represent values that mitigate the crassest forms of purely economic anthropocentrism, thus making the position more acceptable. Norton defines his position as follows:

> A value theory is weakly anthropocentric if all value countenanced by it is explained by reference to some felt preferences of a human individual or by reference to its bearing upon the ideals which exist as elements in a world view essential to determinations of considered preferences.[60]

This position is therefore weak from the standpoint of moral theory as well: it is open to all the charges to which utilitarianism is open in its weakest formulation. Based upon Norton's position, all we can offer to any group, individual, or policymaker intent on advancing her common interests, which might be strongly anthropocentric, is our plea for the support of "values," explained by reference to some "felt or considered preferences of a human individual."[61] Whether these are aggregate rather than individual preferences, and whether they even embody some ideal, the answer is still the same: the result can be purely utilitarian in a time-limited sense (although John Rawls's position might mitigate it to some extent). Choices based on preference satisfaction are often blind to other individual rights and to justice considerations. They can also be culturally relative (for example, in some cultures female genital mutilation is part of a "moral" family-oriented ideal); thus many such preferences may not be universally defensible from a moral standpoint.

The case of the fish wars shows how useless such a position would have been from the standpoint of reaching an environmentally fair and ecologically sound solution. Any position that presents a choice between "considered preference A" and "considered preference B" offers no grounds, other than a counting of heads, efficiency, or (for a policymaker) perhaps political expediency, for the ultimate result. Hence, the proponents of such a position must bear the responsibility for their stance even if, in their individual case, their choice might have been just as sound and prudent as one reached on ecocentric grounds.

The problem is one envisioned by Plato: knowing the road to Larissa without knowing why. In other words, even reaching a right decision on wrong principles may not be sufficient if the principles would permit a morally bad decision on another occasion. This is not based exclusively on a quest for personal moral purity but on the responsibility for consequences to which others, even human innocents now and in the future, may be subjected through our choices, and our choice of principles.

Norton rejects all defenses of intrinsic value in nonhuman nature, whether holistic or individualistic,[62] although he aims his attack primarily at Baird Callicott's own position and his interpretation of the land ethic of Aldo Leopold.[63] Leaving aside for the moment individual grounds for intrinsic value in nonhuman animals, a holistic perspective supports respect for all parts of natural systems, as well as the wholes within which they function. We ourselves are parts, at least physically, of these structures. They also respect system functions—that is, the processes they engender, which involve their biotic and abiotic parts—a necessity when we wish to defend the survival of any species.[64]

An ecocentric position such as the biocentric holism recommended by the principle of integrity (PI) recognizes (1) the interrelationship between human and nonhuman nature and their "connaturality"[65] and kinship;[66] hence (2) the intrinsic value of natural/evolutionary processes;[67] and (3) the foundational value of life-support systems for ecological sustainability.[68] It also acknowledges that (4) ecological sustainability is primary, as it alone supports economic and social sustainability.[69] Therefore (5) at the most basic—that is, at the *life* level—the dichotomy between anthropocentrism and nonanthropocentrism is a false one. I believe that this is true not because anthropocentrism is the only defensible theory but because "preferences" sometimes address want-interests, as well as need-interests, but at the basic level of survival only, we have no interests that are completely separate from those of all other life, so that their "values" and our "values" coincide.[70]

Hence, the argument proposed here is not that humans have interests that are defensible because they are intrinsically valuable beings, unlike any other, but because humans and nonhumans share an interest, a need for a safe habitat, and—whether or not this is consciously acknowledged—the value of survival conditions persists, and it includes the valuable contributions of all participants in ecosystemic processes. This does not render all life equal, but it shows all living things are possessed of value singly and collectively, for themselves and for all else. Rather than relying on preference-satisfaction indicators, a position that has been found morally lacking in risk assessment and technology assessment,[71] my approach defends the general (human and nonhuman) value of integrity and health for various habitats in appropriate proportions.[72]

Norton prefers to isolate another common regulatory and legislative strand, which, like the appeals to ecological integrity, can also be found in many documents: the issue and rights of future generations (of humans, if I understand him correctly). If he is looking for a publicly accepted legislative priority, he is correct. If, however, Norton is seeking a moral basis that is less hard to defend, or less controversial than intrinsic value for nonhumans, then the future-generations emphasis he has chosen is both controversial and debated, and even less easy to sell to the person in the street as a possible preference than ecological life support, with all its prudential implications.[73]

In conclusion, *pace* Norton, there is no clear, obvious, and philosophically defensible difference between the concepts and values that sustain the argument of the WLSA and those that support the intrinsic-value beliefs of the ecocentrist, nor is ecocentrism as vacuous and "exotic" as Norton claims.[74] In practice, Norton claims that holistic/intrinsic-value arguments are impotent. But when dealing with agencies and government bodies (such as Environment Canada or the Great Lakes International Joint Commission) or major organizations like the International Union for the Conservation of Nature (IUCN), it would be no easier to attempt to support environmental action by appealing to the details of philosophical debates regarding future generations than by appealing to intrinsic-value arguments. At the level of scientific evidence and with the support of ecology, the intrinsic-value arguments are not only easier to use, particularly for wholes and processes (though admittedly less so for individual animals, unless endangered), but also by the very same arguments culled from ecology, they are a necessary and integral part of the future-generations arguments Norton prefers. In order to accept a determinant role for duties to future generations, we must understand why we need to respect the life-support function of systemic processes. In other words, if the consequences of unrestrained technological and economic activities were simply various changes in the natural environment requiring changes in preferences and the exercise of our ingenuity and our technological abilities, we would have little or no reason to moderate our activities out of respect for the future, as some argue.[75]

It is only because of the mounting evidence showing the life-support function of systemic processes and the role of their component parts that we must accept that it is not the deprivation of this or that resource that we may inflict on the future but the limitation of the very basis for any life at all. It goes without saying that neither ecology nor biology could make absolute pronouncements about these issues. But the evidence (mentioned in our discussion of agricultural and fishing practices) appears to be on the side of the defense of naturally evolving entities. We affect, severely, the health of all human and nonhuman animals through anthropogenic stress to ecosystems leading to nonevolutionary changes.[76]

Some of the most obvious changes are caused by climate changes, as many have argued. Most of these changes deal with effects on living species and habitats. Yet there are effects that are even more insidious. Cor Van der Weele shows why our present exclusive preoccupation with reductionist causal connections in genes and genetic traits, with the combined impact of our methodological bias toward positivism, blinds us to the reality that "causal choices cannot be avoided."[77] In brief, developmental biology shows the strong effect of environmental conditions, and the time scale for these changes begins before birth: "The ecological environment can be seen as a set of nested structures, beginning with the immediate setting of the developing person, the microenvironment, up to the macro-environment which refers to the cultural or sub-cultural level."[78] The "microenvironment" is the womb or its equivalent in nonmammalian animals. Even small temperature changes (occurring abruptly because of anthropogenic stresses) affect various embryonic traits, including gender, in a number of nonhuman animals. This is similar to the negative impact on reproduction caused by chemicals such as pesticides and herbicides. Temperature changes translate into various effects, one of which, the occurrence of sexual/gender changes, would lead, albeit unintentionally, to the extinction of many species that are documented to be sensitive to such temperature changes.

These effects represent not just the imposition of some substitutions or minor changes that we might impose on future generations, but an almost complete overturning of the most basic support, that of life. It is not only internal factors that affect a fertilized egg or embryo: "when a few pinches of simple salts . . . are added to the water in which a fish (Fundulus) is developing, that fish will undergo a modified process of development and have not two eyes, but one."[79] Hence, internal, reductionist study will yield only a partial cause of development, whereas the external environmental factors are at least codeterminant of future consequences. Without Frankenstein's motivation and determination, we are nevertheless preparing the way for "monsters" for whom we are unwilling to accept responsibility.

Warming trends represent *indirect* global changes that affect reproduction, and thereby individuals as well as species. Recent research has shown that direct effects extending to reproductive function and well beyond it can be traced to certain features of our technological lifestyles and the corporate activities that foster and support them. The groundbreaking research of Theo Colborn and others has shown how man-made chemicals, long known to be hazardous and carcinogenic, and also many others thought to be biologically inert, affect the reproductive organs and related capacities of most species, from fish to birds to mammals, including humans.

As "hormone mimics" they also significantly alter our behavior, intellectual capacities, and parenting abilities.[80] The results of Colborn's research present a clear indictment of the way we interact with corporations and industry. After cataloging a litany of horrors resulting from even minute exposures to polychlorinated biphenyl compounds

(PCBs) affecting women of reproductive age, infants, fetuses, and children, Colborn says of the move to produce PCBs:

> Confident of their safety as well as their utility, the Swann Chemical company, which would soon become part of Monsanto Chemical Company in 1935, quickly moved them into production and onto the market.[81]

It is the corporations who have the resources to research, test, and market these complex and novel products. Even in democratic nations, however, we have no institutional mechanism to oversee, acquire information on (because of trade secrets laws), or debate, let alone impose limits on, these industrial giants. But even the tiniest molecule of a PCB compound is not biodegradable; it is durable, it travels and persists, and thus it has a range of negative effects:

> Researchers studying declining seal populations have found that seventy parts per million of PCBs is enough to cause serious problems for females, including suppressed immune systems and deformities of the uterus and of the fallopian tubes.[82]

Nor are PCBs the only chemicals with far-reaching transgenerational effects. DDT, "PCBs (209 compounds), . . . 75 dioxins, and . . . 135 furans were invented by chemists" in laboratories "to kill insects threatening crops and to give manufacturers new materials such as plastics."[83]

> Inadvertently, however, the chemical engineers had also created chemicals that jeopardize fertility and the unborn. Even worse, we have unknowingly spread them far and wide across the face of the Earth.[84]

These chemicals disrupt the endocrine system, mimic estrogen and other hormones, and block the pathways through which hormones signal normal development of all animals, including humans:

> This is like jamming the line on a cellular phone so it is always as busy and the intended messages are blocked. Without these testosterone signals, male development gets derailed and boys don't become boys. Instead they become stranded in an ambiguous state where they cannot function as either males or females.[85]

In addition, fungicides "inhibit the body's ability to produce steroids hormones, so vital messages are never sent," whereas long-lasting DDE "depletes hormones by accelerating their breakdown and elimination leaving the body short, not just of estrogen, but of testosterone and the other steroid hormones."[86]

As long as our quietism permits the continuation of present practices, and because governments do not appear to be eager to mandate controls in much of the Western world, here and in Europe emphasis is on deregulation rather than on tighter controls.

In that case, although Colborn and her collaborators propose principles of mitigation and change based on the Wingspread Consensus Statement (July 1991), within the present political and institutional system it is hard to envision acceptance of and compliance with her suggestions. The tobacco industry resisted regulation and controls for a long time, although there were unambiguous links between their products and deaths.[87]

It is my argument that we need to understand and accept this responsibility and recognize our obligation to respect life-support systems from a biocentric standpoint in order to support the changes indicated by these hazards. From Norton's point of view, in order to introduce arguments about future generations, we also need to understand the many ways we may negatively affect them. For this task, simple interhuman considerations will not suffice: we will need to expand our consciousness, our understanding, and our respect as required to include these processes and causal links. The holistic position would thus extend Norton's argument to all future generations of both human and nonhuman life.

A Question of Responsibility

For Hans Jonas responsibility was the "key word for the ethics of human conduct in dealing with technology."[88] Our moral responsibility is supported by the grave consequences of many of our choices. Another example of the *interface* between human activities and ecological sustainability may be taken from an area where scientific uncertainty has been manipulated to discourage radical change: global warming and climate changes.[89] Climate changes have been engendered primarily by human-induced stress to natural systems. Their effects, now increasingly documented in scientific journals, show that they give rise to grave problems for human health, wildlife health and species survival, agricultural productivity and land capacity, ocean habitat degradation, and social upheavals due to severe weather conditions and turbulence (including floods and other catastrophes).[90]

At the outset it seems that no aggregate human preference could or would have supported policies intended to curtail the fast spread of the technologies that were eventually banned through the Montreal and the Copenhagen protocols. Only principles of noninterference and general

respect for natural systems, land, air, and water might have made a difference. Dale Jamieson and others argue that "a stable climate, unlike
standard commodities, is irreplaceable."[91] Thus, the basic needs of all
life are at stake and, correspondingly, our responsibility should extend
that far.

If the argument of this chapter can be accepted at least as a reasonable one, then certain consequences will follow, in regard to the evaluation of technology. A reevaluation of the limits of moral theory suggests,
as I have argued, that the *primary* criterion for the evaluation of technology should be environmental and, specifically, ecological integrity. If
this is accepted, then certain questions about our shared habitat must
be raised in our evaluative assessments. They might include some of the
following:

1. Has the uncertainty of post-normal science been incorporated in
   our assessment? Have we applied the precautionary principle?
2. Has the question of the sustainability of natural capital used by the
   proposed technology been asked and answered within the parameter suggested in (1)?
3. Does the technology to be evaluated exhibit any possible aspects
   suggesting a negative impact on life-support systems, that is, on the
   services they provide to all life?
4. Are there obvious or hidden possible threats to biodiversity within
   the proposed technology?
5. Have the technology's possible synergistic effects with other processes or technologies been evaluated together with its own separate
   impact?

These questions would be followed by the necessary questions based
on traditional theories and values mentioned earlier and are therefore
not intended as substitutes but as additional and, in fact, primary questions, followed by still other moral questions. We need to ask ourselves,
in regard to each envisioned technology, whether it permits the preservation of sustainable, biodiverse life, *before* we ask whether it also permits
moral interspecies dealings among humankind. In light of the arguments of the previous two sections, it seems to me these questions may
provide a starting point and stimulate additional thought and research.

The next chapter examines in some detail the case of Ken Saro-Wiwa
and the Ogoni in Nigeria. The case does not occur in a Western democracy, but the ambiguous role played by Western democracies in the case
will emerge. Chapter 6 discusses another so-called technological advance, that is, biotechnology and aquaculture. Once again our aim will

be to argue for the unique and necessary input of a holistic perspective and the ethics of integrity.

Notes

1. Carl Walters, "Fish on the Line," monograph published by the David Suzuki Corporation and the Fisheries Centre, University of British Columbia, Vancouver, BC, 1995.

2. *The Globe and Mail* (Toronto) (March 13, 1995), p. A1.

3. K. Redford and A. Stearman, "Forest Dwelling Native Amazonians and the Conservation of Biodiversity: Interests in Common or in Collision?" *Conservation Biology* 7, 2 (June 1993).

4. Robert Ulanowicz, "Ecosystem Integrity: A Causal Necessity," in *Perspectives on Ecological Integrity*, ed. L. Westra and J. Lemons (Dordrecht, The Netherlands: Kluwer, 1995), pp. 77–87.

5. Walters, "Fish on the Line," pp. 50–52.

6. M. Hammer, A. M. Jansson, and B. O. Jansson, "Diversity, Change and Sustainability: Implications for Fisheries," *Ambio* 22, 2–3 (May 1993).

7. L. Westra, *An Environmental Proposal for Ethics: The Principle of Integrity* (Lanham, MD: Rowman & Littlefield, 1994); see L. Westra "Ecosystem Integrity and Sustainability: The Foundational Value of the Wild," in *Perspectives on Ecological Integrity*, ed. L. Westra and J. Lemons.

8. Reed F. Noss, "What Should Endangered Ecosystems Mean to the Wildlands Project?" *Wild Earth* 5, 4 (Winter 1995/96): 21.

9. RIVM, *National Environmental Outlook, 1990–2010* (Bilthoven, The Netherlands: Rijksinstituut voor Volksgezondheid en Milieuhygiene, 1986).

10. D. A. Brown, "The Role of Law in Sustainable Development and Environmental Protection Decision Making," in *Sustainable Development: Science, Ethics and Public Policy* (Dordrecht, The Netherlands: Kluwer, 1995), pp. 64–76.

11. Robert Goodland, "Environmental Sustainability and the Power Sector—Part I: The Concept of Sustainability," *Impact Assessment* 12, 3 (1994): 276.

12. K. Shrader-Frechette, *Risk and Rationality* (Berkeley: University of California Press, 1991); see Alistair MacIntyre, "Corporate Modernity and Moral Judgment: Are They Mutually Exclusive?" in *Ethics and Problems of the 21st Century*, ed. K. Goodpaster and K. Sayre (Notre Dame, IN: University of Notre Dame Press, 1979), pp. 122–38; Kurt Baier, "Technology and the Sanctity of Life," in *Ethics and Problems of the 21st Century*, ed, K. Goodpaster and K. Sayre, pp. 160–74.

13. L. Westra, "Biotechnology and Transgenics in Agriculture and Aquaculture: The Perspective from Ecosystem Integrity," in *Environmental Values* (Lancaster, England: Lancaster University, White Horse Press, 1996).

14. J. B. Callicott, *In Defense of the Land Ethic* (Albany, NY: State of New York University Press, 1989), especially "Traditional American Indian and Western European Attitudes Toward Nature: An Overview," pp. 177–201.

15. M. Sagoff, *The Economy of the Earth: Philosophy, Law and the Environment* (Cambridge, England: Cambridge University Press, 1988); see Robert Goodland

and Herman Daly, "Why Northern Income Growth Is Not the Solution to Southern Poverty," World Bank Environment Department Divisional Working Paper,
No. 1993–43, May 1993.

16. Sagoff, *The Economy of the Earth.*

17. D. Scherer and T. Attig, *Upstream/Downstream* (Philadelphia: Temple University Press, 1990).

18. Robert E. McGinn, "Technology, Demography, and the Anachronism of
Traditional Rights," *Journal of Applied Philosophy* 11, 1 (1994): 57–70.

19. Walters, "Fish on the Line."

20. Bryan Norton, "Why I Am Not a Nonanthropocentrist: Callicott and the
Failure of Monistic Inherentism," *Environmental Ethics* 17, 4 (Winter 1995):
341–58; see Bryan Norton, "Environmental Ethics and Weak Anthropocentris,"
Environmental Ethics 6, 2 (Summer 1984): 131–36, 138–48.

21. Goodland, "Environmental Sustainability and the Power Sector—Part I:
The Concept of Sustainability," pp. 275–304.

22. McGinn, "Technology, Demography, and the Anachronism of Traditional Rights."

23. Eric T. Freyfogle, *Justice and the Earth: Images for Our Planetary Survival*
(New York: Free Press, Macmillan, 1993), p. 27.

24. Freyfogle, *Justice and the Earth,* p. 29.

25. Freyfogle, *Justice and the Earth,* pp. 24–27.

26. W. E. Rees and M. Wackernagel, *Our Ecological Footprint* (Gabriola Island,
BC: New Society, 1996).

27. M. Sagoff, "Carrying Capacity and Ecological Economics," *Bioscience* 45,
9 (October 1995): 610–20.

28. J. A. Hutchings and R. A. Myers, "What Can Be Learned from the Collapse of a Renewable Resource? Atlantic Cod, *Gadus Morhua,* of Newfoundland,
Labrador," *Canadian Journal of Fisheries and Aquatic Science* 51 (1994): 2126–46;
see Hammer, et al., "Diversity, Change and Sustainability: Implications for Fisheries"; M. C. Beveridge, M. Lindsay, G. Ross, and L. A. Kelly, "Aquaculture and
Biodiversity," *Ambio* 23, 8 (December 1994): 497–502.

29. William Broad, "Creatures of the Deep Find Their Way to the Table,"
New York Times (December 26, 1995).

30. Rees and Wackernagel, *Our Ecological Footprint,* p. 16.

31. Rees and Wackernagel, *Our Ecological Footprint,* p. 4.

32. Rees and Wackernagel, *Our Ecological Footprint,* pp. 14–16.

33. Ibid., pp. 55–57.

34. L. Westra and P. Wenz, *The Faces of Environmental Racism: The Global Equity
Issues* (Lanham, MD: Rowman & Littlefield, 1995).

35. Westra, *An Environmental Proposal for Ethics*; see Freyfogle, *Justice and the
Earth.*

36. Brown, "The Role of Law in Sustainable Development and Environmental Protection Decision Making."

37. Walters, "Fish on the Line."

38. Shrader-Frechette, *Risk and Rationality.*

39. R. Ulanowicz, *Ecology, The Ascendent Perspective* (New York: Columbia University Press, in press).

40. Brown, "The Role of Law in Sustainable Development and Environmental Protection Decision Making."

41. Thomas Muir and Anne Sudar, "Toxic Chemicals in the Great Lakes Basin Ecosystem," Environmental Canada, Burlington, Ontario, *Science Advisory Board Report to the International Joint Commission* 15–41 (1987), p. 18.

42. L. Westra, "Ecosystem Integrity and Sustainability: The Foundational Value of the Wild," in *Perspectives on Ecological Integrity*, ed. L. Westra and J. Lemons, pp. 12–13; Westra, *An Environmental Proposal for Ethics*, pp. 24–27, 41.

43. McGinn, "Technology, Demography, and the Anachronism of Traditional Rights."

44. Bryan Norton, *Toward Unity among Environmentalists* (New York: Oxford University Press, 1991), p. 222.

45. Brown, "The Role of Law in Sustainable Development and Environmental Protection Decision Making."

46. D. Pauly, "Principles of Marine Ecology Applied to the Establishment of Marine Fisheries Reserves." 125th Meeting of the American Fishery Society, Tampa (1995).

47. Westra, *An Environmental Proposal for Ethics*; Westra, "Ecosystem Integrity and Sustainability"; James Karr and Ellen Chu, "Ecological Integrity: Reclaiming Lost Connections," in *Perspectives on Ecological Integrity*, ed. L. Westra and J. Lemons, pp. 34–48.

48. Westra, *An Environmental Proposal for Ethics*.

49. Reed F. Noss, "The Wildlands Project: Land Conservation Strategy," *Wild Earth*, special issue (1992): 10–25; Reed F. Noss and A. Y. Cooperrider, *Saving Nature's Legacy* (Washington, DC: Island Press, 1994).

50. James J. Kay and E. Schneider, "The Challenge of the Ecosystem Approach," *Alternatives* 20, 3 (1994): 1–6; reprinted in *Perspectives on Integrity*, ed. L. Westra and J. Lemons, pp. 49–59.

51. Norton, *Toward Unity among Environmentalists*, p. 246.

52. Gary E. Varner, "Can Animal Right Activists Be Environmentalists?" in *People, Penguins and Plastic Trees*, 2d ed. (Belmont, CA: Wadsworth, 1995), pp. 254–73.

53. Norton, *Toward Unity among Environmentalists*, p. 246.

54. Karr and Chu, "Ecological Integrity"; See Noss and Cooperrider, *Saving Nature's Legacy*; R. Noss, *Maintaining Ecological Integrity in Representative Reserve Networks*, A World Wildlife Fund Canada/World Wildlife Fund/United States Discussion Paper (January 1995).

55. Brown, "The Role of Law in Sustainable Development and Environmental Protection Decision Making," p. 67.

56. B. G. Norton, "A New Paradigm for Environmental Management," in *Ecosystem Health*, ed. R. Costanza, B. G. Norton, and B. D. Haskell (Washington, DC: Island Press, 1992), p. 24.

57. Hans Lenk, "Ecology and Ethics: Notes about Technology and Economic Consequences," with Matthias Maring, in *Research in Philosophy and Technology*, vol. 12 (Greenwich, CT: JAI Press, 1992), p. 210.

58. Norton, "Environmental Ethics and Weak Anthropocentris"; Norton,

"Why I Am Not a Nonanthropocentrist: Callicott and the Failure of Monistic Inherentism."

59. See, for instance, W. Aiken, "Ethical Issues in Agriculture," in *Earthbound: New Introductory Essays in Environmental Ethics,* ed. Tom Regan (New York: Random House, 1984), pp. 247–88; T. Regan, *The Case for Animal Rights* (Berkeley: University of California Press, 1983), to mention but two other opponents of arguments for holism of the ecocentric/biocentric variety.

60. Norton, "Environmental Ethics and Weak Anthropocentris."

61. Norton, "Environmental Ethics and Weak Anthropocentris."

62. Regan, *The Case for Animal Rights,* p. 50; H. Rolston, *Environmental Ethics: Duties to and Values in the Natural World* (Philadelphia: Temple University Press, 1988); K. Goodpaster, "On Being Morally Considerable," *Journal of Philosophy* 75 (1978): 308–25; P. Taylor, *Respect for Nature: A Theory of Environmental Ethics* (Princeton: Princeton University Press, 1986).

63. Norton, "Why I Am Not a Nonanthropocentrist: Callicott and the Failure of Monistic Inherentism."

64. Noss, *Maintaining Ecological Integrity in Representative Reserve Networks.*

65. Klaus Meyer-Abich, *Revolution for Nature,* trans. M. Armstrong (Cambridge, England: White Horse Press, 1993).

66. A. Leopold, *A Sand County Almanac and Sketches Here and There* (New York: Oxford University Press, 1949).

67. Karr and Chu, "Ecological Integrity"; Kay and Schneider, "The Challenge of the Ecosystem Approach"; Ulanowicz, *Ecology, The Ascendent Perspective.*

68. Robert Goodland and Herman Daly, "Universal Environmental Sustainability and the Principle of Integrity," in *Perspectives on Ecological Integrity,* ed. L. Westra and J. Lemons (Dordrecht, The Netherlands: Kluwer, 1995), pp. 102–24.

69. Goodland, "Environmental Sustainability and the Power Sector—Part I: The Concept of Sustainability"; Westra, "Ecosystem Integrity and Sustainability: The Foundational Value of the Wild."

70. Lenk, "Ecology and Ethics: Notes about Technology and Economic Consequences."

71. K. Shrader-Frechette, *Nuclear Power and Public Policy* (Dordrecht, The Netherlands: Kluwer, 1982); Shrader-Frechette, *Risk and Rationality;* McGinn, "Technology, Demography, and the Anachronism of Traditional Rights."

72. Noss and Cooperrider, *Saving Nature's Legacy;* Lenk, "Ecology and Ethics: Notes about Technology and Economic Consequences."

73. E. Partridge, "On the Rights of Future Generations," in *Upstream/Downstream,* ed. D. Scherer and T. Attig (Philadelphia: Temple University Press, 1990), pp. 40–66; Richard De George, "The Environment, Rights and Future Generations," in *Ethics and Problems of the 21st Century,* ed. K. E. Goodpaster and K. M. Sayre pp. 93–105; Ruth Macklin, "Can Future Generations Correctly Be Said To Have Rights?" in *Responsibilities to Future Generations,* ed. E. Partridge (Buffalo, NY: Prometheus Books, 1981); Gregory Kavka, "The Paradox of Future Individuals," *Philosophy and Public Affairs* 2, 2 (Spring 1982): 92–112; Derek Parfit, *Reasons and Persons* (Oxford, England: Oxford University Press, 1984).

74. Norton, "Why I Am Not a Nonanthropocentrist: Callicott and the Failure of Monistic Inherentism."

75. De George, "The Environment, Rights and Future Generations."

76. L. Westra, "Integrity, Health and Sustainability: Environmentalism without Racism," in *The Science of the Total Environment*, for the World Health Organization (Oxford, England: Elsevier, 1990); Rita Colwell, "Global Change: Emerging Diseases and New Epidemics," President's Lecture, February 10, 1996, American Association for the Advancement of Science; Janice D. Longstretch, et al., "Effects of Increased Solar Ultraviolet Radiation on Human Health," *Ambio* 24, 3 (May 1995): 153–65.

77. C. Van der Weele, *Images of Development—Environmental Causes in Ontogeny* (Amsterdam: Free University of Amsterdam Press, 1995).

78. Van der Weele, *Images of Development*, p. 8.

79. Van der Weele, *Images of Development*, p. 9.

80. Theo Colborn, Dianne Dumanoski, John Peterson Myers, *Our Stolen Future* (New York: Dutton, 1996), p. 186.

81. Colborn, Dumanoski, and Myers, *Our Stolen Future*, p. 89.

82. Colborn, Dumanoski, and Myers, *Our Stolen Future*, pp. 88–89.

83. Colborn, Dumanoski, and Myers, *Our Stolen Future*, p. 81.

84. Colborn, Dumanoski, and Myers, *Our Stolen Future*, p. 83.

85. Colborn, Dumanoski, and Myers, *Our Stolen Future*, pp. 85–86.

86. Colborn, Dumanoski, and Myers, *Our Stolen Future*, pp. 251–60.

87. Jon Cohen, "Tobacco Money Lights Up a Debate," *Science* 272 "Special News Report" (April 26, 1996): 488–94.

88. Hans Jonas, *The Imperative of Responsibility* (Chicago: University of Chicago Press, 1984).

89. Dale Jamieson, "Managing the Future: Public Policy, Scientific Uncertainty, and Global Warming," in *Upstream/Downstream*, ed. D. Scherer and T. Attig, pp. 67–89; Dale Jamieson, "Ethics, Public Policy and Global Warming," *Science, Technology and Human Values* 17 (1992): 139–53.

90. Westra, "Integrity, Health and Sustainability: Environmentalism without Racism."

91. John Lemons, R. Heredia, D. Jamieson, and C. Spash, "Climate Change and Sustainable Development," in *Sustainable Development: Science, Ethics and Public Policy*, ed. John Lemons and D. Brown (Dordrecht, The Netherlands: Kluwer, 1995), 167.

5

Development and Environmental Racism: The Case of Ken Saro-Wiwa and the Ogoni

> The environment is man's first right
> We should not allow it to suffer blight
> The air we breathe we must not poison
> They who do should be sent to prison
> Our streams must remain clean all season
> Polluting them is clearly treason
> The land is life for man and flora,
> Fauna and all: should wear that aura,
> Protected from the greed and folly
> Of man and companies unholy.
>
> Ken Saro-Wiwa, "A Walk in the Prison Yard"

Playwright George Seremba writes:

> Last Monday I got news of the five attempts it took before they finally hanged him. In the Wild West they would let you walk at the failure of the first attempt. I will remember the words "Why are you doing this?" I also heard that he said, before they were all martyred: "Lord take my soul, but the struggle continues."[1]

Seremba is speaking of the murder of Ken Saro-Wiwa on November 10, 1995, an unspeakable crime committed by General Sani Abacha and his military tribunal, with the complicity of Nigeria's powerful elites, and with the tacit support of Royal Dutch Shell Oil and all of us in affluent northwestern countries who overconsume and overuse. For the most part, our silent complicity and our responsibility goes unacknowledged. Therefore, after briefly detailing a chronology of Nigeria's history from June 1993 to February 1995,[2] and presenting Ken Saro-Wiwa's case,[3] I

111

argue for the need for a new approach to personal morality and public policy that includes an *environmental* assessment of all technological projects. I also argue that a holistic assessment of all developmental issues is the only approach capable of imposing respect for all life-support systems, hence for all human and nonhuman life.

Nigeria under the Dictatorship of Sani Abacha: Ken Saro-Wiwa and the Ogoni People

The events of 1995 and the killing of Saro-Wiwa may be seen as the culmination of two separate but intertwined historical lines, one tracing the political developments in Nigeria and the other that country's economic interaction with oil companies, primarily Royal Dutch Shell Oil and Exxon.

Political Developments

In June 1993, General Babangida sanctioned presidential elections in Nigeria: Chief M. K. O. Abiola was the clear winner, but Babangida canceled the elections after the fact, claiming fraud. The international community reacted by canceling all but humanitarian aid, suspending military cooperation, and restricting visas to Nigeria. Wole Soyinka describes what happened:

> On June 23, 1993, the day of the annulment of the presidential election, the military committed the most treasonable act of larceny of all time: it violently robbed the Nigerian people of their nationhood.[4]

Through July and August, the country was plagued by demonstrations, and hundreds were killed in clashes. The government in power detained human-rights workers and charged them with sedition, unlawful assembly, and other "crimes." At this time, both Babangida and Shonekan, his intended successor, were ousted by Abacha.

In November 1993, Abacha disbanded all elected bodies, such as the state legislature, thirty houses of state assemblies, and all local councils, and banned all political activity. He also suspended the 1979 constitution, including all provisions for human rights it contained. In April 1994, a Civil Disturbances Tribunal was established with the power to impose the death penalty: capital offenses now included "unrest crimes" and "attempted murder." By May 1994, four Ogoni leaders were murdered and several hundred people, supporters of the Movement for Survival of the Ogoni People (MOSOP) were arrested, including Saro-Wiwa.

The documents of Amnesty International relate that "he was severely beaten, his legs chained."[5] Former senators, governors, and members of the House of Representatives were also detained without charge. From June to September, a major gas and oil union went on strike, causing riots and protests, and President Bill Clinton sent Jesse Jackson as a special envoy to attempt mediation. This effort was not successful, and the whole Nigerian Labour Congress (NLC), representing forty unions and 3.5 million workers, joined the strike. This prompted authorities to dissolve all unions and replace their leaders with government-appointed officials. In September, the strike collapsed, and Abacha issued a series of decrees, retroactive to mid-August, allowing "administrative detention laws, for up to three months, renewable," and specifying further that this particular law could not be challenged in court.

Abacha also fired the attorney general, Olu Onagoruwa, and arrested union officials and leaders. In 1995, a ban on all political activities was enacted; still, no time was set for the present regime's departure. In Ogoniland, hundreds of villages were destroyed and hundreds of villagers killed, while Saro-Wiwa was still detained, suffering ongoing inhumane treatment and often torture: he was expected to be tried by the Civil Disturbances Tribunal for the murder of four officials in Ogoniland.

Economic and Technological Developments

In 1958, Shell discovered oil in Ogoniland, 404 square miles of largely wild, fertile land, home to a variety of flowers, plants, and animals, both terrestrial and, beyond its coast, marine, and to 500,000 Ogoni people.[6] Chevron moved its oil exploration to Ogoniland in 1977, and both companies, jointly, have extracted an estimated US$30 billion worth of oil from Ogoniland. Saro-Wiwa said:

> In return for this we have received nothing but a highly polluted land where associated gas burns twenty-four hours a day, belching carbon monoxide, carbon dioxide, methane and soot into the air; and oil spillage and blow-outs devastate much needed farmland, threatening human existence.
>
> Flora and fauna are all but dead, marine life is destroyed, the ecosystem is fast-changing. Ogoni is a wasteland.[7]

Nigeria's military dictatorship was geographically removed from this devastation, and enjoyed a mutually supportive relationship with the oil companies, as it depended on the wealth the oil companies provided.

In turn, the oil companies depended on the dictatorship to ignore the environmental disasters they continued to create, and not to impose restraints or demand remediation or compensation for the land and people affected. Throughout this increasingly distressing state of affairs, Saro-Wiwa maintained that "the environment is man's first right. Without a safe environment, man cannot live to claim other rights."[8] He also steadfastly opposed the devastation of Ogoniland, demanding remediation of environmental problems and royalties to assist his people. The Ogoni desperately needed help, as families could no longer depend on the land and the sea but required financial and medical aid to mitigate the many ills destroying not only their livelihood but also their health, as they were now living in "absolute poverty."[9] They had no access to safe water, electricity, telephones, or any educational or health facilities.[10]

Examples of the harms inflicted on the Ogoni people from Shell's economic exploitation abound. In one case, Grace Zorbidon was walking near her mud hut one night in January 1994, carrying a kerosene lantern to light her way. She did not see "the oil slick oozing from a rupture in a pipeline that runs hard up against her tiny village."[11] When she put down her lantern, she was engulfed by flames, and in May 1994 was still lying on the floor of a healer's hut in terrible pain, treated only with traditional potions made from leaves. Shell neither inquired after her nor saw to her treatment or to the fate of the eight children of this "subsistence farmer." Its excuse? Shell said it was "hazy" on the accident and could not substantiate Zorbidon's report because of the "tensions in the area." Shell was much quicker to respond to protests and demonstrations that had forced it to close its operations in early 1994. Shell's reaction was to "ask for assistance" from the military authorities, who responded with swift and brutal retribution against the protesters.

The Nigerian government was not prepared to tolerate any interference with its business relations with Shell: neither human rights nor environmental concerns could be allowed to interfere. The *Wall Street Journal* reports:

> Nigeria's government depends on oil for 80% of its income, and sees any threat to the industry as imperiling its shaky hold on power. Oil produced by Shell accounts for about half of these revenues.[12]

Nigeria's military dictatorship and Shell operate as a joint venture in which Shell holds a 30 percent interest, the Nigerian government holds 55 percent, Elf Aquitaine of France, 10 percent, and Agip Française, 5 percent. Further, the United States was also benefiting from the arrangement: it imported 36 percent of Nigeria's oil production in 1993, which accounted for about 11 percent of all U.S. oil imports.

In all these large business transactions, what if any benefits have the Ogoni reaped from their land's exploitation? When large multinationals interact with impoverished developing countries, the benefits accrue primarily to their constituents in the affluent Northwest. The usual trade-offs offered are employment; improvements such as roads, hospitals, and schools; and remediation of any environmental impact. Shell's record appears dismal on all counts. "Of Shell's 5000 employees in Nigeria, only 85 are Ogoni."[13] There are "96 oil wells, two refineries, a petrochemical complex and a fertilizer plant" in Ogoniland, but the only available hospital is described as an "unfinished husk," and the promised schools are seldom open, "because there is no money available for teachers' salaries."[14]

In addition, Shell's spokesman claimed that Shell "deplored" the military's "heavy-handed clampdowns and the pain and loss suffered by local communities." However, there is no record of Shell initiating any policy to ameliorate the Ogoni's lot or to mitigate the damage it had perpetrated. Given the strength of their economic interests in Shell's operations, the military continued to organize raids to "punish" the Ogoni for obstructing Shell, and responded to protests by shooting into the crowd, killing and maiming civilians, using any pretext to lay "entire villages to waste." The raids were often conducted by a mobile police unit, "nicknamed Kill and Go." On Easter Sunday in 1994, villagers who had fled the raids were felled by random shootings. "One ten-year-old girl says she was gang-raped. Three days later, the whites of her eyes were bloodshot the flesh around them purple and swollen." She explained that the soldiers attempted to gouge her eyes out, so "that she would not be able to identify them."[15] Health facilities, says a European nurse, are minimal, and Shell refused even to pave the roads to prevent patients' having to walk through the mud to reach the clinic.

What of the "economic benefits"? In response to increasing protests from the Ogoni, the government ostensibly offered 3 perent of its oil revenues to them. In practice, these percentages never reached the Ogoni, as the money was spent in the tribal lands of the ruling majority instead or vanished "in corrupt deals."[16] As far as remediation is concerned, one example will suffice. A spill more than twenty years ago, near the village of Ebubu, has never been cleaned; today, in "an area the size of four football fields, cauliflower shaped extrusions of moist black tar cover the ground to a depth of about three feet."[17] Shell claims that while unrest continues, it is not prepared to do any cleanup work: it is worth noting that the spill occurred in the late 1960s.

Along with the government's role in the economic development by the oil companies, foreign observers are denied access, and even a fact-finding mission from the Netherlands was denied permission to visit; "checkpoints" were set up instead "to monitor Western travellers." The *Wall Street Journal* reporter who compiled most of the information summarized in this section concludes by relating her own experience:

> When I approached an army officer to ask for the military's account of a violent incident, I was handed over to the secret police, held and interrogated for two days, and then deported "for security reasons."[18]

Although the U.S. government commissioned a human rights report on the Ogoni in 1993, the report only admitted "some merit" to the Ogoni's claims and refused to accept the designation of "genocide" urged by Saro-Wiwa to describe the Ogoni's plight. Saro-Wiwa remarked that "one thousand dead Ogonis out of five hundred thousand" is comparable to five million dead U.S. citizens, which surely would be considered genocide.

In essence, the annihilation of human rights and the clear presence of racism (or even of attempts at "ethnic cleansing") that was manifested by the oil companies with the support of the military dictatorship of Nigeria was more than a particularly lethal case of environmental racism. It was and is no less than an "ecological war"; Saro-Wiwa called it "omnicide," adding: "men, women and children die unnoticed, flora and fauna are threatened, the air is poisoned, waters are polluted, and, finally, the land itself dies."[19]

Again a Question of Responsibility

So far we have pointed to joint activities of Shell Oil and the military regime under Abacha as the primary source of the crimes committed against the Ogoni and their land. But are they the sole culprits? We can learn a lot from Shell's public relations response to Saro-Wiwa's murder and the international revulsion and anger that followed. After all, Saro-Wiwa was well known as the recipient of several prizes and grants (the 1995 Goldman Environmental Prize, the 1994 Right Livelihood Award). One of the 1995 Bruno Kreisky Human Rights Awards, the Goldman Environmental Prize, was deliberately given to him in advance of its appropriate date, in the hope of drawing international attention to him, as he had already been declared a prisoner of conscience by Amnesty International. As Saro-Wiwa was a well-known poet, writer, and activist, his death had an impact that Shell attempted to offset by buying prime space in international newspapers, in an effort to shift blame for its actions and omissions, disclaiming any responsibility for either the environmental devastation or the murder.

In a carefully worded message[20] entitled "Clear Thinking in Troubled Times," Shell explicitly allied itself with "clear thinking" and patronizingly dismissed a "great wave of understandable emotion over the death of Ken Saro-Wiwa," together with the anger and disapprobation it faced from all nations. "The public have been manipulated and misled" was one of its statements, as Shell attempted to whitewash itself because it had spent millions in "environmentally related projects." The environmental problems were due, they claimed, to "over-farming"(!), soil erosion, deforestation, and population growth, in areas where only the most meager subsistence farming existed: Geraldine Brooks of the *Wall Street Journal* describes it as "pulling tubers from the earth with sticks."[21] Shell further appealed to a World Bank survey to support its position, but the World Bank was one of the few major powers who, together with the Royal Geographical Society, withdrew all their support from Nigeria in protest and categorically denied Shell's allegations.

Shell also remarked that, after all, it was not the only one at fault, as all humanitarian protests and even international sanctions could not (and in fact did not) succeed. One can speculate that no other "sanctions" could prevail, as they would not carry the same clout for a money-hungry military clique as would the continued cash-producing presence of Shell and other oil companies.

Finally, Shell raised a question and a veiled threat common to all industries that are the target of environmental protests worldwide. The ad continued, "What if we were to withdraw from the project" and with it, all employment the project entails? "The oil extraction would continue," the ad asserted, "and it might not be done any better." One could respond that other companies elsewhere have in fact done much better. For instance, Conoco DuPont, which drilled a well in Gabon between 1989 and 1992,

> flew in much of its equipment to avoid pushing a major road through the rain forest. When trees had to be felled, the company hired scientists to cultivate cuttings so that sites could be replanted with exactly the same species that had been removed.[22]

Hence, a technology assessment based on a holistic management perspective would have made a large difference at the outset rather than to demand remediation after the fact, a largely useless procedure from the environmental standpoint and, as we saw, in light of the military regime's disrespect for human rights.

Even more appalling from the moral standpoint was the final paragraph of Shell's page-long ad:

> Some campaigning groups say we should intervene in the political process in Nigeria. But even if we could, we must never do so. Politics is the business of governments and politicians. The world where companies use their economic influence to prop up or bring down governments would be a frightening and bleak one indeed.[23]

It is both "frightening" and "bleak" to read such a vicious travesty of the facts: Shell is a partner in the joint venture with Nigeria's ruthless and inhumane military regime and knew full well the impact its financial support had on the latter's existence. Further, when negotiations and consent *both* originate from nonelected, nonrepresentative authorities, one is clearly already "meddling" in the politics of the country with which one deals.

Environmental Ethics and Responsibility

Ascribing responsibility for the gross miscarriage of justice and the environmental devastation of Ogoniland to Shell and the military regime of Nigeria is necessary, but it is not sufficient for a serious ethical evaluation of the situation. Shell and others like it could quickly point out that they have a profitable market for their operations only because we, the affluent northwestern consumers, are hungry for abundant, low-cost oil and gasoline products. It is not enough to point the finger at Shell and other corporate exploiters. It is also necessary to confront the morality of our lifestyle and our policy choices.

This is the raw, evil side of technological progress. It is eco-violence perpetrated against the most vulnerable people: it shows the worst face of environmental racism in a most deadly form. Retaliation against pro-environmental protest ended in a murder, orchestrated by a kangaroo court: Ken Saro-Wiwa was murdered by hanging. The dictatorial regime that plotted and executed his murder on a trumped-up charge was heavily dependent on the oil revenues generated by Shell's operations. The question now is, how should that technology have been evaluated before its impact on Nigeria was felt?

Traditional moral theories could and should indict the gross abuse of human rights that took place when Saro-Wiwa was murdered; they could decry the lack of justice and due process in his trial and sentencing and appeal to Rawlsian principles in defense of all the Ogoni people; finally, they could appeal to Bullard's "five principles of environmental justice" to combat environmental racism.[24] But all these arguments are end-of-pipe attempts at mitigation, after the fact. The fundamental question remains: how should the introduction of a large technological system such as oil extraction have been evaluated in that particular geographical area? From the ecocentric point of view, the environmental impact should have been anticipated, if not precisely, at least with enough accuracy to discourage Shell, unless an impartial international commission, including appropriate scientists and environmental ethicists, with veto powers, could be put in place to oversee all Shell's plans and activities. In contrast, if we would counsel a purely anthropocentric position for our starting point, we might still be able to put in place some restraints based on risk assessments of the situation. But without knowing the actual results of Shell's operations, it would have been extremely difficult to stop them or establish tight limits on their activities, *before the fact.*

Hence, if we had simply appealed to traditional moral principles, we might not have been able to stop the violence that followed. This also would have rendered us guilty of complicity, as would have our isolating ourselves from the information and simply averting our eyes while enjoying these products' easy availability.[25] The question is one of moral responsibility, one that Hans Jonas, for instance, viewed as the most important question to be asked in regard to technology.[26] Jonas said, "The new kinds and dimensions of action require a commensurate ethics of foresight and responsibility, which is as novel as the eventualities which it must meet." And when foresight is difficult because of science's lack of predictive capacities, since "care for the future" is the "overruling duty," we must face the fact that the only possible moral choice might be the careful application of the precautionary principle, or even abstention from certain nonbasic lifestyle and technological choices.

A question remains. Had a democracy been in place, and had the citizens of Ogoniland been polled about their wishes in regard to the projects of Shell and other corporations, would that have been enough to save the environment on which they depend? One problem is that even if a technology impact assessment had been required and openly publicized, it is unlikely that a community of subsistence farmers would have been well informed enough to foresee the irreversible ecological damage that would be their lot eventually, even if they would have received a fair percentage of the oil royalties and roads, schools, and clinics were built for their use. Saro-Wiwa would have known, but it is at least an open question whether he would have been listened to before the fact.

This remains a routine problem whenever hazardous operations move into minority or economically depressed areas in their home countries, although both education levels and standards of living might be higher, comparatively, than those of the Ogoni.[27] Hence, I suggest that even in an ideal situation, where legal restraints on environmental hazards are in place and where democratic institutions prevail, the environmental and health protection of all is by no means guaranteed, when the need for sustainability does not govern public policy.

Thus, although it is both easy and even necessary to indict (1) the military rule and the despotism that was instrumental in the killing of Ken Saro-Wiwa and the devastation of his land and (2) the large corporations that wreaked havoc on the environment and their callous and unjust exploitation of a vulnerable people, this is not enough.

On November 13, 1995, the *Wall Street Journal* reported that, although "sanction threats" were issued and the United States cut military aid, and although the United Kingdom banned arms sales and the European Union recalled its ambassadors and suspended all aid, *no nation* had "halted purchases of Nigerian oil or sales of drilling equipment, as a result of the hangings."[28] Halting the oil trade would bring Nigeria to its knees, as oil represents 90 percent of its exports and 80 percent of its revenue, but the United States would also be hard hit, as it imports 40 percent of Nigeria's oil. The United States recalled its ambassador but did not make the principled stand made by the World Bank. The International Finance Corporation (private-sector lending for the World Bank) withdrew its support in the form of a US$100,000 loan to Nigeria from a liquefied natural gas project.[29]

The problem is that as long as we elect leaders and governments on the basis of promises of low taxes and low prices, as well as the "right" to development, without any consideration of the size of our "ecological footprint," let alone its location (that is to say, without considering who is to pay for our choices), we cannot claim to be free from responsibility. Each one of us is to some extent a contributor to the evil deeds perpetrated in Nigeria.

It is both what we *do* and what we *fail to do* that are at issue. In essence, we cannot continue to consume and to waste as though we had the right to take from the poor and the vulnerable just because we can afford it. We must reconsider our political choices when they are explicitly isolationist and segregationist in intent, and when they are both supported by and supportive of big business, such as oil companies, tobacco producers, or manufacturers of chemicals or transgenics—all of which, in their present forms, often spell death for our environment and severely threaten our health and the persistence of our species on earth.[30] Thus the problem is a question of personal as well as ecological integrity: it is a moral problem to which no facile solutions now exist. In some sense, Ken Saro-Wiwa died because of our moral failures, our negligence, and our lack of commitment to justice and a moral ideal.

Notes

Note: I am extremely grateful to Dr. Owers Wiwa for reading this chapter for factual accuracy.

1. George Seremba, "Playwright Grieves for Saro-Wiwa and Africa," *The Globe and Mail* (Toronto) (November 18, 1995), p. H3.

2. Amnesty International, "Nigeria Historical Fact Sheet: June 1993, February 1995" (Washington, DC).

3. Goldman Environmental Foundation Documents package on Ken Saro-Wiwa (San Francisco, 1995); see also Goldman Environmental Prize Foundation, Duane Silverstein, Executive Director, San Francisco, "Nigeria's Ken Saro-Wiwa On Trial for His Life" (February 23, 1995) (a publication on the Goldman Environment Foundation).

4. Wole Soyinka, "Nigeria's Long, Steep, Bloody Slide," *New York Times*, August 22, 1994.

5. Amnesty International, "Nigeria Historical Fact Sheet."

6. Ken Saro-Wiwa, "Human Rights, Democracy and an African Gulag," unpublished talk, New York, March 2, 1994.

7. Saro-Wiwa, "Human Rights."

8. Ken Saro-Wiwa, "Right Livelihood Award Acceptance Speech," Stockholm, Sweden, December 9, 1994.

9. Vandana Shiva, *Staying Alive* (London: Zed Books, 1988).

10. Saro-Wiwa, "Human Rights"; Saro-Wiwa, "Right Livelihood Award."

11. Geraldine Brooks, "Slick Alliance: Shell's Nigerian Fields Produce Few Benefits for Region's Villagers" and "How Troops Handle Protests," *Wall Street Journal* (May 6, 1994), pp. A1, A4.

12. Brooks, "Slick Alliance."

13. Brooks, "Slick Alliance."

14. Brooks, "Slick Alliance."

15. Brooks, "Slick Alliance."

16. Brooks, "Slick Alliance."

17. Brooks, "Slick Alliance."

18. Brooks, "Slick Alliance."

19. Saro-Wiwa, "Human Rights."

20. *The Globe and Mail* (Toronto) (November 21, 1995), p. A17.

21. Brooks, "Slick Alliance."

22. Brooks, "Slick Alliance."

23. *The Globe and Mail* (Toronto) (November 21, 1995), p. A17.

24. L. Westra and P. Wenz, *The Faces of Environmental Racism: The Global Equity Issues* (Lanham, MD: Rowman & Littlefield, 1995).

25. K. Shrader-Frechette, *Risk and Rationality* (Berkeley: University of California Press, 1991), especially chapter 10.

26. Hans Jonas, *The Imperative of Responsibility* (Chicago: University of Chicago Press, 1984).

27. Westra and Wenz, *The Faces of Environmental Racism*.

28. Thomas Kamm and Robert Greenberger, "Nigeria Executions Raise Sanction Threat," *Wall Street Journal* (November 13, 1995), p. 10.

29. Kamm and Greenberger, "Nigeria Executions"; see also Howard W. French, "Nigeria Executes Activist Playwright," *San Francisco Chronicle* (November 11, 1995), pp. A1, A13.

30. L. Westra, "Integrity, Health and Sustainability: Environmentalism without Racism," in *The Science of the Total Environment* (Oxford, England: Elsevier, 1996).

6

Biotechnology and Transgenics in Agriculture and Aquaculture: The Perspective from Ecosystem Integrity

In the previous chapter we analyzed a specific case of environmental racism in which consumerism and the profit motive collided with justice. Here we examine a particular area of technology from the standpoint of the ethics of integrity and of morality in general. Biotechnology represents a fairly recent technological development, and its possible impact on integrity is a grave one, at both the macro and the micro levels. I show the urgent need for regulations, and I argue that biotechnology would best be regulated from the standpoint of the ethics of integrity defended in this work.

After introducing the issue of biotechnology in agriculture and focusing on the hazards engendered by the use of biotechnology in food production, the discussion turns to aquaculture and examines the impact of biotechnology in that context, followed by the role of climate change in regard to biotechnology. My conclusion is that the present regulatory framework that places the burden of proof on those who suffer harm may need to be reversed. Biotechnology may have to be judged as a prima facie contributor to disintegrity. In that case, it ought to be up to those who manufacture, market, and distribute those products to show in situ whether each new introduction of a transgenic is ecologically sound. Additionally, they should be prepared to establish their good faith and accountability by open labeling of all technologically engineered products.

Introduction to Biotechnology

When we face moral and social questions about the commercial uses of biotechnology and transgenics, we need to ask ourselves two important

123

questions *before* consenting to their use: (1) Are these technologies equal
to the task they are intended to accomplish? (2) Even if it can be shown
that they are the means to some common good, can it also be argued
that they are right in themselves, or a morally defensible means to a
morally right goal? Biotechnologies and transgenics are proposed as
means to the universal good of alleviating hunger worldwide. Hence, in
relation to food production, the multinational corporations that push
to develop, patent, and commercially distribute technologically altered
organisms do so for profit; at the same time, however, they claim that
their products are environmentally sounder than those produced by
present practices and, in fact, that they provide the only solution to hunger in the Third World in the face of exploding populations.

Increasing scientific evidence about the problems arising out of the
high-tech approach to agriculture, such as soil erosion and increased
use of pesticides (with its accompaniments, pesticide-resistant insects
and contaminated food), points to reduced productivity in the near future and fosters poor long-term prospects as well. On one hand, these
pressing concerns suggest the need for new agricultural techniques; on
the other, public unease in regard to the widespread use of toxic chemicals also appears to point to the need for new solutions to the hunger
problem. Hence, the drive to quickly introduce new products and technologies, ostensibly to solve the previous problems and to produce better results.

The newly engineered plants, animals, and fish look as they always
did, but they are different in specific ways. A plant may have been bred
with a virus so that the new creation is both animal and vegetal (an
"aniplant" perhaps?), and it possesses traits the predecessor plant did
not. These traits are desirable from the standpoint of economics and
production: on the plus side, they increase yield and thus promise to
feed more people more efficiently. On the minus side, the new plant
has now evolved into one with an inbred resistance to a specific herbicide. The result is that the bioengineered species—heralded as a step
forward for environmental safety and a step away from chemicals—
actually represents a permanent, inescapable link to chemicals, as the
new creation has a built-in tolerance for a specific herbicide.

Therefore, the corporation gains twice: once when it sells the biotechnology, and again when it ensures the product's permanent addiction
to its own patented herbicide. At the same time, however, the people
and the environment lose twice: once because the proposed "safe"
product ultimately is not, and again when other possibly safer, organic,
and sustainable choices are preempted. The producers' strategy entails
appealing to shared principles of the good for the majority in order to
defend their aggressive pursuit of these novel technologies and their

intensive marketing. Despite this side of their operations, corporations could still operate according to shared moral principles.

But these so-called shared principles of justice, fairness, and the pursuit of the common good are not necessarily present once both the technologies and their dissemination are scrutinized more closely. If the expected consequences are either nonexistent or vastly different from the results envisioned, then the "countervailing benefits" may not be overwhelming enough to justify neglecting the problems and risks involved.[1]

Therefore, we need to reexamine the questions posed at the outset. Is the claim advanced on behalf of new biotechnologies and their superior capacity in regard to food production a correct one? Is it true that these new products are not only instrumental in resolving the problem of world hunger, but that they also represent the *only* possible solution to that problem? It would be easier to dismiss the whole enterprise as nothing but another corporate moneymaking scheme if these questions could be answered with some degree of certainty. To feed the hungry is a morally worthwhile goal, and if it could be shown that the achievement of that goal depends on the use of biotechnology, then we would need to attempt to mitigate its negative effects, and to find ways to control and modify the way engineered products are manufactured, marketed, and distributed, but not to question their very existence.

In contrast, if a careful examination were to indicate that the widely touted benefits of biotechnology are doubtful, or simply outweighed by their negative effects, then its moral status as a means to a desirable end would be seriously in doubt. The next sections discuss the claims made on behalf of biotechnology and the use of transgenics in the areas of agriculture and aquaculture and carefully examine their negative impact. These negatives will not only be practical and ecological, but also will include problems that might be raised by their use, in regard to traditional moral theories as well as from a holistic environmental perspective. I conclude that once the impact of these technologies is unmasked, the principle of integrity provides the strictest criterion on which to base our assessment of their moral viability.

Agricultural Food Production, Biodiversity and Biotechnology: The "Perils Amidst the Promise"

What are "transgenic plants," and what is their application and use in commercial agriculture? "Transgenic plants are crops that have been genetically engineered to contain traits from unrelated organisms."[2] In practice, "adding novel genes to crops means adding new traits and abilities. Genetic engineers can move genes from any biological source—animal, plants or bacteria—into almost any crop," and it is this novelty that ensures that these "aliens" will simply not fit in with the rest of the system's naturally evolved biota. Traditional breeding techniques have a built-in safety net, as they will fail unless the organisms that are joined are similar (in the sense of coming from similar species) in ways that are relevant to their function within their joint habitats. If they were incompatible for some reason, they could not be successfully joined. In this sense then, earlier, traditional techniques ensure that the breeding's result will fit within the natural habitat of both organisms used. From this perspective, therefore, traditional breeding is different *in kind* from genetic engineering.

In the past, food scarcity, the desire for new products, or the presence of agricultural problems has been mitigated by the importation of alien species (for example, the introduction of the potato in Europe). From this perspective, there is a difference in degree between biotechnology and this occasional introduction of nonnative species. Biotechnologies are many, uncontrolled, widespread, and ubiquitous in many areas without any attempt to coordinate and study the effects of their presence as a whole. They are added to complex systems already subjected to multiple anthropogenic stresses, under hazardous conditions of global change.

Thus, the introduction of biotechnologies gives rise to a number of environmental problems. These problems affect the claims about increased agricultural productivity on which biotechnology's manufacturers rely in order to justify their enterprise.

The environmental problems—major as they are, as we shall see— inspire only one set of questions that needs to be raised in this regard, and although many of the problems raised by biotechnology are related, a list of problem clusters may help us to understand the concerns many express in their regard:

a. The introduction of novel organisms into natural ecosystems, with unpredictable effects on both humans and nonhumans
b. The lack of controls comparable to those imposed on the manufacture of new drugs, cosmetics, and medications
c. The lack of labeling, hence, the denial of the public's right to know
d. The absence of independent professional interventions, to ensure safety to humans
e. The lack of support for our right to choose, to consent, and to freely practice a chosen religion, which follows upon the denial in (c)
f. The increase of threats to biodiversity and to natural systems

A brief discussion of these points will place us in a better position to reconsider the claims about increased productivity and the industry's right to be viewed as the only answer to world hunger.

The major point at issue is the introduction of *novel* organisms (a) into natural systems, in the senses discussed earlier. Corporate manufacturers respond that by combining what is already available in nature, transgenics are neither novel nor alien in the sense intended by this objection. This response ignores the fact that each natural system is geared to function optimally through and for certain species that are appropriate and native to it. The evolutionary unfolding of various systems through almost two thousand years has ensured that certain processes will support a diversity of life appropriate to each landscape. Any change is at least a risk. The introduction of novelty represents a risk without precedent, leading to unpredictable effects that are unlikely to be benign. We are learning, by trial and error, the results of these new anthropogenic stresses on natural systems, but we do so only at the cost of using all the earth's biota (including ourselves) as the unconsenting subjects of giant experiments.

Another point worthy of note is that (b) like the pharmaceutical industry, biotechnology is research intensive. It tends toward expensive products that can be sold "at premium prices to cover the cost of research."[3] But unlike the drug industry, biotechnology is (1) under no tight controls similar to those imposed by the medical establishment on new drugs and medications; (2) not forced to label its products clearly for content, indications, and possible side effects; and (3) because it targets global mass markets, without the intervention of a medical professional to protect the public, free to examine the industry claims, and to tailor the use of a product to the specific requirements of each individual patient.

In other words, the introduction of alien substances may produce different effects in different natural systems; similarly, both the medication and its quantity must fit specific patients. One example will illustrate this problem and the related issue of the right to knowledge and consent (c). In the late 1980s, an amino acid, tryptophan, was produced and sold through health food stores as a sleep medication. Eventually, a Japanese firm, Showa Denko Company, changed the process and started to produce it with genetically engineered bacteria—with disastrous results. Particularly in the United States, where, in contrast with Canada, it was sold as food, and thus not subject to testing, regulations, and labeling, people started to sicken and die from eosinophilia-myalgia syndrome. After thirty-one deaths, injuries to over a thousand people, and a rash of lawsuits, Showa Denko closed for business. This made it impossible to test either the substance or the manufacturing/engineering process.

Nevertheless, as the substance was over 99 percent pure, the procedure involving genetic engineering appears to be the most likely cause of the terrible toll of death and suffering.[4]

Even if absolute proof is not available of the direct causal connection between genetic engineering and this case's morbidity and mortality, several points emerge. (1) There was no required labeling to alert the public to the changed processes and the genetic engineering involved in the manufacture of the product. (2) The product was sold as food, rather than as a drug, and therefore neither testing nor medical advice was required for its use. (3) The U.S. government itself was "unaware of the introduction of tryptophan made by genetically engineered bacteria" so that, under present regulations, the tragedy was unavoidable, even in principle.[5]

It can be argued that the *institutional* setting of biotechnology is hostile to any concern for the public interest, beyond public relation efforts designed to allay public fears without, however, imparting information about the manufacture of products (because of the legal protection of trade secrets) or about possible effects (because of the lack of available research, scientific imprecision, and the lack of time to develop appropriate research projects).

Some of these problems appear similar to those affecting the nuclear power industry, although the latter has a much longer history and its problems and risks have been amply documented.[6] The similarities are mainly institutional: neither industry is subject to outside reviews of its practices,[7] and in neither case can scientific experts be found who are not supported or employed by their respective industries or by government bodies that have a vested interest in each industry's continued viability.

Further, as Margaret Mellon points out,[8] other novel, expensively researched new products capable of imposing risks can be found among pharmaceuticals (c). But these products are controlled by strict governmental regulations, including labeling and disclosure requirements, and they are subject to checks by dispensing pharmacists and prescribing medical professionals (d). For medications and drugs, these factors tend to minimize the public risk exposure, although even with all such regulations in place, tragedies like the damage suffered by infants who were exposed in utero to thalidomide can still happen.

One might object that pharmaceutical products are ingested, but in one form or another so are agricultural biotechnologies. It is also increasingly clear that the industry as a whole resists all efforts on the part of the public and other concerned scientific organizations to regulate it. Monsanto, for instance, has recently expanded aggressively into Canada, funding a "food research institute" at the University of Toronto, and taking out a full-page advertisement about milk additives (BGH) in the Canadian national newspaper, *The Globe and Mail.* Monsanto's position is, "as it's perfectly safe, we don't need to label it," a circular argument that does nothing to prove its claim of safety or defend the company's refusal to comply with the public disclosure regulations to which all food is subject. There is no direct evidence linking the use of BGH to human health threats, but a recent event in England indicates that not all possible links have been properly explored. The recent outbreak of mad cow disease (arising from sheep scrapie, and linked to Creutzfeld-Jakob disease in humans[9]) is a case in point. When milk-producing cows are put on a BGH regimen, they require a great deal of protein in their diet, to support their increased productivity. The only cost-efficient way to introduce the additional protein into their feed has been to feed animals to animals, that is, to use ground sheep carcasses in cattle feed, which led to the transmission of the disease between the two species. The fact that Creutzfeld-Jakob disease carries an incubation period of up to thirty years and that its symptoms in humans are very close to those of Alzheimer's makes it very hard even to diagnose let alone predict. Furthermore, no cure exists. This case was briefly mentioned in chapter 1 because it clearly demonstrates that the present regulatory framework and institutional procedures are insufficient to protect the public globally from serious threats to life and health.

We can therefore argue that, whatever the risk of physical harms arising from biotechnology and transgenics, *moral harms* are clearly imposed as breaches of human rights. Through corporate activities, we are not permitted to know exactly what we eat or what we feed our children; under such conditions of deliberate secrecy, informed choices are not possible (d). This situation fosters physical harms as well (for instance, from possible allergic reactions), and it precludes the possibility of complying with personal lifestyle and religious choices (e) in connection with food.[10]

Finally (f), what about the biotechnology industry's connection to the chemicals its products are intended (ostensibly) to avoid? We are now increasingly aware of the degradation intensive petrochemically supported agricultural practices entail. I have argued that the call to integrity is foundational for sustainability in food production in at least two senses: (1) the loss of ecosystems' capacity (that is, disintegrity) that follows upon intensive petrochemically based agricultural practices; and (2) intrusive and manipulative activities such as the introduction of exotics and aliens (such as transgenics) into ecosystems, both of which affect integrity at the macro level (ecosystems) and at the micro level (single organisms).

Wild areas support sustainable agriculture directly and indirectly. Directly, the biodiversity they foster remains a supply depot in which alternatives may be found for lost species; indirectly, wild areas provide the only exemplar or benchmark for comparable areas, for what is appropriate and necessary within an ecosystem to support its health and foster its function. Thus, if we continue to exploit certain areas without reference to integrity and wild areas, sustainability will be lost through the scientific incapacity to understand and predict the effects of technical interference and alterations.

Agricultural examples abound. Studies concerning chemically based agriculture show the dangers of reliance on short-term solutions.[11] Other environmental concerns about biotechnology are no less grave. Two major points need to be emphasized at the outset: (1) the commercialization of transgenic crops carries serious environmental risks in itself; and (2) transgenic crops have both initial effects and "cumulative and cascading effects." Underlying both problems is the lack of stringent regulations governing these products, at least in North America. For example, the U.S. Department of Agriculture, which governs transgenic crops as food, requires only that the corporations that research and manufacture them be prepared to do their own testing and submit the results.[12] The tests are performed under controlled circumstances that may be quite different from those of the landscapes where the products will be introduced, many of them in the Third World.

The importance of the changed conditions of the ecosystem/habitat where these plants will grow cannot be overemphasized. Recently, over twenty plants imported into nonnative ecosystems have invaded their own and other adjacent areas as weeds: Kudzu and purple loosestrife are just two of the better-known ones. Weeds are plants "whose undesirable qualities outweigh [their] good points." They invade crops and other habitats, play havoc with the native plant and animals species, and often produce toxic and allergenic side effects, when unintentionally mixed with crop seeds. They also compete with native species, choking growth and producing toxic chemicals.[13] Transgenics often "convert non-weedy crops to weeds"; once they are established, many undesirable and unanticipated effects will come into play. Their "cascading effects" may include deleterious effects on nontarget organisms, wild birds, insects, arthropods, amphibians, fish, and the like. Their effect on the ecological integrity of ecosystems is thus simply unknown.

When the transgenics are pesticidal, they often kill "non-target and even beneficial insects and fungi," and the "loss of fungi involved in resource cycling could impede the flow of nutrients vital to ecosystem functioning."[14] Similarly, the ultimate results of the evolution of pest resistance are not known. Hence appropriate testing (before commercialization), both long term in scope and carried out by impartial parties, appears to be vitally important to the decision on whether the safety of human and nonhuman animals and habitats has been protected. Moreover, the weediness that appears to be an unavoidable consequence of the use of transgenics may also threaten centers of biodiversity in the Third World on which global agriculture is utterly dependent.

Transgenic virus-resistant crops add yet another risk, that is, the threat that new viral strains may arise. Some manufacturers (for example, Upjohn Company in 1992) have objected that "coinfection of plants by multiple viruses," because it is already present naturally, makes this risk negligible.[15] But there have been no experimental investigations of these claims, as no outside specific testing is ever required before patenting applications for a transgene are approved. Unforeseen effects of technologies, such as the loss of the ozone layer, coupled with the lack of precise predictive capacities of the biological sciences in particular, render the existence of these unknowable risks very serious indeed. Moreover, as we will note later in this chapter, changed climate conditions also aggravate both the risks and the uncertainty.

Additionally, there is no uncertainty whatsoever about the unpredictable results of introducing nonnative, natural species into ecosystems, so that the introduction of *alien* species, that is, of species that did not exist in earlier times, into complex systems under drastically changed climate conditions is as potentially hazardous as the introduction of other chemical and toxic man-made unnatural substances. *Beyond the Limits*, the second book presenting the research of the Club of Rome,[16] argues that both sources and sinks on earth are limited; thus, every time we introduce a substance that has not evolved slowly and naturally and is not a native to the ecosystem into which it is introduced, we are imposing an anthropogenic stress that is hazardous to the system. This becomes, implicitly, a stress to the earth's life-support systems in general.

Biotechnology is primarily geared to produce herbicide-tolerant crops, thus increasing significantly both the use of pesticides and herbicides and the profits of the corporations producing the engineered crop. The consequences of these practices should thus raise grave concerns for both environmental and human health reasons.

For example, the California biotechnology company Calgene, in conjunction with the multinational company Rhone-Poulenc, is seeking U.S. government approval to sell a cotton plant genetically engineered to tolerate bromoxynil, a Rhone-Poulenc herbicide. Bromoxynil has been shown to cause birth defects in animals and has been classified as a developmental toxicant for humans. Use of these transgenic crops will result in substantial increase in the use of bromoxynil.[17]

Another problem arises because the same toxin (gene) is used by several companies to induce insect tolerance in crops. When a toxin is widely used, resistance in insect pests may develop and farmers may once again be driven to increased use of chemicals.

What remains to be addressed is the question of the alleviation of hunger worldwide. Is it a real enough "benefit" to offset the global risks involved? In general, while northwestern countries are technologically (and in general) richer than developing countries in the Southeast, the latter are much richer in biodiversity, as they possess "centers of crop diversity":

> They are the source of the new genes that plant breeders and genetic engineers use to adapt crops to changing environmental conditions . . . most of the centers of diversity for food crops are in developing countries.[18]

Hence it is fair to say that no practice that may eventually threaten these centers can be truly sustainable, and thus successful in the fight against world hunger in the long term.[19] Not every attack on biodiversity or lessening of the genetic pool is a portent of future global tragedy, but "these localized insults, repeated countless times around the globe, eventually weaken the earth's unique life-sustaining system."[20]

Therefore, the appropriate U.S. agencies, as well as U.N. organizations, must develop biosafety protocols that are both strict and globally valid and enforceable. Biotechnologies and transgenics are not the "promise of the future"; they offer no guarantee of alleviating world hunger. Thus, the threats they present far outweigh the promise, even if we consider them only from the standpoint of our use. The perspective of integrity instead suggests that the hazards and the concomitant moral problems engendered by these practices are also equally present for those who view nonhuman individuals, species, and ecosystems as *intrinsically* valuable, and thus worthy of respect.[21]

Of course, one could object that all technologies may impose some degree of risk, and that life in earlier times was even more hazardous than the life we live today. But biotechnologies are virtually unregulated. They attack our life-support systems, they impose unresearched and unmitigated hazards on us, and at the same time they disregard many of the freedoms and rights that we take for granted in modern democracies. In some sense, as only large, powerful multinationals can normally undertake the manufacture and distribution of transgenics and biotechnologies, their operation appears to be above the law and beyond public control, an unnerving combination when coupled with the risks and uncertainties discussed here.

Environmental Impact on Water Bodies: Is Sustainable, Ecological Aquaculture Possible?

In the previous section the question of world hunger was addressed together with the usefulness and morality of biotechnology, given that intensive petrochemical agriculture is responsible for both reduced productivity and many grave environmental problems. Since present systems of agriculture are failing to keep up with both present and projected demands for food, the promise of transgenics appears, ideally at least, to fill that gap. But, as was noted, both moral and practical problems beset these technologies, and these problems persist for aquaculture as well.

The urgent need for food drives agricultural production. Some aspects of that production, for instance, intensive animal production, can be indicted on both moral and environmental grounds. I have also argued that our Western-style dietary habits are as inappropriate to our health as they are to an ethic of environmental concern. But the same argument cannot be made for fish, as it is both healthful and, at least normally, "free range," so it escapes some of the problems outlined by defenders of animals' rights and interests. But our wasteful, profit-driven lifestyle has resulted in depleted fish stocks and even in species extinction in many cases. For instance, Canada has recently been the site of major fish wars, discussed in chapter 2, when the cod population became depleted beyond recovery. This may well become a common occurrence if ecological requirements such as the ones suggested by the principle of integrity are not followed.[22]

In fish we have a nontoxic and nonhazardous product. We also have traditional lifestyles at stake, as people have lived by fishing from time immemorial. But recently fish stocks have disappeared, not only because of increased quotas but also because of advanced and far-reaching fishing technologies and increasing pollution in streams, lakes, and oceans. In that case, the only alternative for some sort of fish-dependent commerce and for a healthier diet for all might be aquaculture. Unfortunately, its environmental prognosis is not good. In essence, if we turn away from natural fisheries and their losses, and try to supplement them through aquaculture, we open the door to another set of possible environmental problems. Thus, on top of the possible ecosystem collapse engendered by species loss and pollution, overfishing may force us to yet another hazardous and unsustainable option. "Aquaculture is the aquatic counterpart of agriculture,"[23] and probably because of the problems of natural fisheries over the past twenty years, it has increased exponentially; it now accounts for 17 percent of the world's fisheries.

Unfortunately, like agriculture, aquaculture has potentially deleterious effects on the environment and human health. It is not a natural process, and it affects biodiversity in several ways: (1) through the consumption of resources; (2) through the transformation process itself; and (3) through "the production of wastes."[24] Its effects on biodiversity are both direct and indirect. Releasing "exotic genetic material into the environment" is a direct impact, which effects changes "to the biotic components of an ecosystem," thus causing possible loss of habitats or alterations in systems' function, which is an additional indirect impact.

It is worth looking at some of these problems in more detail. As we saw, environmental impact from aquaculture is unavoidable, but because it is a novel procedure, even less is known with certainty about this impact than is known about those of agriculture. Moreover, in direct contrast with the latter, most often mariculture, for instance, "is frequently conducted in public waters"; hence, from the standpoint of the environment the public is directly involved and affected at every level of production.

Major problems in aquaculture parallel the problems present in transgenic agriculture. Side effects of aquaculture involving transgenic fish are the introduction of pathogens and parasites, the alteration of habitats, and even worse, gene pool deterioration, which may compromise the "fitness or even the genetic integrity of the indigenous species."[25] These conditions affect both wildlife and their habitats and human populations as well. Effects on humans include the possible spread of parasites and disease, as the conditions necessary for the practice of aquaculture (particularly the cage culture of fishes) create conditions favorable to disease, while the introduction of additives and antibiotics into the food chain foster drug-resistant strains of bacteria when residues affect human consumers.

It is easy to see the appeal of aquaculture, a technological fix to help us adjust to the results of our own overconsumption. But it is neither logical nor morally right to deal with the results of our carelessness through a short-term remedy that will ultimately *add* ecological stress. If we turn to aquaculture to seek solutions to fish stock depletion and species extinction—both caused in part by pollution and ecological disintegrity—then aquaculture must avoid contributing to the problems that led us to it in the first place. Further, even aquaculture operations are themselves often constrained by increased aquatic pollution from other sources, habitat degradation, and reduced access to appropriate land and water resources.

Thus, aquaculture must be managed very carefully so that it will neither receive nor cause negative environmental effects. In this regard ecological integrity (including biodiversity) is particularly relevant:

> While most of the wild relatives of domesticated terrestrial livestock have already been lost, the majority of aquatic genetic diversity is found in wild undomesticated species.[26]

Moreover,

Certain techniques, such as culture-based fisheries or ranching and cage and pen culture in natural waters, constitute greater risks to wild populations or natural diversity.[27]

Some Aggravating Environmental Problems: Climate Changes and Global Warming

The litany of problems and difficulties described in the previous two sections is still incomplete, because global climate changes further aggravate the present complex problems. Hence, the present environmental conditions add to the general problems outlined in the previous sections, in ways that are deleterious not only to human health but also to both fisheries and agriculture. Their decline leads in turn to increased dependence on aquaculture and novel forms of agriculture, thus spurring corporate interests to produce quickly without appropriate testing. But if a strong ecocentric position were adopted, then the preservation of the wild would be mandated as primary, and this would eventually help to ameliorate the present environmental degradation, and eventually reverse climate changes.

As we saw, the link between climate changes/global warming and the imperative of maintaining and protecting ecosystem integrity is present in two separate senses. On one hand, deforestation of large, biodiverse areas would be prohibited from the standpoint of integrity, and the role of forests in regard to global climate would be preserved. These landscapes would be largely protected as "core" areas, and they would be kept in their wild state, in sizes large enough to ensure safety (prudential principle). Further, the major contributors to the problem—the "global warming brought about by the injection of greenhouse gases (i.e., carbon dioxide, methane, nitrous oxides, and chlorofluorocarbons) into the atmosphere"[28]—would not be permitted even in areas beyond the wild, such as buffers or culture/urban areas. No "risky business" should be allowed to operate if it could be reasonably anticipated that it would have an adverse impact on wild/core areas, buffers, or areas of "culture" themselves.[29]

Although considerations of global climate changes are not specifically related to biotechnology, these changes cannot be ignored, given their effects. A discussion of the effects of biotechnology, central to the understanding of the veracity of the claims made on their behalf, would remain incomplete without some mention of the aggravating external factors introduced by climate changes. Only then might we have a more complete picture from which to attempt to answer the first question raised: are these technologies equal to the task they are intended to accomplish? The task projected was that of feeding the world's hungry while ameliorating the loss of environmental integrity and capacity brought about by intensive petrochemical agricultural practices. For this project to succeed, it would need to be sustainable globally. Hence, it is appropriate to examine the actual conditions under which it must unfold to produce the practical results it claims.

Intended as it is to aid in combating environmental degradation, biotechnology cannot involve practices that might increase it instead. In the previous two sections we noted several problems linking biotechnology to environmental problems, in principle. We also need to consider the role of climate change in practice; this problem was discussed in detail in chapter 2.

Moreover, just as climate changes have negative and unpredictable effects on agriculture and fisheries, so we can also anticipate correspondingly unpredictable effects on genetically altered organisms and the systems that house them. We can therefore take for granted that the problems and difficulties discussed earlier do not tell the whole story, because recent ecological damage due to climate changes is not factored into the research and findings cited.

Conclusion

Although the previous sections did not argue explicitly for one or another moral theory, appeals to moral concepts were often made, particularly in regard to human rights. But are the criteria that arise from traditional morality—that is, considerations of rights, utilities, and justice—sufficient to assess biotechnology? There is no question that these standards are necessary: we are first alerted to the possibility of problems arising from biotechnology when we notice the difficulties it brings to some human value or human good. At this stage, our concern is already moral rather than prudential. We are not worried only about possible risks or harms to ourselves our families: we speak in universal human terms.

The problem with this approach and the traditional moral theories is that these doctrines cannot give precise moral guidance for such novel questions. For instance, do we have global, collective "rights" to increased productivity, however obtained and of whatever duration? Is our good to be based on any condition for survival, notwithstanding possible negative effects on less-developed countries or on future generations? Questions regarding biotechnology are, like other novel practical ethics questions, almost guaranteed to force a reexamination of the meaning and reach of our moral beliefs. Thus it might be argued that, in addition to evaluating these technologies based on traditional theories, it might be best to subject them to an ecological/environmental evaluation.

Our final aim should be to regain a measure of control, through appropriate public policy, over what affects us. A holistic environmental ethic perspective will offer the strictest criterion, as it is not open to the balancing of preferences or purely human interests. Some argue that provided we are governed by "weak anthropocentrism," we can implement desirable environmental policies without recourse to holism or doctrines based on the intrinsic value of natural entities.[30] I have argued that weak anthropocentrism is powerless in the face of many of the grave environmental issues that face us, primarily because it is simply a reaffirmation of majoritarian preferences, without the capacity to ground these choices in values beyond these human preferences, as all nonhuman values are excluded a prior from the argument (see chapter 4).

In the final analysis, weak anthropocentrism boils down to a counting of heads. In contrast, a holistic position based on the principle of integrity (PI) permits a wider recognition of natural value and a corresponding condemnation of hazardous and disruptive practices. The 1992 climate treaty called for global research by epidemiologists: environmental monitoring is mandatory for "the atmosphere, the oceans and terrestrial ecosystems." It is for this reason that an imperative of integrity was proposed imposing limits on human activities, in order to protect and restore natural life-support systems in certain proportions, but also imposing limits on certain kinds of human activities wherever these may occur, even outside wild areas, in order to minimize the catastrophic risks noted above.

Unlimited, uncontrolled technological/economic activity causes disruptions in natural systems, and its effects are not accurately predictable. It almost appears to be the sort of reversibility that is present in Kantian ethics. But it is not a truly Kantian form of reversibility, as the moral responsibility is not reciprocal. Humankind is immorally affecting natural systems. But natural systems are not equally immoral when they respond with harm; the reciprocity that follows our interventions is amoral instead. On the other hand, humankind's initial causative activity is doubly immoral: (1) it affects natural systems, and (2) it affects humankind *through* natural systems. Hence, the superficial critique often levied at ecocentric ethics as antihuman, drawing an inappropriate cleavage between humans and other biota, is mistaken. Respect for ecosystems is ipso facto respect for all natural entities, both human and nonhuman animals, and for both biotic and abiotic components of natural systems.

Thus, to take a "deep ecology" position and to support some preservation of the wild does not force humans outside the natural environment; it simply recognizes the limits within which humankind must operate in it. Of course, it is simply "human," not "techno-human," beings who belong in natural systems, as claims about an ecological niche can only be made for an animal in its natural state. For instance, a transgenic plant or fish no longer belongs *naturally* in an ecosystem, as it did before it was technologically altered and manipulated. The biotech fish, like the "techno-human," no longer performs its function as part of the system's biota; it now often wreaks havoc, as it disrupts and alters the system's natural functioning.[31]

I have argued elsewhere from the perspective of integrity, stating that all human culture, activities, and institutions conform to the requirements of a buffer zone in relation to core or wild areas. If the central necessity is to protect wild areas in relatively sizable proportions, say 20 percent to 45 percent of the earth's surface, as areas of ecological integrity (I_a), then it is our obligation to dwell in the remaining 55 to 80 percent (varying according to particular landscape requirements) in ways that produce no adverse impact upon these areas. This absolutely demands that we consider ourselves as living in "buffers." I have termed areas of ecosystem health, where many natural evolutionary processes persist, areas of I_b, and used I_c to refer to urban areas, where little evolutionary processes persist relative to the core areas.

True buffers (I_b) entail that most natural ecologically evolutionary processes be present, although these areas may be manipulated for basic needs (agriculture, forestry, and perhaps careful aquaculture). All of these may utilize land and water, but without imposing degradation and disintegrity either on their own landscapes or on those of core areas. In practice, this would mean the elimination of all hazardous and toxic substances from those pursuits, as well as the imposition of bans on the introduction of exotics of all kinds. Even in areas where human culture predominates, thus where natural evolutionary processes are restricted or minimal (that is, in urban or industrial centers), the centrality of wild integrity will need to be constantly emphasized in public policy in order to avoid harmful interference with it. Hence I have argued that while we need to utilize and manipulate some landscapes, wild areas are required to support healthy areas through their natural functions. Despite the abundant scientific material supporting the foundation role of wilderness and biotic integrity for conservation biology, much less has been said about its role in regard to human health, although recent material confirms and supports much that has been said here.[32] The effects of climate changes on both aquatic and terrestrial/agricultural ecosystems have also been documented.[33]

What does the perspective of integrity recommend in regard to transgenes and biotechnology? First, by recommending the preservation of large wild areas and also mandating restrictions on human activities so that these wild areas are treated as central and primary, the principle of integrity (PI) proscribes any interference that would result in a system's loss of integrity. But any unnatural or partly man-made organisms, when introduced into a system or landscape, affect its structure and its natural function, hence its integrity.

Thus, from the standpoint of integrity, any genetically altered organism is at least prima facie undesirable. In order to view it as acceptable, its creators would bear the burden of proof that (1) the organism does not have adverse effects on the system, even in the long run (and this proof should be through testing *in situ*, not simply on controlled assays under laboratory conditions), and (2) the organism *itself* is not affected in its natural development. The Netherlands already has such a rule in place in regard to genetically altered animals, which cannot be altered if the additional gene or genes would change an animal's natural functioning and behavior.

Hence the ethics of integrity recognizes the intrinsic value of both the natural structure of organisms, which defines these organisms' identity as well as their function within an evolutionary whole, and that of natural wholes, for the same reasons and, additionally, for the life support they provide for all organisms.

A deep and holistic position based on respect for intrinsic value can be opposed to management goals, whose basic question is how to manipulate and control natural systems. But once manipulation and alteration are viewed as prima facie acceptable (in contrast with the PI), it becomes hard to draw the line on a continuum, and a special case needs to be made to explain why this particular kind of manipulation may need to be restricted. Such a claim can probably be supported on anthropocentric grounds, by appeals to the unacceptability of causing unconsented and uncompensated harms to individuals.[34] But it is difficult to provide clear and uncontroversial *legal* proof of harm in the case of substances that have not existed as such until recently, although their component parts may have. I have argued in a similar vein for the public's right to know not only because of risk of harm, but also because of the right to religious freedom (in regard to dietary laws), both of which would require, minimally, clearly labeling all transgenics as drugs, rather than treating them as food. The tryptophan example cited earlier also supports a purely anthropocentric argument against the easy acceptance of biotechnologies.

Unfortunately, the lack of clear-cut scientific evidence restricts the possibility of strong legal evidence, and thus militates against the possibility of clear causal arguments against transgenics. Of course, the fact that both the money and the power to support new research are not in the hands of the public, but in those of the multinational corporations that control the production of these new substances, indicates at least one reason the necessary impartial research is not available and is not likely to be.

The conceptual basis of our approach to these novel substances and organisms will determine their fate and ours. If one views their creation as different only in degree from other forms of acceptable manipulation of natural entities and systems, then our assent to their use may at most be conditional, but it is assured. If, on the other hand, we start from a strong position of respect for natural evolutionary systemic processes (supported by the PI)—hence, for both the structure and the function of landscapes and all the biota within them—then our first reaction will clearly be negative and all our future responses governed by caution. Manipulation of any sort needs a clear defense, primarily in the form of evidence of no harm, as well as of expected benefits.

The imprecisions and unpredictability of science[35] will also need to be factored into our decision, leading to a call for additional precaution.[36] Further, respect for individuals within systems, both humans and nonhumans, dictates that interference and alteration are always, prima facie, wrong, especially when no consent is available (from humans) or possible (from nonhumans).

Respect is based on the recognition of intrinsic value, which in turn is based on the existence on individual life projects and the natural tendency of all organisms to carry out their actualization, culminating in reproduction, as individual and species goals.[37] For humans, we can add autonomous will, not only tendencies and propensities but also intended goals, supported by life. For natural wholes and systems, intrinsic value is found in their own evolutionary development and the life support they provide to all within them and without, globally (as forests and oceans and their functions reach well beyond their own limits).[38]

Therefore, taking seriously the human right to life and to the noninfliction of harm,[39] in an ecologically aware world, demands recognizing and respecting natural evolutionary paths in systems and all their component parts as proposed by the PI. It also demands that nonhuman individuals and wholes be respected in the same way, and that when confronted with biotechnologies and transgenics, we deem them "guilty" of breach of integrity, minimally, in the absence of thorough and unbiased evidence to the contrary.

Mark Sagoff argues:

We need models—including meso- and microcosms, sentinel species, and other ecological indices that will provide some assurance that we can protect the integrity of natural ecosystems from changes owing to biotechnology.[40]

But Sagoff views integrity as "a cultural, moral and aesthetic concept" exclusively, and denies its "biological significance." In contrast, both culture and morality have an important *historical* component that Sagoff himself would not deny. Biotechnologies, like other alien or hazardous forms of interference with the optimum evolutionary capacities of natural systems (central to my definition of ecological integrity), destroy these systems' history by destroying vast numbers of individual organisms and species, eliminating not only the biological connectedness of these systems, as Edward Wilson argues,[41] but also their whole genetic history, along with their genetic capacities. Holmes Rolston argues that a species has no "right to life apart from the continued existence of the ecosystem with which it co-fits."[42] But he adds, "Artificial extinction [of species] shuts down tomorrow because it shuts down speciation."[43] What is eliminated through extinctions, including the historical dimensions of natural systems and their "history" as well as the evolved capacities of ecosystems, is the primary concern of the ethics of integrity.

Notes

1. K. Shrader-Frechette, *Risk and Rationality* (Berkeley: University of California Press, 1991).

2. Jane Rissler and Margaret Mellon, "Perils Amidst the Promise," *Ecological Risks of Transgenic Crops in a Global Market* (Cambridge, MA: Union of Concerned Scientists, 1993); Margaret Mellon, "Comments on Discussion Paper on Food Labelling and Biotechnology," Union of Concerned Scientists, October 13, 1994, p. 29.

3. Rissler and Mellon, "Perils Amidst the Promise"; Mellon, "Comments on Discussion Paper on Food Labelling and Biotechnology."

4. A. N. Mayeno, and G. J. Gleich, "Eosinophilia-myalgia Syndrome and Tryptophan Production: A Cautionary Tale," 12-TIBTECH 346-52 (1994); see also Mellon, "Comments on Discussion Paper on Food Labelling and Biotechnology"; National Wildlife Federation, Fact Sheet on "Tryptophan," National Wildlife Federation Biotechnology Policy Center, June 1992.

5. Mellon, "Comments on Discussion Paper on Food Labelling and Biotechnology."

6. K. Shrader-Frechette, *Nuclear Power and Public Policy* (Dordrecht, The Netherlands: Kluwer, 1982); see also K. Shrader-Frechette, *Burying Uncertainty* (Berkeley: University of California Press, 1993).

7. Shrader-Frechette, *Nuclear Power and Public Policy.*

8. Mellon, "Comments on Discussion Paper on Food Labelling and Biotechnology."

9. *The Economist,* as reprinted in *The Globe and Mail,* Canada, March 25, 1996.

10. L. Westra, "A Transgenic Dinner? Ethical and Social Issues in Biotechnology and Agriculture," *Journal of Social Philosophy* 24, 3 (Winter 1993): 215–32.

11. D. Pimentel, et al., "Environmental and Economic Effects of Reducing Pesticide Use," *Bioscience* 41, 6 (1991); see also D. Pimentel, C. Harvey, P. Resosudarmo, K. Sinclair, et al., "Environmental and Economic Costs of Soil Erosion and Conservation Benefits," *Science* (February 24, 1995): 1117–23; K. Shrader-Frechette, *Risk and Rationality* (Berkeley: University of California Press, 1991); L. Westra, K. Bowen, and B. Behe, "Agricultural Practices, Ecology and Ethics in The Third World," *Journal of Agricultural Ethic* 4, 10 (1991): 60–77.

12. Westra, "A Transgenic Dinner? Ethical and Social Issues in Biotechnology and Agriculture."

13. Rissler and Mellon, "Perils Amidst the Promise"; Mellon, "Comments on Discussion Paper on Food Labelling and Biotechnology."

14. Rissler and Mellon, "Perils Amidst the Promise"; Mellon, "Comments on Discussion Paper on Food labelling and Biotechnology."

15. Rissler and Mellon, "Perils Amidst the Promise"; Mellon, "Comments on Discussion Paper on Food labelling and Biotechnology."

16. D. H. Meadows, D. L. Meadows, and J. Randers, *Beyond the Limits* (Post Mills, VT: Chelsea Green Publishing, 1992).

17. Rissler and Mellon, "Perils Amidst the Promise"; Mellon, "Comments on Discussion Paper on Food Labelling and Biotechnology."

18. Rissler and Mellon, "Perils Amidst the Promise"; Mellon, "Comments on Discussion Paper on Food labelling and Biotechnology."

19. Rissler and Mellon, "Perils Amidst the Promise"; Mellon, "Comments on Discussion Paper on Food labelling and Biotechnology."

20. L. Westra, *An Environmental Proposal for Ethics: The Principle of Integrity* (Lanham, MD: Rowman & Littlefield, 1994).

21. J. A. Hutchings and R. A. Myers, "What Can Be Learned from the Collapse of a Renewable Resource? Atlantic Cod, *Gadus Morhua,* of Newfoundland, Labrador," *Canadian Journal of Fisheries and Aquatic Science* 51 (1994): 2126–46; see also L. Westra, "Ecosystem Integrity Health and Sustainability: The Canadian 'Fish Wars,' " *Journal of Aquatic Ecosystem Health* (Dordrecht, The Netherlands: 1996).

22. M. C. Beveridge, M. Lindsay, G. Ross, and L. A. Kelly, "Aquaculture and Biodiversity," *Ambio* 23, 8 (December 1994): 497–502.

23. Beveridge, et al., "Aquaculture and Biodiversity."

24. Final Draft—*Performance Standards for Safely Conducting Research with Genetically Modified Fish and Shellfish,* Document No. 95–01, April 15, 1995. Prepared by the U.S. Department of Agriculture, Agriculture Biotechnology Research Advisory Committee, Working Group on Aquatic Biotechnology and Environmental Safety.

25. FAO, 1995.

26. Barry A. Costa-Pierce and H. T. Peters, *Environmental Impacts of Nutrients Discharged from Agriculture: Towards the Evolution of Sustainable, Agriculture Systems.* Plenary Talk, Ecological Institute of Agriculture, University of Stirling, Scotland (June 21, 1993).

27. Dale Jamieson, "Managing the Future: Public Policy, Scientific Uncertainty, and Global Warming," in *Upstream/Downstream*, ed. D. Scherer (Philadelphia: Temple University Press, 1990), pp. 67–89.

28. Westra, *An Environmental Proposal for Ethics.*

29. Bryan Norton, "Why I Am Not a Nonanthropocentrist: Callicott and the Failure of Monistic Inherentism," *Environmental Ethics* 17, 4 (Winter 1995): 341–58; see also Bryan Norton, *Toward Unity among Environmentalists* (New York: Oxford University Press, 1991). (See discussion in chapter 4, this volume.)

30. Beveridge, et al., "Aquaculture and Biodiversity."

31. Janice D. Longstretch, et al. "Effects of Increased Solar Ultraviolet Radiation on Human Health," *Ambio* 24, 3 (May 1995): 153–65; see also M. Soulé, "Health Implications of Global Warming and the Onslaught of Alien Species," *Wild Earth* (Summer 1995): 56–61; Rita Colwell, "Global Climate and Infectious Disease: The Cholera Paradigm," President's Lecture, February 10, 1996, American Association for the Advancement of Science, in *Science* 274 (December 20, 1996): 2025–31.

32. M. Caldwell, et al., "Effects of Increased Solar Ultraviolet Radiation on Terrestrial Plants," *Ambio* 24, 3 (May 1995): 166–73; see also Donat-P. Häder, et al., "Effects of Increased Solar Ultraviolet Radiation on Aquatic Ecosystem," *Ambio* 24, 3 (May 1995): 174–80.

33. Shrader-Frechette, *Risk and Rationality.*

34. S. Funtowicz and Jerome Ravetz, "Science for the Post-Normal Age," in *Perspectives on Ecological Integrity* (Dordrecht, The Netherlands: Kluwer, 1995), pp. 146–61.

35. D. A. Brown, "The Role of Law in Sustainable Development and Environmental Protection Decision Making," in *Sustainable Development: Science, Ethics and Public Policy* (Dordrecht, The Netherlands: Kluwer, 1995), pp. 64–76.

36. P. Taylor, *Respect for Nature: A Theory of Environmental Ethics* (Princeton: Princeton University Press, 1986); see also T. Regan, *The Case for Animal Rights* (Berkeley: University of California Press, 1993).

37. Westra, *An Environmental Proposal for Ethics.*

38. Alan Gewirth, "Human Rights and the Prevention of Cancer," in *Human Rights* (Chicago: University of Chicago Press, 1982), pp. 181–217.

39. M. Sagoff, *The Economy of the Earth: Philosophy, Law and the Environment* (Cambridge, England: Cambridge University Press, 1988).

40. E. O. Wilson, "Threats to Biodiversity," *Scientific American* (1989); reprinted in *World Scientists' Warning Briefing Book* (Cambridge, MA: Union of Concerned Scientists, 1993), pp. 155–60.

41. Holmes Rolston III, *Environmental Ethics: Duties to and Values in the Natural World* (Philadelphia: Temple University Press, 1988).

42. Rolston, *Environmental Ethics.*

PART III

7

The Greeks and Kant: The Quest for Compatible Ethics

In the third and final part of this work, we need to attempt to reach solutions for the conceptual and practical problems discussed earlier. If present and future human health, life, and capacities are at risk, as well as life-support systems including all their biota, we need much more than slightly modified or "greened" public policy. We need a changed perspective, a new way of living, and a new ethic of environmental and social interaction, or, as William McDonough puts it, a "new design."[1] To support these changes, I do not propose a new interhuman ethic: instead I suggest a return to much earlier positions, as these appear both compatible with and supportive of the changes indicated. Ecological integrity (as point C)[2] was understood not as a completely definable state or condition but as a point of *return*, prior to regeneration and rebirth in an ongoing evolutionary cycle. Its value did not lie in its specificity or in the details of present circumstances as much as in the vast potential it carried for future development, incorporating creatively both the past history of the system and the somewhat unpredictable trajectory and configurations of the future.[3]

Perhaps our quest for a compatible ethic should manifest a parallel movement: rather than leaving the past behind, it might be best to return to a point rich in significance and history, but also pregnant with creative possibilities. I argue that "virtue ethics," primarily as instantiated in the work of Greek thinkers such as Plato and Aristotle, but also including Kantian ethics (following Margaret Paton),[4] represent such a point well. The "ethics of integrity" were intended as ethics, *simpliciter*, in view of their far-reaching effects, not purely as environmental ethics. But no clear argument or evidence supporting that claim was offered. It is time then to make good on that promissory note, by showing how the requirements of the principle of integrity (PI) may drive us back to earlier principles and doctrines, in order to move forward.

Paradoxically, the move to greater acceptance of individual differences, and of our right to pursue these differences in character and talent, preference, and lifestyle, has not led to a greater emphasis on recognizing and respecting the dignity of humankind, singly and collectively. To say that everything is equally good and valuable is to say that nothing truly is. If glass, crystal, and stones were given parity with diamonds and other gems, nothing would be considered truly valuable, and only the numbers of those having one or another preference would bestow value on the "trinket of the month." Nothing would be deemed to be truly valuable in itself; neither human nor nonhuman animals, neither systems nor specific landscapes would possess intrinsic value.

In order to avoid the so-called danger of hierarchical thinking and the supposed danger of unfairness it harbors, we seem to have embraced a flattened vision of all that exists. In order to treat everyone and everything with political correctness, we truly value and respect nothing. From a logical point of view, if everything is equal, then everything is potentially exchangeable for everything else and there is no reason to respect the integrity of either individuals or systems, other than the abstract respect for majoritarian choices, whatever these might be. This approach upholds form, not content; hence, by implication, it defines as good or better and valuable whatever is chosen, with no reference to its intrinsic value. The quest for what might be good or better and valuable in itself is foreclosed, with grave implications not only for morality but for health and security as well.

Hence I argue that we ought to return to earlier positions in ethics and to a perspective that argues for what is "a human," without necessarily accepting the limits that the Greeks, for instance, posited on the capacities of groups and classes of individuals, but starting from a defensible understanding of the nature and dignity of human beings in Plato, Aristotle, and—eventually—Kant. The disadvantages of accepting the existence of a human nature, or what it is to be human, have been argued throughout the history of philosophy, especially in recent times, and I do not revisit those arguments.

I instead attempt to find an ethic compatible with the PI, through an initial step back to virtue ethics. This recreated doctrine is not patterned precisely on the unchangeable form of the "good" of Platonic ethics, for instance; I simply treat Platonic, Aristotelian, and Kantian ethics as a seminal starting point, as I believe they possess the optimal capacity for future development and regeneration that denoted the parallel optimum ecological capacities at point C in our earlier definition of integrity.[5] As in the case of point C, the recognition of these capacities

includes all their future unfolding; hence it is not limited to the histori-
cally defined parameters encountered at the time to which I propose to
return. Therefore, while referring closely to the textual grounds of my
argument, I only show where Plato, Aristotle, and Kant defend positions
that are (1) compatible with the ethics of integrity and (2) superior to
present approaches (contractarian and utilitarian for the most part), in
the sense that they can offer answers to the problems raised in the previous chapters. While it is important to be textually accurate when invoking another philosopher's insights in support of one's argument, it is
not necessary here to present in detail all of Plato's, Aristotle's, and
Kant's arguments in support of their doctrines. My discussion assumes a
certain degree of familiarity with Plato's basic text in the *Republic*, with
Aristotle's *Nicomachean Ethics*, and with Kant's basic principles, although
I will devote more time to his position on "duties to oneself," as those
texts are less familiar than his Categorical Imperative.

Contractarian and utilitarian positions fail in the face of environmental problems because of certain lacks in their respective arguments; in
contrast, I argue that virtue ethics are more successful precisely as they
have answers in response to those lacks. I start with Plato's discussion of
the "good" in relation to the best *polis* in the *Republic*, before turning to
Aristotle's *Nicomachean Ethics*, and several aspects of that work that add
constructively to the Plato section. Finally, I argue that Kant's position
on "duties to oneself" yields valuable insights to help us recover an
ethical position where optimum human capacities and the optimum capacities of natural systems support one another.

Plato on the "Good," Liberal Democracy, and Environmental Ethics

Corporate business practices and legal but otherwise unrestrained
human choices have been wreaking havoc on the environment and,
through it, on our lives, and there have been increasing efforts on the
part of most nations to band together to enact regulatory protocols to
impose limits on our consumer lifestyles and technological excesses.
These limits, apparently, cannot be imposed easily or thoroughly by either democratic or nondemocratic regimes, but they have become necessary and even urgent. One person in three will die of environmentally
caused cancers;[6] asthma and other respiratory diseases are on the increase even among children, particularly in cities and other industrial
centers.[7] Global climate change is having an almost incalculable effect
on the health of all living things, including human and nonhuman ani-

mals; the list of negative effects includes skin cancers, old reemerging infectious diseases, as well as new ones emerging, as viruses, bacteria, hosts, and vectors correspondingly change in quantity, location, and characteristic behaviors.[8] Hazardous wastes and persistent chemicals (including hormone mimics) endanger the reproductive functions and capacities of animals (contributing to the disappearance of many species) and humans—robbing our children and hence our species of a future.[9]

In the face of mounting threats and encroaching risks, it would be easy to point the finger at this or that corporate villain, perhaps Union Carbide in Bhopal, India, or Royal Dutch Shell Oil in Ogoniland in Nigeria, for a more recent example.[10] Both of these examples are also cases of "environmental racism,"[11] and they happened in places where modern democracy might not have been well implemented.

But what are we to say of Monsanto Corporation's aggressive marketing of bovine growth hormone (BGH), which makes ruminants require a protein-enriched diet of feed containing other ground-up animals and leads to the incidence of spongiform encephalitis (mad cow disease) in animals and humans?[12] What about the continued productions of "risky" businesses,[13] creating products that remain hazardous from "cradle to grave," and even after they are trashed, affecting our environment, and, through it, our health in North America and Europe?[14] In the affluent Western world, democracy is well in place, and we cannot blame tyrannies or military regimes for our ills.

In fact, it is most often taken for granted that democratic institutions are not only necessary but also sufficient to ensure respect for human rights (such as the right to life and health). Generations of students taking introductory philosophy or Greek philosophy classes almost bristle with indignation when presented with Plato's arguments in the *Republic* that philosophers should be kings or queens, and—as in the myth of the metals—that our *nature*, not our enterprise or our efforts, should be allowed to limit the role we play in the polity.

In this chapter, I return to Plato and argue that, in contrast to the tenets of "political correctness" and individualistic modern liberalism, we may be able to cast some serious doubts on the capacity of our institutions, at least in their present form, to do better in both theory and practice than the Platonic philosopher. The question is, what is lacking in modern democracies? In the light of Plato's discussion of justice, the "good," and the best city in the *Republic,* I suggest at least three major missing components: (1) any common conception of the "good," that is *not* open to revision and rejection, based on utilitarian preferences and majoritarian choices; (2) a *holistic approach* to the good, in contrast with the enshrinement of extreme individualism and the worship of what Robert McGinn terms "technical maximality";[15] and (3) a belief in the necessity for both *reason* and *universality* in both personal morality and, as in our main focus here, public policy.

Plato on the Less-Than-Ideal Constitutions

In Book VII of the *Republic*,[16] Socrates returns to his discussion of the best constitution for the city. He names four as "illnesses" of the city (544c) and treats democracy as the last regime before the worst, that is, before tyranny. In line with the rest of the *Republic*, he also proposes the existence of four corresponding forms of individual character, as these are basic to their respective cities' makeup. The ideal city is, of course, the focus of the *Republic*'s argument, and all other cities are described as progressively worse than the ideal. They are, in descending order: (1) a timocracy, (2) an oligarchy, (3) a democracy, and (4) a tyranny. A timocracy is "ruled by people . . . themselves ruled by the spirited part of their soul"; their main focus is to achieve fame, honor, and a good reputation based on military successes and victories in battle (561a–b). A tyranny is under the power of someone who is ruled by "lawless, unnecessary appetites" (571a).[17]

Leaving aside Plato's understanding of a timocracy and the reasons why it is placed so close to the ideal city, the analysis of an oligarchy merits attention as, together with the tyranny, it is best understood by contrast with democracy, to which it is deemed superior. Plato's oligarchy sounds quite close to a capitalist regime coupled with free-market ideology and without the benefit (and restraints) of Rawlsian fairness to balance it. Oligarchy is "the regime founded on a property assessment . . . in which the rich rule and the poor man has no part in ruling office" (550c). It originates, Socrates suggests, in the soul of sons dispossessed because of the fortunes of war and the great losses sustained by their fathers. This leads them to prize security above all else.

It is, however, the need for *necessary* security that drives them, but this also turns them into misers and hoarders, who "enshrine" wealth above all else. When wealth becomes primary, these "squalid" men, who aim to get "a profit out of everything" and who aim always at "filling up their storerooms," pursue neither education nor virtue. Hence there are serious problems with this city, and Plato explains them—"When . . . the wealthy are honoured . . . virtue and the good men are less honourable" (551a). It is not possible to choose the best "pilot" on the basis of "property assessments" (551c); that is, the highest capacities and the best skills to perform a task cannot be found on the basis of men's financial holdings. The regime fosters a divided city, "the city of the poor and the city of the rich . . . ever plotting against each other" (551d). Finally, this form of rule permits one man to sell all his belongings to

another, thus rendering the former a citizen with neither task nor affili-
ation, "neither money maker . . . nor a craftsman, nor a knight" but
simply a poor man *in* the city but not *of* the city in any appropriate sense.

The man with the oligarchic soul does not truly value virtue, justice,
or education, but at least he is pursuing *necessary* needs (to excess). This
is what makes him somewhat better than the man who supports democracy, who is ruled by the pursuit of *unnecessary needs* (or, as we might say
today, by "wants" instead). Martha Nussbaum, for instance, observes
(citing the *Gorgias*) that Callicles is not disturbed by the fact that instrumental goods form a large part of a "good life": "replenishment" and
"ministering to the exigencies of a body" may both have positive value,[18]
though they do not possess intrinsic value "merely" because they are
"replenishments."

When we turn to *unnecessary* needs, the situation is quite different,
although democracy has its origin from oligarchy, "as a result of the
insatiable character of the good that oligarchy proposes for itself," the
necessity of "becoming as rich as possible" (555b). Socrates notes the
basis for the change from one bad regime and character to an even
worse one:

> Isn't it by now plain that it's not possible to honour wealth in a city and at
> the same time adequately to maintain moderation among all citizens, but
> one or the other is necessarily neglected? (555c)[19]

This is precisely the root of the environmental threats described at the
beginning, at least from the social/psychological point of view: under
the relentless assault of corporate marketing strategies and our own desire to *have* rather than *to be*, moderation and restraint have no chance
to prevail, and democracy itself remains impotent.

Practically, Socrates sees the inception of democracy in the battle between the rich and the poor, whereby the poor fight the fat, unprepared
rich and win, now sharing "ruling offices," which are, in these circumstances, "given by lot" (557a). The result is a regime under which the
greatest freedom of choice and the greatest variety of human beings can
be found. This varied, multihued city "decorated with all dispositions"
might appear to be the fairest, like a garment of many colors. But it
would only be judged to be the most beautiful, Plato asserts, by "boys
and women." It should not be judged in that way, however: it is a system
without true rulers, and it only supports officials "dispensing a certain
equality to equals and unequals alike" (558c).

Rulers and officials are not chosen according to skill or to nobility of
character, and a man is chosen and honored only "if he says he's well-
disposed toward the multitude." In democracy, the "ruled" will be "full

of pleasures and desires." The desire for "bread and relish" or the necessities of life is appropriate, but beyond that, it is the unnecessary pleasures and desires that characterize the democratic man, in contrast with the stingy, oligarchic one (559c–d).

Socrates sketches a portrait of the democratic individual; in the description, we recognize the individual living in an affluent modern country and the reason our democratic institutions can and should be brought into question. What do these early "democrats" do? Socrates says:

> . . . naming shame simplicity, they push it out with dishonour, a fugitive; calling moderation cowardliness and spattering it with mud, they banish it; persuading that measure and orderly expenditure are rustic and illiberal, they join with many useless desires in driving them over the frontier. (560d)[20]

Neither the common good nor the good of his own soul and character limits the pursuit of "unnecessary desires." This man is not governed by the "good" or by the pursuit of perfection: he is guided only by "the law of equality" (561e); thus "there is neither order nor necessity in his life, but calling his life sweet, free and blessed, he follows it throughout" (561d).

It is clear that Plato is not in favor of democracy, and he makes the reasons for his belief equally clear. But, one may object, we believe in human rights, beyond what Plato might have found acceptable. Hence we can invoke human rights to life and health as universally valid and, we believe, unavoidably inherent in democratic institutions. But in the next section I argue that even without reference to Plato's theory, modern democracy is insufficient to protect the human rights it is intended to protect as primary.

Plato, the Good, and Democracy

For Plato the ideal city is ruled by an aristocracy; the ruler, a philosopher, has no personal interests and clearly sees the moral failure of timocracy, oligarchy, and democracy as well as tyranny, and is therefore able to avoid all their respective pitfalls. Further, in Book IV he neither seeks nor depends on the favor of the multitude and thus is ideally able to ensure that civic (that is, public policy) choices are purely derived from the "good," instead of attempting to make this or that group happy at the expense of another. Further, not only is it untrue that every desire one entertains is equal and thus entitled to equal consideration, but Plato proposes as the fundamental task of education to effect the *radical* change of desires, as their unqualified pursuit necessarily eclipses the need for education and for the pursuit of the good.

It is important now to consider whether these lacks are, as it appears, also at work in modern democracies, and whether the reintroduction of the good might mitigate the problems that beset us as well as the similar ones Plato perceived many years ago. Without any knowledge of modern technologies, nor of toxicology, epidemiology, or ecology, Plato nevertheless pointed to the crux of the problem. When we enshrine wealth and economic success, we correspondingly depreciate or even eliminate the centrality of the common "good"—thus of a universalizable morality—from our public policy; when we compound our error by making freedom and majoritarian preferences co-primary with it, we open the door to an endless variety of people's lifestyles and choices and their unlimited need to satisfy unnecessary desires. But, like a good human being, a good *polis* must function like an organism: it must be centrally organized around a *telos* that supports the organism itself and permits it to thrive.

In contrast Theo Colborn argues, describing the behavior of breast cancer cells in an experiment exposing them to either natural hormones or "hormone mimics" in the form of man-made chemicals: "If those cells start multiplying continuously the way bacteria do, the organism will rapidly turn into little more than a big disorganized tumor."[21] Disorganized growth, without the check provided by a uniting inhibiting factor, is a natural ecological disaster. Our own organism permits or limits growth according to our genetic plan, unless its natural pathways are disrupted by man-made substances that block these natural inhibitors. Notwithstanding the fact that Plato may not countenance an "Aristotelian turn," such as the example I have cited, it is important to emphasize that the deep philosophical meaning of Plato's thought on this question should not be trivialized by relegating it to a purely historical point.

What is the role and function of the "good" for Plato? It is the primary criterion according to which all human action, thought, and endeavor are to be judged. However, this criterion is not immediately available to all, like a sample of paint by which we might judge how close our color might be to the "original." Martha Nussbaum says:

> Plato's standpoint of perfection is not immediately available to any creature who wishes to assume it. It is a long and difficult matter to learn to detach ourselves from our human needs and interests, or to get to a point at which we can do so.[22]

Education and the right social organization are vital to achieve this point of view; hence Nussbaum adds:

... the *Republic* is, for more than half of its length, a book about education, i.e. about the strategies for "turning the soul around" from its natural human way of seeing, to the correct way.[23]

In contrast, not only are we not living in a homogeneous, morally oriented "city," but we also are not the product of a common education based on common beliefs, and for the most part we ignore community and commonality in favor of individuality and personal freedom in both lifestyle and education. Plato separates the visible from the noetic in the "divided line" example (509d–511e), but at one point he links them in a way that might permit us to attempt the analogy between the corrective and saving role of the "good," and the foundational role of life-support systems and their integrity, as a guiding criterion superior to the relentless pursuit of unnecessary desires. Socrates says:

> You'll be willing to say, I think, that the Sun not only provides visible things with the power to be seen but also with coming to be, growth and nourishment, although it is not itself coming to be. (509b)[24]

And even if this unusual, somewhat "scientific" approach cannot be accepted as anything other than either an anomaly in Plato's work or simply an analogy, the force of his major argument remains completely relevant. Perhaps Plato did not accept the existence of an intimate connection between "the good" and decisions that are good in virtue of being life supporting and ecologically based, but the rest of the argument I propose remains independent of this point and thus defensible in any case.

I have argued that individualistic free choices fostered by democracy, without the imposition of checks based on a philosophical commitment to the "good," are intellectually, morally, and in our world, even physically harmful to all.

It is grossly immoral to pursue one's preferences (desires) without considering of the general good. Plato often uses health as the example of indisputable good, to which justice runs parallel in the soul, rather than the body. He says, for instance, "Healthy things produce health, unhealthy ones, disease" (444c); he also asks, "don't just actions produce justice in the soul and unjust ones, injustice?" (444d). Health in turn can be produced by establishing "the components of the body in a natural relation of control, one by another, while to produce disease is to establish a relation of ruling and being ruled contrary to nature" (444d). The same holds true about the parts of the soul, so that "virtue seems, then, to be a kind of health ... while vice is disease" (444e).

Hence we can say that the lack of physical health, like the lack of virtue, is not a good or a benefit. When imposed on another, it may therefore constitute a harm. Socrates had argued earlier against Thrasymachus, contrasting "doing or having one's own" with Thrasymachus's understanding of justice as real power, in the sense of "outdoing" (*pleonektein*) (343e) everyone else. The notion of "pleonexia" or the desire of possessions to outdo others can be easily related to the immoderate pursuit of the unnecessary, typical of the modern as well as the Platonic democracy.

Even earlier, in Book I, Socrates had also argued against Polemarchus that injuring or harming even one's enemies is never right or just and concluded that "it is never just to injure anyone" (335e). The subject of the discourse is clearly "virtue," in fact, "justice"; thus it is possible that the harm intended may not be physical. Yet the sense of the dialogue at this point appears to include physical harms, as "enemies" are not normally taken to be opponents in philosophical debates whom one is attempting to best (an intellectual harm?) or people whose character one is trying to corrupt (moral harm?), but physically threatening persons who wish to harm us, which prompts Polemarchus to argue that we should harm them in turn, justly.

Hence we can accept as given that those who are *not* harmful to us and who cannot be defined as "enemies," are, a fortiori, *not* people whom we can harm, while remaining just. Even if we eliminate the general health- and life-giving aspects of the sun and view it simply as a metaphor on other human, moral, and intellectual grounds, diminishing the health, and thus, the capacities of *anyone* is an immoral act, whether it is the result of a single person's activity or permitted as a policy in the "city" in order to promote other goods, such as affluence or even personal freedom.

Despite his disdain for individual "freedoms" beyond that of perfecting one's character, Plato has some important things to say about the relation between the good and the polity. In fact, his indictment of democracy might be reexamined and reevaluated. It might then act as a clarion call to alert us to what we lost, singly and collectively, when we embraced a self-centered vision in which the "good" played no part.

Aristotle, Man's "Function," the Good Life, and the Golden Mean

> Nevertheless it is evident that *eudaimonia* stands in need of good things from outside as we have said: for it is impossible or difficult to do fine things without resources. (NE 1099a31, 1–3)[25]

Aristotle shares Plato's background, hence his emphasis on the need for a community that is political but also based on common principles and a common understanding of what is right. He also shares Plato's belief in the rationality and universality of the definition of the good and of human nature. Additionally, Aristotle's philosophy is based on and incorporates scientific observation and a deep respect for what is "natural." His thought is invaluable to help understand (1) the ecological value of integrity, (2) the relation between parts and wholes, (3) the intrinsic value of life-support systems,[26] and (4) the future-oriented sense of "being eternal" discussed in chapter 3. In addition, others have argued for Aristotelian aspects of ecological science connected with ecosystemic hierarchies[27] and his major contribution to the study of causality.[28] Finally, I have proposed that the Aristotelian "golden mean" may provide another useful tool to help us understand what is needed for an ethic that is compatible with the ethics of integrity.[29]

Leaving aside the aspect of Aristotle's thought for which I have already argued, or those that are defended in other works, this section focuses on additional insights from Aristotle: (1) the function (*ergon*) argument, (2) the argument about the good life, or *eudaimonia*, and (3) some additional aspects of the "golden mean," as all build on Plato's vision and enrich it in various ways.

The Function "Argument"

Much of Aristotle's work in the *Nicomachean Ethics* is devoted to an analysis of what it means to live a "good life" and to achieve *eudaimonia*. The latter is a difficult term to translate: its meaning is not simply "happiness," as it is often translated. Happiness is a psychological state, quite different from the activity of *eudaimonia*.[30] Translations such as "living a good life for a human being"[31] or "human flourishing,"[32] both understood as "living well and doing well," are far more accurate. The reason why that is so is precisely the reason we are reaching back to Aristotle's thought here: *eudaimonia* only makes sense in relation to the proper understanding of what man does and what man is, his "function" and his excellence. In an earlier section we noted how dangerous it is to propose a public policy that is detached from a defensible, logically coherent "public good," as Plato argued in the *Republic*. Further, since, as Plato also argued, the *polis* is only as good as its citizens, the "good" has to be consonant with man's natural excellence in order to be logically and morally defensible, that is, in order to be that "for the sake of which" everything must be done.

Aristotle's "function" argument starts, as is his custom, from observations about the natural world. Everything has a natural excellence, and all that is done or happens naturally is also for the sake of something. All natural species pursue the eternity of being in the way available to them, that is, not individually and separately but through their species' reproduction. The physical "function" that supports this quest for "eternity" is shared with all life, from plants to nonhuman animals. In the well-known discussion in the *De Anima*,[33] Aristotle acknowledges our link to all other life, even plants. But what we share with plants is simply being alive; in contrast, we share motion and sentience with nonhuman animals: in both cases their respective function lies in the specific capacities and excellencies of each kind.

Therefore, our function and excellence cannot lie in anything that we share with other species; it must lie in that which is particularly ours—our rational nature, shared by neither plants nor other animals, for Aristotle. Hence our function embodies our "difference" and indicates the basis for our excellence, and Aristotle's argument provides the tie between the "good," the "good life," or *eudaimonia*—and our own nature: the good is not the choice of the majority, as such, nor one preference among others. The real good for humans is the only choice that is at once logical, practical, moral, and natural. It represents the only way that "flourishing" is meaningful for humans, our most proper function. Aristotle concludes the *ergon* argument as follows:

> The human good turns out to be activity of soul in accordance with virtue, and if there is more than one virtue, in accordance with the best and most perfect. (NE 1098a16–18)[34]

The good—that is, not one among many—is the pursuit of an activity in accordance with virtue; hence, given our nature, "the virtuous activity equated with the human good in the function argument is virtuous activity of the reasoning part of the soul."[35] In contrast with J. L. Ackrill, who believes that virtuous activity of the moral kind is the best,[36] Richard Kraut believes that the good "consists in intellectual activity and nothing else."[37] This apparent conflict may not be as stark as it appears, that is, either intellectual *or* moral value. Kraut suggests that in the *Nicomachean Ethics*,[38] "Aristotle makes a distinction between perfect happiness and a secondary form of happiness. He says that the former consists in contemplation; but that by exercising the practical virtues, the politician can also be happy."[39]

From the point of view of the environment and the ethics of integrity, the "lesser" sort of happiness provides the most appropriate emphasis. When life and health are present, contemplation is "self-sufficient," according to Aristotle; in fact, that is what makes it superior to the "other" *eudaimonia*, that is, the one that needs external circumstances and other goods to flourish. Hence, minimally, we can argue that life and health are primary in Aristotle, as they are in the PI, although they are not argued for; their primacy is implicit. But the main point that can be drawn from Aristotle's argument is the necessary connection between human nature and the good.

The difference between Aristotle and modern thinkers like John Rawls, for instance (see chapter 3), is that for Aristotle not only must the good must be universalizable and logically defensible, but also the existence of a universal human nature is beyond question; it represents the basis and justification of the "good" itself.

The Meaning and Role of *Eudaimonia*

If human flourishing means moral and intellectual activity in accordance with reason, and if excellence in this activity represents the highest goal in human life, then we must inquire into the prerequisites (or other "goods") necessary for the attainment of that goal. Nussbaum argues that the good life is extremely "vulnerable" to disaster, and hence other circumstances beyond our moral character may be concomitant with or instrumental to *eudaimonia*, or an intrinsic part of it.

In the previous section we saw that Aristotle relies on a twofold interpretation of *eudaimonia*, as the term encompasses the highest intellectual and moral virtues, although the former is primary, and the latter secondary:

> If happiness is activity in accordance with virtue it is reasonable that it should be in accordance with the highest virtue; and this will be that of the best thing in us. (NE X. 7. 1117a12–14)

Aristotle adds, "That this activity is contemplative we have already said" (NE X.7.1177a17–18). Why is this so? He proposes a twofold answer: first, it is the best (rational) activity, directed at the best objects knowable; second, it is "most continuous." But there is another aspect of this primary form of *eudaimonia* that cannot be ignored, as it is equally important: the contemplative use of reason is self-sufficient, hence less vulnerable to both negative chance happenings and the lack of other goods. In contrast, Aristotle himself recognizes that this sort of life, devoted purely to the philosophical contemplation of truth, "would be too high for men," as it is the exercise of the "divine" in them, that is, this way of life would allow a part (though admittedly the best one) to take over, in a sense, the entire human capacity for activity.

In contrast, the "secondary" form of happiness is entirely suitable to humans, and as Aristotle points out, it is here that we find the need for specific circumstances and additional "goods" beyond one's life and moral character.

Nussbaum argues that activity is required for the secondary form of
eudaimonia as well, as a state of character is not sufficient for it. In that
case, however, the activity must not be "impeded."[40] Aristotle says:

> No activity (*energeia*) is complete if it is impeded; but *eudaimonia* is some-
> thing complete. For the *eudaimon* person needs the goods of the body and
> external goods, and goods of luck in addition, so that his activities should
> not be impeded. (NE 7.1153b16)

Examples of such "impediments" are lack of a good birth or "good
looks," children, or friends. In that case, we can start by noting the obvious—that is, that life and unimpaired rationality and health are necessary preconditions of "living well"—and then add a few candidates to
the broad category of possible "impediments." For instance, environmental conditions might render one too weak to interact with one's
friends or, through climate changes and powerful infectious diseases,
make one ill and thus contagious to such friends; or perhaps the sort of
environmental "hormone mimics"[41] discussed in earlier chapters might
render one incapable of fulfilling one's human destiny because of the
loss of normal reproductive capacities. (See also the discussion of this
question in chapter 10.)

Such contemporary "impediments" are far more than difficulties and
possible reductions of our capacity for full achievement of *eudaimonia*.
They constitute instead extreme threats to the very aim of our lives, that
of achieving our own excellence. Today we tend to view such problems
simply as threats to human health or physical well-being, or even as part
of the modern human condition. But, insofar as both health and physical well-being are intrinsic components of the natural capacities of humans, Aristotle would view anything impeding such capacities as far
more significant than that. Anyone who interferes with the capacities of
a man is guilty of preventing him from pursuing his natural goal, that
"for the sake of which" all his activity unfolds. The "impeder" would
take away, essentially, his reason for living and the very role he is intended to play within the universe. It is a grave harm that attacks at the
same time the universal, essential nature of man, and through it, his
final goal. In principle, and prima facie, an attack on an individual's
microintegrity is at the same time an attack on the function the individual performs within her habitat, and hence it is also an attack on the
integrity of the systemic whole.

What about other relational goods? How many or how much is necessary for *eudaimonia*? Aristotle simply says that we must be "sufficiently
equipped with other goods."[42] This point deserves careful attention.
While other external goods are absolutely necessary, it is not true that

the more of these we acquire, the better our virtue, or the closer our achievement of *eudaimonia*. Kraut explains:

> we should wish for that level of fortune that enhances our virtuous activity. More generally, the right level for any good other than happiness is the level at which it best contributes to one of the ultimate ends in which happiness consists.[43]

As in our examination of the good in Plato, Aristotle uses his conception of *eudaimonia* as the criterion for the need for external goods in general, but also for the quantity of external goods required:

> to determine the extent to which music, drawing, gymnastics or any other subject should be studied, politics must look to the ultimate end of human life.[44]

Hence, external goods have a limit (*horos*), as Aristotle is applying the doctrine of the mean to both this topic and the understanding of virtue. The mean must be sought between the extremes of a complete lack of external goods and an excess, or a limitless amount, which would be equally wrong.[45]

The appropriate amount of goods is to be found in the mean between too little and too much; further, it is not defined in terms of preferences but must be limited according to the two criteria we have encountered: the criterion of our rational human nature and its function, and that of the ultimate good, the good of human life. In addition, all other goods can be understood as both intrinsic and instrumental goods in regard to the final goal and the two criteria. Not only are external goods necessary prerequisites of the good; they are also, without doubt, components of it. This interpretation is based on the "inclusivist" conception of happiness in Aristotle[46] and, Kraut observes, is not accepted by some commentators.[47]

One further point will clarify the relation between Aristotelian moral doctrine and the principle of integrity. Although both Plato and Aristotle seek *universal* goals and rationally defensible arguments to link the goals to human nature, a great difference emerges. Aristotle, according to Nussbaum, "defends a conception of the city as a plurality, an association of free and equal citizens who rule and are ruled by turns."[48] Where Plato views the *polis* as a single, organic unit, one family, in order to avoid the possibility of conflict, Aristotle defends the importance of both "philia" and "political justice," both of which require separate elements, different parties and interests, for their existence and therefore permit opposition and even conflict among groups.[49]

But before we return once again to the acceptance of democracy, we need to recognize the foundational difference between Aristotelian democracy and its modern, liberal counterpart. For Aristotle, the two criteria discussed in this section can never be set aside by democratic choices, as democracy, or any desirable form of government, must be based on the right understanding of the nature of man and of his final goal.

Virtue and the "Golden Mean"

The concepts of "human function" and "excellence" and the "good life" provide important insights about the limits they impose on individual human choices and on democratic choices in public governance. In the previous section, we saw that although other "goods" besides intellective and moral virtue were required for *eudaimonia*, they themselves were subject to certain criteria to ensure that they would not be either too much or too little. The ideas of limit and balance in all things are typical in Greek thought. Aristotle adds his own particular sense to the meaning of moral virtue, through the doctrine of the golden mean. As is his custom, Aristotle bases his theory on what happens in the case of natural (bodily) virtues. Health, like strength, is negatively affected by both excess and deficiency or, as Kraut puts it, "too much or too little exercise, too much or too little eating, and the same holds true of such virtues of the soul as temperance and courage" (NE 1104a11–19).[50]

We need to aim at "a mean between deficiency and excess" in our virtuous activities, just as a craftsman would aim at producing something that is just right, complete as it stands. This requires the exercise of practical reason, as Aristotle emphasizes in his definition of moral virtue as:

> a state concerned with choice, being in a mean that is relative to us, as determined by reason by which the practically wise person would determine it. (NE 1106b36–1107a2)

But "hitting the mean," as Kraut has it, is not an easy task: it is much easier to do too much or too little, and Aristotle recognizes the imprecision of his criterion. Clearly, the emphasis is on moderation in our practical endeavors, as our goal is to become good, not simply to contemplate moral truths (NE 1103b26–28). To do so, one cannot simply quantify excess and defect and mathematically calculate the mean between the two. Aristotle advances the use of "right reason" and introduces another helpful component into our deliberative process—the criterion of the *phronemos*, the wise man—as we keep in mind what his experienced choice might be in similar circumstances.

Both actions and emotions are at issue, but only those that are morally relevant, that is, those that (1) advance our general goal of achieving *eudaimonia*, and (2) are consonant with the excellence of which our natural "function" is capable. *Horos*, as "limit, standard, boundary or definition" of the mean,[51] is thus a foundational part of Aristotle's moral doctrine. Therefore, the doctrine of the mean is helpful in two ways. The first and most important is the conceptual sense in which it establishes the need for clear boundaries to democratic rule, as all choices must be limited by reference to the two clear and universal criteria, not by collective preferences.

This sense of the mean is particularly important because, unlike other ancients, such as Cynics, Stoics, and later some Neoplatonists and even Plato himself, Aristotle emphasizes the need for other, external goods to achieve *eudaimonia* through the moral life. For Aristotle, the "wise man on the rack" is neither happy nor an example of moral perfection. The second sense I have suggested might be to use the value of the mean as a limit of the right, as a solution to present global problems. This approach requires extending Aristotle beyond the scope of the community, the morally homogenous *polis* of which he spoke. Through this extension, we can apply Aristotle's doctrine to the problem of overuse of natural resources and overconsumption on the part of northwestern countries at the expense of southeastern developing areas and future generations.

Aristotle's doctrine of the golden mean provides a helpful perspective from which to approach this complex problem. If the poor and the underdeveloped have a right to better their lives and those of their children, we in the North cannot continue to produce and consume at our present pace.[52] What would be the morally right choice? Aristotle's mean between excess (our present state) and defect (the present state of developing countries) might be achieved by reflection on the two criteria Aristotle used: the "function" and excellence of humankind and the final aim of life.

From that perspective the right and rational thing to do is to aim for a "mean" that lies within clear-cut limits: limits to *our* excess, and limits to *their* lack. It requires that we eliminate overuse and overconsumption in order to actualize our natural potential, so that others may alter their *under*use and *under*consumption accordingly and so finally come to achieve their potential as well. Suffering from famine, attacked by disease and by enemies in violent conflicts, and living in constant dread and anxiety for one's children do not create a state conducive to actualizing one's potential, and Aristotle, within his realm of examples, is quite explicit on the need for sufficient means for health and for relaxation.

But the actualization of our capacities requires precisely the *same limits* as those required by the actualization of the capacities of others. Virtue is as hard to achieve with too much as it is with too little. All of us equally must be virtuous by aiming at the mean, according to right reason, as the wise man would do. Riches and excesses are not the right path to *eudaimonia*: the natural "function" of rich and poor alike must strive for excellence under equal conditions.

Virtue ethics in Plato and Aristotle, I believe, provide a perspective long lost in our comfortable (for some) modern world. They also provide an interhuman ethic that not only is compatible with the ethics of integrity but also affords a much sounder basis for the protection of the Earth. It is time now to turn to the last of the virtue ethics philosophers we will consider, Immanuel Kant.

Kant's Virtue Ethics: The Value of Life and Duties to Oneself

The basis for including Kant among "compatible ethics," aside from the categorical form of his doctrine and the infinite value he ascribes to life, both of which were acknowledged in my earlier work,[53] is the fact that, not unlike Plato and Aristotle, Kant believes that we have duties to ourselves. Margaret Paton argues that the importance of duties to oneself in Kant is not always recognized. She adds:

> When this is realized, it becomes apparent that his central concern is with virtue and the perfection of moral agents, rather than with the abstract concept of duty.[54]

Kant's second formulation of the Categorical Imperative provides the main basis for the duties to self. "Act so that you treat humanity, whether in your person in the person of another, always at the same time, as an end, and never only as means." The concepts present in this formulation—"Humanity, obligation, means, personality, dignity and self-respect"—are used by Kant in his discussion of duties to oneself in the *Metaphysics of Morals* and in the *Lectures on Ethics*.[55] Although Kant's respect for humanity is based primarily on our capacity to be autonomous, that is, to exercise our rationality and free will, our life and our physical integrity appear to be equally (and unconditionally) worthy of respect.

> I maintain that to every rational being possessed of a will we must also lend the idea of freedom as the only one under which he can act.[56]

In a later section in the same work, Kant separates the pursuit of morality from that of happiness, characterizing the latter as governed by "the law of nature governing desires and inclinations," in contrast with the Greek doctrines whereby the two pursuits are joined, as we have seen. Nevertheless Kant admits the need to regard himself "from one point of view as a being that belongs to the sensible world."[57] In this sense as well as in the sense that Kant employs in his discussion of suicide, our body is the locus of great value, as the necessary basis for the employment of our rationality. As Ruth Chadwick puts it, "It is because human beings should be treated in a certain way that we have obligations to ourselves as human beings."[58]

We are told to respect ourselves, so that all acts that degrade us as humans are impossible. I showed in chapter 3 the importance of Kant's argument in relation to the risks to which we are exposed. In this section I add the Kantian perspective as another form of virtue ethics, in order to enrich the moral side of the argument of chapter 3; in chapter 8 I return once again in more detail to laws and public policy.

Whether or not Kant holds seriously a doctrine of duties to oneself has been debated. I believe that much of that scholarly debate hinges on a disagreement about the difference—if any—between legal and moral obligations and the alleged absurdities that might follow if we took Kant to say that we do have obligations to ourselves (for example, would I take myself to court for failure to comply, and how would I divide my "self" into "obligated" and "obligating" self, in order to make sense of such duties?).[59] Without focusing on the details of the debate, it is sufficient to acknowledge that it exists, and that, by listing Kant as a representative of the "virtue ethics" tradition, it is clear that I am more convinced by the arguments supporting the existence of self-directed duties. Warner Wick says:

> Without a moral obligation to develop a certain sort of character in ourselves . . . the moral sphere appears so flattened as to be unrecognizable.[60]

In Kant, as in Aristotle, a human being "flourishes" when certain conditions are met. This flourishing entails the development of a character appropriate to the dignity of humanity in ourselves: the flourishing of our capacity for such a character is—together with the possession of life and rationality—what renders "each man a being of infinite value or worth and an end in himself."[61] In contrast, actions that violate the prerequisite circumstances and the conditions for this flourishing are forbidden. These include such attacks on the self as "arbitrary limitations of one's personal liberty, self-degradation, and . . . self-deception."[62] Kant is quite clear about the most extreme case of such impermissible behavior, that of suicide, as it eliminates the body through which any and all flourishing might take place, and it does so through our defining characteristic, our autonomous will.

Kant also offers other examples. From Paul Eisenberg's list, for instance, selling oneself into slavery is clearly wrong, but "self-degrada-tion" and "self-deception" are far more obscure. What might count as self-degradation? Eisenberg suggests "voluntarily becoming a prosti-tute" or "taking drugs for non-medical reasons." Self-deception is par-ticularly difficult to describe. Does it simply mean not understanding or not knowing something, and acting in accordance with our wrong be-liefs? It seems that self-deception about our duties represents a flawed first step toward the performance of other duties; however, it involves "not faulty cognition, but faulty evaluation."[63]

The application of these categories, especially self-deception, appears to be particularly relevant to the case of modern, affluent democratic states, when full information about the implications and consequences of what we plan to do is eliminated and—following on our faulty evalua-tion of the situation and of our role in it—we perform actions that are not consonant with the value and the integrity of the beings that we are. In this case self-deception is doubly immoral: intrinsically, as a form of lying, and instrumentally, as a wrong first step in fulfilling our duties to humanity, through the neglect of our character. Kant supports this interpretation: "a lie is more a violation of one's duty to oneself, than one's duty to others."[64] Through both aspects, we do an injury to our-selves. Although we are not using our liberty and our free will to elimi-nate ourselves altogether (a self-contradictory endeavor), in the case cited we still contradict who we are, essentially, as our moral character is at stake.

In addition, in the *Lectures on Ethics*, Kant argues for respect for our own bodies. He says:

> If a man for gain or profit submits to all indignities and makes himself the plaything of another, he casts away the worth of his manhood.[65]

He adds:

> Moreover, if a man offer his body for profit for the sport of others—if, for instance, he agrees in return for a few pints of beer to be knocked about—he throws himself away, and the perpetrators who pay him for it, are acting as vilely as he.[66]

This is particularly relevant from our point of view. If Kant says that "our actions must be in keeping with the worth of man," and if "the legal maxim, *Neminem laede*" (Harm no one) can be said to apply to this case in the form *Noli naturam humanam in te ipso laedere* (Do not harm human nature in your own self), then the argument proposed in chapter 3 rests on solid textual ground. We cannot agree to be harmed in exchange for any benefit, nor can we collectively agree to be harmed as a group or allow another group to be harmed, even for "countervailing benefits."[67]

We have double duties to ourselves: first, to promote the flourishing of our moral character and respect our essential freedom and rationality; second, to support and respect our physical humanity, never using our bodies merely as means even for some perceived gain. In the first sense, Kant provides strong moral arguments against consenting to any trade-off that might harm humanity in our person, as our bodies are "the embodiment of persons."[68] Hence Kant's point of view is in stark contrast with the view that we have complete sovereignty over our own bodies, including the right to sell them. For Kant, we have no right to sell even "one finger," and we have the duty "to deny the use of our bodies by others when they are needed for the pursuit of social goals."[69]

Therefore, we can support the conclusion of our argument in chapter 3, against consent to harms, even knowingly, for economic or other reasons; from the philosophical/moral point of view, we can appeal to Kant's emphasis on virtue and character; and from the practical/moral point of view, we can turn to Kant's emphasis on a human beings—as a "unity," to whom we owe an absolute duty of respect. As Paton argues, "What Kant appears to be saying is that the moral goodness of individuals has priority over the performance of social obligations";[70] but our duty to others is also a duty to humanity and its infinite worth, in each individual instantiation. Hence it is immoral to inflict harm on others (with or without their consent), either in the sense of harming their "physical unity" or in the sense of harming their character, whatever social utility might ensue.

Moreover, both our physical integrity and our essential humanity depend on the functions of life-support systems. Therefore we can argue that Kant's moral doctrine, like those of Plato and Aristotle before him, is entirely compatible with the ethics of integrity; and we can also then argue, from the virtue ethics perspective presented in this chapter, that for all three thinkers neither direct harm to humans nor harm to humans through ecosystems is morally permissible. Further, in contrast with the accepted tenets of liberal democracy, no social benefit or other trade-off can make it so.

Conclusion

Chapter 9 expands on the second-order principles that comprise the ethics of integrity in order to turn the principle of integrity's general imperatives[71] into a moral approach that can provide practical guidance for individual and collective activities. These activities, in order to fit into the ethics of integrity, will have to be directed by a new "design," as William McDonough proposes.[72] McDonough is an architect, not a philosopher, yet his paper "A Boat for Thoreau"[73] has deep philosophical implications. He argues that even our present "greening" practices, our efforts to "minimize waste," and the like are fundamentally misguided: we cannot reach our true goal of a totally changed life (not lifestyle) merely by "slowing down," while still traveling in the wrong direction. We also need to stop believing that even a 50 percent reduction in toxins and other endocrine disrupters might be a sufficient or even laudable goal to pursue. More will be said about the specifics of McDonough's proposal in chapters 9 and 10. For now it is important to note that even "eco-efficiency" is not enough:

> That is the problem with eco-efficiency from a designer's point of view: it does not tell you to re-imagine the world, it just tells you to leave the world the way it is. Eco-efficiency is not revolutionary—it is still a linear process headed for zero and never getting there, like Zeno's paradox.[74]

This radical "re-imagining" McDonough terms the "Strategy of Change." In some sense, that has been the goal of this chapter as well. To propose a return to the demanding tenets of virtue ethics is another such strategy, and one without which the ethics of integrity are hard to embrace. Our usually accepted moral doctrines look at what to do in cases of quandaries and problems, such as the "prisoner's dilemma."[75] But all such "action ethics," as Louis Pojman argues, are "minimalist ethics":

> The accent is on *social control.* Morality is largely preventive, safeguarding rights and moral space where people may carry out their projects unhindered by the intrusion of others.[76]

Louis Pojman cites Daniel Callahan's characterization of a "moral minimalist ethic": it represents only a modest proposal and lacks the richness of eudaimonistic ethics. In contrast, eudaimonistic ethics are "inspirational."[77] Their approach proposes precisely a new design for life. Virtue ethics do not ask us to refine a rational contractor's position or to find some other "self-interested" considerations:

> The crucial factor in classical aspiration ethics is the duty to grow as a moral person, so that one may be able to take on greater moral responsibility.[78]

The Greeks and Kant

But that is exactly the major requirement of the ethics of integrity. It is our duty to grow and develop in character and responsibility. Our growth may then help us re-form (in the sense of redesigning) our life to include the ethics of integrity, with their truly radical and demanding message (see chapter 9).

Before expanding the second-order principles in order to show the import of the ethics of integrity, in the next chapter I return to a discussion of compatible and defensible public policy. That discussion is firmly anchored in present laws and regulations. I argue that if these are properly examined and understood, they may be sufficient to suggest public policy decisions compatible with the PI. As with the regulations, legislation, and various acts using the language of integrity, I argue that much of present legislation simply needs to be coordinated, analyzed and applied consistently in order to provide the global protection the public needs and that new regulatory acts, such as the *Earth Charter*, may provide the required holistic basis for public policy.

Notes

1. William A. McDonough, "A Boat for Thoreau," in *The Business of Consumption: Environmental Ethics and the Global Economy*, ed. L. Westra and P. Werhane (Lanham, MD: Rowman & Littlefield, in press).

2. L. Westra, *An Environmental Proposal for Ethics: The Principle of Integrity* (Lanham, MD: Rowman & Littlefield, 1994), see chapter 2, especially pp. 27–51.

3. Westra, *An Environmental Proposal for Ethics*. See chapter 2, especially pp. 27–51.

4. Margaret Paton, "A Reconsideration of Kant's Treatment of Duties to Oneself," *Philosophical Quarterly* 40, 159 (April 1990): 222–32.

5. Westra, *An Environmental Proposal for Ethics*.

6. K. Shrader-Frechette, *Risk and Rationality* (Berkeley: University of California Press, 1991).

7. RIVM, *National Environmental Outlook, 1990–2010* (Bilthoven, The Netherlands: Rijksinstituut voor Volksgezondheid en Milieuhygiene, 1986).

8. Rita Colwell, "Global Climate and Infectious Disease: The Cholera Paradigm," President's Lecture, February 10, 1996, American Association for the Advancement of Science, *Science* 274 (December 20, 1996): 2025–31; see also Intergovernmental Panel on Climate Change (IPCC), 1996: Summary for Policymakers, "Climate Change 1995": *The IPCC Second Assessment Report, Volume 2: Scientific-Technical Analyses of Impacts, Adaptations, and Mitigation of Climate Change*, ed. R. T. Watson, M. C. Zinyowera, and R. H. Moss (Cambridge and New York: Cambridge University Press, in press); Dale Jamieson, "Managing the Future: Public Policy, Scientific Uncertainty, and Global Warming," in *Upstream/Downstream*, ed. D. Scherer (Philadelphia: Temple University Press, 1990), pp. 67–89; Dale Jamieson, "Ecosystem Health: Some Preventive Medicine," *Environmental*

Values 4, 4 (November 1995), special issue on ecosystem health, 333–44; Janice D. Longstretch, et al., "Effects of Increased Solar Ultraviolet Radiation on Human Health," *Ambio* 24, 3 (May 1995): 153–65.

9. Theo Colborn, Dianne Dumanoski, and John Peterson Myers, *Our Stolen Future* (New York: Dutton, 1996).

10. See chapter 5.

11. L. Westra and P. Wenz, *The Faces of Environmental Racism: The Global Equity Issues* (Lanham, MD: Rowman & Littlefield, 1995).

12. See chapter 6.

13. L. Westra, "On Risky Business," review of *Risky Business*, by E. Draper, *Business Ethics Quarterly* 4, 1 (January 1994): 97–110.

14. Colborn, et al., *Our Stolen Future*; see also Carl F. Cranor, *Regulating Toxic Substances* (Philosophy of Science and the Law) (New York: Oxford University Press, 1993).

15. Robert E. McGinn, "Technology, Demography, and the Anachronism of Traditional Rights," *Journal of Applied Philosophy* 11, 1 (1994): 57–70; see also chapter 4, this volume.

16. Plato, *The Republic*, tr. A. Bloom (New York: Basic Books, 1968).

17. Marc S. Cohen, Patricia Curd, and C. D. C. Reeve, *Ancient Greek Philosophy* (Indianapolis: Hackett, 1995)—*The Republic*, tr. G. M. A. Grube and C. D. C. Reeve, pp. 253–431.

18. Martha C. Nussbaum, *The Fragility of Goodness* (Cambridge, MA: Cambridge University Press, 1986).

19. Plato, *The Republic*, p. 233.

20. Plato, *The Republic*, p. 239.

21. Colborn, et al., *Our Stolen Future*, p. 123.

22. Nussbaum, *The Fragility of Goodness*.

23. Nussbaum, *The Fragility of Goodness*, p. 157.

24. Cohen, et al., *Ancient Greek Philosophy*.

25. Aristotle, *Nicomachean Ethics*, ed. R. McKeon (New York: Random House, 1992).

26. Westra, *An Environmental Proposal for Ethics*, see chapter 4.

27. R. O'Neill, D. De Angelis, J. B. Waide, and T. F. Allen, *A Hierarchical Concept of Ecosystems* (Princeton: Princeton University Press, 1986).

28. Robert Ulanowicz, "Ecosystem Integrity: A Causal Necessity," in *Perspectives on Ecological Integrity*, ed. L. Westra and J. Lemons (Dordrecht, The Netherlands: Kluwer, 1995), pp. 77–87; see also R. Ulanowicz, *Ecology, The Ascendent Perspective* (New York: Columbia University Press, in press).

29. L. Westra, "Ecosystem Integrity and Sustainability: The Foundational Value of the Wild," in *Perspectives on Ecological Integrity*, ed. L. Westra and J. Lemons (Dordrecht, The Netherlands: Kluwer, 1995).

30. Nussbaum, *The Fragility of Goodness*.

31. Nussbaum, *The Fragility of Goodness*, p. 6.

32. Nussbaum, *The Fragility of Goodness*, p. 6; see also John Cooper, *Reason and Human Good in Aristotle* (Cambridge: Cambridge University Press, 1975).

33. Aristotle, *On the Soul*, tr. R. McKeon (New York: Random House, 1992), Book II, chapters 3 and 4.

34. Aristotle, *Nicomachean Ethics*.

35. Richard Kraut, *Aristotle on the Human Good* (Princeton: Princeton University Press, 1989).

36. J. L. Ackrill, "Aristotle on 'Good' and the Categories," in *Islamic Philosophy and the Classical Tradition: Essays Presented to Richard Walzer*, ed. M. Stern, et al. (Oxford, England: Oxford University Press, 1972), pp. 17–25.

37. Kraut, *Aristotle on the Human Good*.

38. Aristotle, *Nicomachean Ethics*, Book X, chapters 7 and 8.

39. Kraut, *Aristotle on the Human Good*.

40. Nussbaum, *The Fragility of Goodness*, see pp. 343–45.

41. Colborn, et al., *Our Stolen Future*; see also Theo Colborn, "Plenary Address" to International Association of Great Lakes Researchers (May 27, 1996) Erindale College, Toronto, Ont.

42. Kraut, *Aristotle on the Human Good*; see also Nussbaum, *The Fragility of Goodness*, chapter 12.

43. Kraut, *Aristotle on the Human Good*, p. 159.

44. Kraut, *Aristotle on the Human Good*, p. 159.

45. Aristotle, *The Politics*, ed. and tr. Ernest Barker (New York: Oxford University Press, 1973).

46. J. Rist, *The Mind of Aristotle* (Toronto: University of Toronto Press, 1989).

47. Kraut, *Aristotle on the Human Good*, especially chapter 5, pp. 267–311.

48. Nussbaum, *The Fragility of Goodness*, see pp. 343–45, 352.

49. Nussbaum, *The Fragility of Goodness*, p. 353.

50. Kraut, *Aristotle on the Human Good*, pp. 158–62, "Too Much and Too Little."

51. Kraut, *Aristotle on the Human Good*, p. 160.

52. Westra, "Ecosystem Integrity and Sustainability"; see also Robert Goodland and Herman Daly, "Why Northern Income Growth Is Not the Solution to Southern Poverty," World Bank Environment Department Divisional Working Paper, No. 1993–43, May 1993; R. Goodland and H. Daly, "Universal Environmental Sustainability and the Principle of Integrity," in *Perspectives on Ecological Integrity*, ed. L. Westra and J. Lemons, chapter 8, pp. 102–24.

53. Westra, *An Environmental Proposal for Ethics*.

54. Margaret Paton, "A Reconsideration of Kant's Treatment of Duties to Oneself," *Philosophical Quarterly* 40, 159 (April 1990): 222–32.

55. Immanuel Kant, *Metaphysics of Morals*, tr. James Ellington (New York: Bobbs-Merrill, 1981); see also Immanuel Kant, *Lectures on Ethics*, tr. Louis Infield (Indianapolis: Hacket, 1979), "Duties to Oneself," pp. 116–26.

56. Immanuel Kant, *Groundwork of the Metaphysics of Morals*, tr. H. J. Paton (New York: Harper Torchbooks, 1964), chapter 3, p. 101.

57. Kant, *Groundwork of the Metaphysics of Morals*, p. 111.

58. Ruth F. Chadwick, "The Market for Bodily Parts: Kant and Duties to Oneself," *Journal of Applied Philosophy* 6, 2 (October 1989): 129–39.

59. Warner Wick, "More about Duties to Oneself," *Ethics* 70 (1960): 158–63; see also Marcus George Singer, "Duties and Duties to Oneself," *Ethics* 73 (1962–63): 133–42; Mary Mothersill, "Professor Wick on Duties to Oneself," *Ethics* 71

(1960–61): 205–8; Frank Knight, "I, Me, My Self, and My Duties," *Ethics* 71 (1960–61): 209–12.

60. Wick, "More about Duties to Oneself"; Warner Wick, "Still More about Duties to Oneself," *Ethics* 71 (1960–61): 213–16.

61. Paul D. Eisenberg, "Duties to Oneself: A New Defense Sketched," *Review of Metaphysics* 20 (June 1967): 604.

62. Eisenberg, "Duties to Oneself: A New Defense Sketched," p. 610.

63. Eisenberg, "Duties to Oneself: A New Defense Sketched."

64. Kant, *Lectures on Ethics*, "Duties to Oneself" and "Duties towards the Body Itself."

65. Kant, *Lectures on Ethics*, p. 118.

66. Kant, *Lectures on Ethics*, p. 199.

67. Shrader-Frechette, *Risk and Rationality*, chapter 10.

68. Chadwick, "The Market for Bodily Parts."

69. Chadwick, "The Market for Bodily Parts," p. 136.

70. Paton, "A Reconsideration of Kant's Treatment of Duties to Oneself," p. 228.

71. Westra, *An Environmental Proposal for Ethics*, see chapter 3.

72. McDonough, "A Boat for Thoreau."

73. McDonough, "A Boat for Thoreau."

74. McDonough, "A Boat for Thoreau."

75. Louis Pojman, *Ethics—Discovering Right and Wrong*, 2d ed. (Belmont, CA: Wadsworth, 1995), chapter 10, p. 225; see David Gauthier, *Morality by Agreement* (Oxford, England: Clarendon Press, 1986).

76. Pojman, *Ethics*, p. 252.

77. Pojman, *Ethics*, p. 251.

78. Pojman, *Ethics*, p. 253.

8

Integrity, Public Policy, and the Law: A Question of Sustainability

For Aristotle, all ethical questions were also political, and this close connection between the two areas also underlies the move from ethics compatible with integrity to the global dimensions of compatible public policy. Public policy implies the existence of policymakers, usually understood to be the government officials of a region, group, country, or state. And this is the first major hurdle that must be faced. We argued that democracy as presently instantiated in various countries is not only largely impotent in the face of environmental problems, but also often has contributed to them. Hence, although when we speak of public policy we mean the body of regulations and laws a democratic government enacts and enforces in order to protect its citizens' interests, we need to look critically at this idealized picture of the relation between public governance and the governed.

Integrity and the Law

In chapters 3 and 7 we discussed some of the serious problems that are present because of the manner in which democracy is implemented today. In addition, even if present democratic institutions were radically altered through new regulations with veto powers over all unsustainable and ecologically unsound choices, it is still important to consider the "bottom up" aspect of the problem as well as its "top down" or regulatory dimension. Regulations need to be acceptable and convincing in order to gain general support beyond that of legislative bodies. But concerns that appear to be purely ecological may be viewed by many as secondary to economic concerns.

When the link between human health and the wild is understood, then the spurious division between "human interests" and "environmental/ecological interests" can be shown to be a false dichotomy and the life and ecological services the wild can provide will be accepted as more basic to human interests than any economic consideration. Anthony J. McMichael, a well-known epidemiologist at the London School of Hygiene and Tropical Medicine, says:

> After a quarter-million years as *Homo Sapiens*, we humans seem now to have come close to overloading the habitable world with people, their social, industrial and agriculture accouterments, and their effluent. If this sounds melodramatic, we should recall . . . that Earth is a closed system which we are, in effect, filling up.[1]

This means that limits are being reached for all our activities. Hence limits should be enforced much earlier, before it is too late to take steps to correct the effects of our shortsightedness. This also means that environmental problems are not simply problems "out there." They affect our lives in serious ways, so that they should be viewed as attacks on our own organic integrity (c), our health, and our natural capabilities (see chapter 2).

The appropriate response to these attacks is not what actually happens, even at best, in modern democracies. What happens, in fact, is compromise, mediation, requests for compensation, or even civil proceedings against the perpetrators, which lead to fines if they are convicted. I believe, however, the appropriate response is immediate criminal prosecution under laws and regulations that are not open to compromise, even if "consent" to the harmful practices can be proven (see chapter 3). These are the responses and procedures appropriate to murders, attacks causing bodily harm, and other forms of causing "reckless endangerment" to individuals.

Nor can it be objected that, by living in a modern society, we somehow give permission, a priori, to whatever may happen to us as a side effect of the lifestyle we have "chosen" (see chapter 3 for a discussion of the constraints to our choices), except when the ills that may befall us are intended with malice aforethought. Canadian law (inspired by British law) provides an answer: when someone is harmed, those who harmed him cannot claim that, by placing himself in a situation conducive to harm, he has thereby given a priori consent.

An example is that of a man who sought redress in law for the harm suffered through his participation in a barroom brawl. The defense claimed that by his presence in a bar, his drinking, and his own admitted participation in the brawl, the plaintiff had in some sense "consented" to his injuries. But this line of defense was not allowed, and he received appropriate compensation for his injury. For the harms imposed by a technological lifestyle in affluent northwestern societies, one can in addition argue that not all citizens in North America, for instance, are equal participants in the hazardous lifestyles of those who are better off: many are exposed to disproportionate shares of the burdens imposed by that lifestyle but do not reap their fair share of the benefits. Chapter 7 advanced the argument that, on the whole, consent may not be given either explicitly or implicitly (tacitly) to injury or harm to ourselves, even if such consent is both free and informed (see chapter 3). What follows is that rights such as the right to life or to freedom from bodily harm cannot be traded or given away: they are inalienable from the standpoint of Kantian moral theory (see chapter 7) as well as political theory from Hobbes to Rousseau to Kant. In turn, we must take seriously our natural inclination to self-preservation and, having acknowledged the existence of serious risks of harm to which we are all exposed, we need to oppose these in the best way available to us: by a changed lifestyle. What is needed is a lifestyle that embodies the model of living in a buffer area, complementary to the required core/wild area necessary to support all life within its own landscape, as well as to provide the services needed for our survival there.

A Question of Sustainability

We do not live today, as we should, as in buffers: our lifestyle, at least in affluent northwestern countries, is neither sustainable nor safe. Although safety and health issues have been discussed in this work, *sustainability* has been left undefined, as it often is in public documents. Some have attempted definitions,[2] but a definition of sustainability from the standpoint of integrity is necessary here.

From the perspective of ecological integrity and the principle of integrity, sustainability may be defined as follows:

1. In regard to the natural systems on earth, sustainability pertains to those systems that possess optimum undiminished capacity for their time and location for sustained evolutionary development. Hence only systems possessing integrity as we have defined it are truly sustainable, without qualifications.
2. Specifically, if our concern is with sustainable biophysical production including sustainable activities in support of human interests, then we can say that those activities (interests or forms of production) are sustainable that do not interfere with or detract from truly sustainable systems as in (1). Hence my position not only ar-

gues for ecological integrity but also ultimately defends sustainability as well.

Accordingly, the primary sense of the concept, sustainability (S-1), is
protected and respected every time integrity is. The secondary sense of
sustainability (S-2), like the secondary sense of integrity (I_b, or ecosystem
health), is derivative.[3] The latter aspect of sustainability indicates the
limits of our human pursuits and activities, and it outlines their parameters.

Hence, there is a close relation between integrity and sustainability,
and both are enshrined in laws and regulations, both local and global,
although neither is seriously implemented today. Once again, with regard to integrity and sustainability, we need not completely reinvent for
public policy what has been done already. But we do need to take seriously what has been done and to render it operational and global, instead of treating those regulations as optional features of the regulatory
acts within which they appear.

There are both ecological and moral reasons for ensuring that ecological sustainability should be our primary consideration. This is equally
true in the case of the habitat of wild nonhuman animals. Ecologist
James Karr recently commented that the U.S. Endangered Species Act
is nothing but a "Band-Aid solution" to the problems it is intended to
solve.[4] I argue that legislation protecting human rights to life, health,
and, in Canada, "security of persons" is rendered a travesty as well, if
our common habitat is unsafe and unprotected. Hence, even when our
primary concern is not with the preservation of wild species, the unregulated activities that affect their habitat also affect ours. An unsustainable
lifestyle is an attack on (1) life-support systems everywhere; (2) groups
and whole nations that are unfairly burdened by the choices and preferences of other groups; (3) the future, including human and nonhuman
generations; and (4) the organic integrity and the potential (natural)
capabilities possessed by (or that ought to be possessed by) present and
future generations.

Group (4) is divisible again into two subgroups: (4a) individuals and
groups in the more affluent and developed countries of the Northwest
and (4b) individuals and groups in the impoverished developing countries of the Southeast. The former, on the whole, may be more protected
from the consequences of global climate changes, for instance: they may
live in areas where readily available medical and other services may help
them deal with floods, heat waves, and other natural disasters. This protection, however, may not be equally available to minorities even in
northwestern countries, as in (2).[5] On the other hand, the same institutional infrastructures that provide medical, social, and technical assis-

tance (such as air conditioning during heat waves) also, at the same time, put these more affluent citizens at comparably higher risk through the many man-made chemicals that are part of their daily lives. Since the end of World War II, as noted in chapter 2, more than 100,000 chemicals have been introduced; most of these have never been tested separately, and none of these have been tested synergistically.[6]

Some Problems with Existing Legal Principles

Present laws do not provide a strong defense for the integrity of individuals and wholes against these substances. These chemicals are not only an imminent and present threat to our lives, they are also a long-term assault on our children and on our species.[7] For all the harm they perpetrate daily, "self-defense" against these threats is almost impossible now. And while the legal system in North America demands clear proof of harm, as argued in chapters 2 and 3, such proof is not available *in principle*. Low-level exposure to toxicants may not even show its effect on the persons exposed but only in their offspring.[8] Further, clear legal proof would require evidence tying a specific harm (result) to a single chemical (cause). As humans do not live under laboratory conditions, in which experiments are constructed separately for each substance, humans' cumulative exposure to toxicants, many of which have never been tested, is such that a single causal link can never be established with precision.[9]

Moreover, one's genetic makeup plays a role as well, as it may involve a predisposition to certain diseases, which are often triggered by environmental stimuli. The predisposition will vary from one individual to another, as will the response to "living with contaminants":

> The responses of organisms to high contaminant exposure concentrations are fairly obvious (e.g. gross morphological or physiological change or death). Responses to low level exposure may be less easily discernible, involving more subtle responses.[10]

In that case, it is, to say the least, disingenuous to continue to support laws that require clear proof of harm, knowing full well that this demand cannot be met.

The issue is further complicated by the presence of climate changes. As we saw in chapters 2 and 3, all biological processes are affected by temperature changes; chemical processes are not immune. Hence, climate changes not only foster the reemergence of infectious diseases[11] but also aggravate the effects of many toxicants. In this area, however, northwestern citizens fare somewhat better than their southeastern counterparts. The same "technical maximality"[12] that affects them in one sense seems to provide some protection in another, as social services and affluence in general may serve to buffer us from the worse ravages of many infections. In the Southeast, abject poverty, with its concomitant lack of hygiene and social services, renders the threat of infection even more lethal. The same scenario is replayed in many North American localities where minorities dwell.[13] The present concern with public policy is supported by the connection between integrity and sustainability on both moral and scientific grounds. The link between integrity and human health indicates a better way of pursuing and implementing tough environmental legislation in order to address the threats posed through the environment.

The better way I propose is simply the appeal to self-defense. As we saw earlier, threats can be stopped before they become real harms more easily from the point of view of self-defense than from the standpoint of environmental regulations. The next section reviews the example of Canadian environmental protection laws and the severe limits of their protective reach. In contrast, if the regulation is not one that deals purely with the environment and thus neglects the latter's impact on our existence, it is far easier to deal both legally and morally with the assaults to which we are subjected when they are recognized as such. Self-defense provides, arguably, the strongest position from which to enact regulations or seek injunctions demanding that the attackers cease and desist. In self-defense, or in the case of defense against bodily harms, even the lack of malicious intent on the part of the attackers only reduces the crime and the corresponding penalty it generates; it does not eliminate the crime altogether, as is the case with infractions of the Environmental Protection Act.

Arguments based on self-defense date back at least as far as the philosophy of Thomas Aquinas, who argued that if our aim is to preserve our own life, not to destroy the enemy, then the use of force in our defense is not only permissible but morally obligatory.[14] Therefore, the extensive legal and philosophical framework supporting self-defense provides a strong basis for coercive laws aimed at protecting not only humans but also all life that is both intrinsically and instrumentally valuable and indirectly necessary for all. It seems that an appeal to self-defense is the best option available to stop those who would use the present loose regulations to pursue their negligent and hazardous course with impunity.

The Limits of Existing Laws and Legal Processes to Implement Ecological Integrity

I have shown elsewhere that the concept of integrity and the mandate that ensues to "respect and restore integrity" have been embedded in

U.S. and Canadian legislation for about twenty years, and in U.S. internal legislation for twenty-five; further, both appear in many regulations, declarations, and protocols from those times to the present. The issue that needs to be examined now is whether present legal processes are sufficient to implement their own recommendations in regard to integrity. Many questions exist, for instance: (1) Are all environmental problems covered under existing environmental laws? (2) Are existing laws too vague for present environmental problems? (3) Would civil or criminal laws be more appropriate to promote integrity?

Freedom and the Common Good

A major transition, almost a revolutionary move, is required at this point. In Western democracies we have become accustomed to thinking of freedom as a universal ideal. Songs are sung to it; people who fight for it are heroes; for many, even their national identity can be traced to it: U.S. citizens speak of their country as the land of the free. But if freedom is commonly viewed as the greatest good, and its support as the most defensible and admirable goal of public policy, how can we even begin to retrench and start to view freedom as a possible enemy of the common good instead?

An answer to this question can be found in *On Liberty* by John Stuart Mill: liberty *can* legitimately be restrained on behalf of the defense of liberty itself. One can argue that exposure to life- and health-threatening conditions represents the worse kind of coercion; in that case the "freedom" of those who would impose those conditions on us ought not to be supported. The descriptive part of this work has traced the results of the modern emphasis on individual freedom of choice, with the corresponding disinterest in the common good at the regional, national, and global levels. In some cases, either the regional or the national level will bear some weight in public policy decisions, but if a conflict between the two should arise, the, local interests would usually prevail over national or global ones (see the discussion of the Canadian fish wars in chapter 4).

The global good is, typically, impossible to support through national democratic votes; it requires rules imposed by treaties and other forms of worldwide regulation. These regulations should be the strongest and provide the best possible defense for environmental cases. But, in practice, they are powerful only in the sense that the Biodiversity Convention and the Montreal Convention on CFCs, for example, are known and respected everywhere. The problem is that although national and local laws can be enforced through penalties and are supported by clear institutionalized infrastructures, there is a U.N. tribunal but no U.N. police or jail. There is a U.N. army, but it is used only for protective purposes, not to enforce regulations. By contrast, the laws and regulations that have the required infrastructure are designed to address *local* problems or those that are *perceived* to be local. For instance, if corporation X releases toxicants at location Y, Y's legal apparatus may seek to penalize X through the civil courts, provided the evidence of "harm" or monetary loss (harm to property) is clearly present locally, but it will not consider long-range or long-term effects. The limits of democracy and predictivity in science have both contributed to the importance of reconsidering present regulations and laws, both national and international. In chapter 1 we suggested a switch to a new paradigm, that is, to the adoption of the precautionary principle (PP). Peter Taylor outlines the difference this strategy would make, in contrast with the current and previous assumptions about science and the corresponding failed strategies for public policy:

> In summary, therefore, we can say that with respect to the dispersal of hazardous substances, the premise of past pollution control strategies has been fundamentally unsound: that premise is that sufficient data and scientific understanding exists both to predict effects and to detect any effects that are not predicted. Waste "management" is based upon that premise. It would be rational and scientific to argue the assumption *that the possibility of management* may ultimately prove the greatest environmental risk. The alternative is to assume that management of wastes is problematic and to be avoided. . . . This can be achieved by *the closure of open systems in industry and agriculture, the elimination of toxics in product lifecycles,* and a *target of zero emissions for persistent synthetic substances capable of being dispersed* (whatever their toxicity or hazard profile).[15]

These points are equally relevant for national and international laws. Given the global nature of environmental hazards, the international aspects of the problem represent an even graver source of threats than the national ones. Some specific examples will help to flesh out this claim.

Problems in Transnational Justice

> . . . all princes and people of the world . . . [are subject to] the laws of God and Nature.[16]
>
> Jean Bodin

Jean Bodin also held "that sovereignty is merely legislative . . . its principal point being the giving of laws unto subjects in general without their consent."[17] Traditionally, sovereignty is deemed to reside in "a well-ordered Commonweal."[18] In the light of the interconnectedness of today's environmental problems, the existence of "absolute" atomistic sovereign power must be reconsidered, and Bodin himself, unwittingly, indicates the reason for this change. In modern times, humankind has for the most part eliminated its belief in the laws of God. It appears that the laws of God as well as those of nature are no longer considered either as absolutes or as limits to national powers. Hence the absolute sovereign power of independent nations and states was always tacitly understood to be itself subject to powers beyond its control: the "arrogance of humanism"[19] is a new phenomenon in regard to nature.

It is ironic that one can appeal to original, traditional political theory in order to find an account of state power compatible with the PI—and to find in this account a reason for limiting individual states' powers in the interest of international justice. In contrast, many acknowledge the diminished autonomy of independent nations, but the source of this phenomenon is found elsewhere than in the "laws of God and Nature." Charles Beitz argues:

> nobody would deny, for example, that states do, in fact, make rules binding on their citizens and such social and economic entities as corporations and the like.[20]

This is true but unfortunate, as it may and often does interfere with the "legal . . . [and] moral principles for the international realm"; for instance, it is clear that political "sovereignty effectively sanctions the existing international distribution of wealth as well as that of power."[21] It is a characteristic of moral "liberalism" that states have a right to protect the property rights of their citizens and the corresponding right to prevent foreigners from sharing in that property. Many philosophers in fact have defended the primary obligation of a state (and citizens) to protect its own, before considering those beyond a state's border.[22]

When we consider environmental problems, the line between "our citizens" and "others" becomes blurred. Not redistributing wealth from North America to citizens living in the Amazon area of Brazil could lead to the continuing destruction of those resources and services upon which *our* citizens depend as well. Similarly, intervention and aid to victims of floods and famine in developing countries ought not to be considered a praiseworthy charitable enterprise as much as an absolute moral duty, to the extent that the damage results from Western and Western-supported policies concerning global climate change.

We therefore must seek to understand what might constitute transnational justice today, in light of altered circumstances, rather than view it as a notion needing a simple update but still arising from the accepted sovereignty of individual states. The redistribution of wealth might be effected within the status quo (doubtful though that might be), but the protection of one state's citizens is inextricably connected with the protection of all life through our common life-support systems.

What we need is an understanding of transnational justice that includes consideration of basic human needs, that is, the need for environmental safety and some measure of economic justice. Onora O'Neill, however, remarks:

> Much modern ethical thought makes no use of the category of needs. In utilitarian thinking needs can be considered only if reflected in desires and preferences; and this is an imperfect reflection. Discussions of human rights often take no account of needs at all; and when they try to do so, strains are placed on the basic structure of rights theory, and the identification of needs is sketchy.[23]

In chapter 3 we noted that even the Rawlsian principles of justice, allied as they are with democratic considerations, do not fare much better in defense of a good based upon needs. When Rawls extends his principles of justice beyond individual states, only his first principle of justice is used. O'Neill cites what aspects of justice can follow, internationally, for Rawls: "non-intervention, self-determination, *pacta sunt servanda*, principles of self-defence and of just war."[24] In contrast, distributive justice is not carried into the international arena in the same way, and no provision is made to clearly support "welfare" rights.

It would be easy to extend (or even to understand) the notion of welfare to include environmental safety, as "faring well" even for humans is entirely dependent on living in a healthy habitat. O'Neill proposes seeking a Kantian framework in order to secure some principle of obligation; she writes, "The first way in which a Kantian approach via obligations yields more than theories of rights can be that it offers an account of virtue as well as of justice."[25] The emphasis on virtue in Kantian theory agrees with our interpretation of Kant in chapter 7. The interpretation O'Neill proposes includes two principles of "imperfect obligation," predicated on the understanding of human beings as "beings of limited capacities." The first such principle she suggests is based on the recognition of our own limited abilities, inadequate to achieve our ends without aid. This realization would commit us to offer help to other beings, equally rational but equally limited, based upon reversibility and a universal perspective. The second principle would recognize that:

> Rational beings whose desires, unlike those of creatures of instinct, standardly outrun their own resources and those of their fellows will (regard-

less of the specific content of their desires) discover that they cannot universally act on principles of neglecting needs.[26]

Hence, the commitment to enhance human potential and human development will have to be present in principle; and those who would ignore these two principles would "act wrongly even if their victims cannot be identified," precisely as was argued in defense of the risk thesis in chapter 3. Against this background, we need to reexamine the interface between science and international laws and regulations.

Science and International Laws

Many have written on the difficulties arising from seeking legal proof against a background of imprecise science,[27] unclear risk-assessment procedures,[28] and value-laden scientific research.[29]

I argue that there are several additional foundational problems that are not often addressed in the literature. For instance, one question that must be asked is why environmental and economic issues are invariably coupled, so that problems and disputes are automatically viewed as civil disputes and therefore never accorded the grave status they deserve. This approach leads to viewing development and economics as the primary life issues, in direct contrast with biotic reality. Another related question is the general acceptance of the anthropocentric/nonanthropocentric dichotomy discussed in chapter 4. This acceptance allows even serious environmentalists to ridicule as impractical, or as "living in an ivory tower,"[30] those who attribute intrinsic value to all biotic and abiotic components of our natural systems and to their requirements for survival.

A purely anthropocentric position, no matter how "weak" or "enlightened" it might be, does not permit us to give proper consideration to our shared habitat and thus renders difficult the rejection of hazardous and unsustainable lifestyles and practices. Even global regulatory documents like *Agenda 21* attempt at best a clumsy reconciliation, as they speak of "development" and of "protecting the integrity of the Earth," without an apparent understanding of how these two goals might coexist.

Donald Brown[31] examines the interface between law and "sustainable development." The latter probably represents the only area of concern that is clearly addressed by global legislation and is recognized as a common goal, requiring common regulations. For instance:

Chapter 39 of *Agenda 21* calls for a review of international environmental law "to evaluate and promote the efficacy of that law and to promote the integration of environment and development policies. . . ." International environmental law consists of: (1) bilateral or multilateral treaties, (2) binding acts of international organizations, (3) rules of customary international law, and (4) judgments of international courts and tribunals. Over a thousand treaties deal with international matters. These treaties have been the most frequent methods of creating binding international rules pertaining to the environment.[32]

Brown adds that "despite this large body of international and national environmental law," sustainability is not commonplace internationally for several reasons.

In general, developing nations see a conflict between "development" and "sustainability," and deeply resent developed nations that are now attempting to check their "progress." Additionally, anything that limits national sovereignty is viewed as suspect. Finally, there is no completeness or coherence in existing environmental regulations, so grave hazards are still imposed on many; hence, regulations are also viewed as ineffective, and this discourages local acceptance. *Agenda 21* was written in part to render environmental law a unified, coherent whole.[33]

However, neither treaties nor conventions have the enforcement infrastructure they require. Even if infractions occur, the response takes the form of sanctions or fines, so that these regulations are viewed, at best, as *civil* laws. The emphasis on consent as the criterion by which to judge the legitimacy of hazardous activities also contributes to an approach based on adjustments, compromise, and compensation (see chapter 3). I have argued that this is a travesty of justice. Humans and nonhumans alike are not simply exposed to compensable risks that need to be found so that a fair trade-off might be made. The reality is that we are exposed to attacks of varying severity; they are not always lethal, but they invariably endanger and diminish our habitat and our specific capabilities, whatever our species.

Many of the problems of scientific evidence Brown and others have discussed[34] might become less paralyzing if we moved from the relatively tame realm of civil and tort law to the more regulated one of criminal law covering assaults and bodily harm, as these represent a far more accurate description of what is taking place. Criminalizing environmental harms carries its own difficulties, however, as we shall see in the following section.

Canadian Environmental Laws

How does the Canadian Environmental Assessment Act define sustainable development?

"Sustainable development" means development that meets the needs of the present, without compromising the ability of future generations to meet their own needs.[35]

The meaning of "needs" is certainly ambiguous. The "needs" of famine-ridden developing countries and the needs of northwestern blue-collar workers affected by an economic downturn are not the same. Individual health, based on a healthy habitat, might be a good example of a common, universal "need," equally appropriate to North and South, East and West, human and nonhuman life. The Canadian Environmental Protection Act is intended to help the appropriate ministries deal with the environmental effects of proposed activities, but unclear definitions such as this one do not help to actualize their goal. Note that "future generations" is left undefined as well, so it is not certain that nonhuman life is also included. These imprecisions, whether or not they are deliberate, are equally present in all legislation in regard to the "environment," as we noted for *Agenda 21*.[36] In another example, even the basic term *environment* is defined is a controversial way by the (Provincial) Canadian Act:

"environment" means,
a. air, land or water,
b. plant and animal life, including human life,
c. the social, economic and cultural conditions that influence the life of humans or a community,
d. any building, structure, machine or other device or thing made by humans,
e. any solid, liquid, gas, odor, heat, sound, vibration or radiation resulting directly or indirectly from human activities, or
f. any part or combination of the foregoing and the interrelationships between any two or more of them, in or of Ontario.[37]

Point (c) is worth noting. Although in (b) "plant and animal life" are deemed to include humans, in (c) the *ecological* question, that is, the condition of the joint habitat of plant, animal, and human life and its impact on "the life of humans or a community," is not clearly indicated. The definition of *environment* also appears to be overinclusive, as many of the categories listed are not normally taken to be "environment," at least from the standpoint of ecology. It is likely that (d) through (f) here are chosen to facilitate the protection of workers or other affected stakeholders who might be affected by certain conditions in their surroundings.

Despite its overinclusiveness, the act's definition is not specific enough to cover serious global damage. For instance it does not specify how far into the atmosphere air is to be protected, and the same is true of water and land, particularly because (f) refers specifically to Ontario; hence it might exclude threats spreading beyond Ontario's borders. Another difficulty is that (b) and (c) may be in conflict, and the act does not offer any basis for the resolution of conflicts between its separate mandates. One problem is that the act, like its counterparts in other provinces, states, regions, or nations, is not global in its reach. Because of this, the true results of environmental disintegrity and the threats it represents to all life and life-support systems are not truly captured by the act's protective function.[38]

The terminology of the act is neither precise nor capable of stopping the damage of environmental threats before they start. In this it resembles all acts and regulations that use the language of integrity and leave it undefined.[39] As we saw earlier, one of the effects of this lack of specificity is that the concept of integrity is viewed by many scientists and philosophers as "merely stipulative,"[40] and this adds to the difficulty of giving it clear support in the law, whether local or global.

The way the act is applied is equally problematic, even at the local level. Beyond the problems of definitions and the act's lack of precision, problems of application arise in at least three areas: (1) the question of *mens rea*; (2) the conflict between the public's right to security and the offending corporation's or other polluter's right not to incriminate itself by divulging damaging information; and (3) the problem of the burden of proof. As an example, some recent Ontario cases demonstrate the impact of all three areas. Christopher Barnes[41] describes some of these problems.

In 1988, Weil's Food Processing Ltd. spilled at least nine million liters of waste water near Windsor, Ontario, "from a holding pond into two creeks and killed thousands of fish, mostly carp and catfish."[42] The company was charged under the Ontario EPA and the Ontario Water Resources Act. On April 19, 1990, Judge C. E. Perkins of Chatham dismissed the case against Weil, accepting the constitutional arguments of defense lawyer Patrick Ducharme.[43] The judge's ruling included the following elements:

1. The section of the EPA requiring polluters to report spills violates the accused's right to avoid self-incrimination.
2. A recognition of the need to report spills as valid, although the judge said that "a free and democratic society" required that no reporting law would be justified unless the polluter were protected against self-incrimination.
3. Regarding the standards of proof the government must not only

prove the responsibility of the accused for the pollution but also must also show "illegal intent, negligence or willful blindness." Basically, the government must show criminal intent, or *mens rea*, a standard and important element in any criminal proceeding.
4. The standard of proof required under the EPA violates the constitutional rights of the accused guaranteed in the Charter of Rights and Freedoms.[44]

The judge's decision has two main portions. The first is that the reporting element violates the accused's right to avoid self-incrimination. This issue arises because the Crown uses the polluters' spill report as evidence against the polluter himself at the trial. Clearly, this is a problem because, as Jim Drummond says, "if there is no requirement to report, then a lot of spills would go without the ministry being aware of them."[45] Second, as to intent, placing the onus of demonstrating wrongful intent would make it harder to prosecute offenses under the EPA.[46] Before this case, one of the defenses available to the accused charged under the EPA was the onus of proving due diligence to present a discharge. However, Judge Perkins ruled that "requiring an accused to prove due diligence is a denial of the right to the presumption of innocence guaranteed by the charter."[47]

Criminalizing environmental offenses introduces more stringent standards of proof. Canadian Law is confusing on this point. In *R v. Sault Ste. Marie*, Justice Dickson recognized three categories of legal offense: *mens rea* offenses, strict liability offenses, and absolute liability offenses.[48]

First, let us look at the category of *mens rea* offense. As the term suggests, the key to the nature of this offense is the accused's state of mind. Justice Dickson said:

> Offenses in which *mens rea*, consisting of some positive state of mind such as intent, knowledge, or recklessness, must be proved by the prosecution either as an inference from the nature of the act committed, or by additional evidence.[49]

An obvious example of a *mens rea* offense would be a criminal act. However, *mens rea*, or the mental element, does not, based on Justice Dickson's phrasing, merely mean intentional acts. *Mens rea* involves "some positive state of mind" of which "intent" is but one example.[50] He also includes "knowledge" and "recklessness" as examples of positive states of mind that may constitute *mens rea*. And further, this list is not necessarily exhaustive of the positive states of mind which may constitute *mens rea*; Justice Dickson merely says *mens rea* offenses are those "consisting of some positive state of mind such as intent, knowledge, or recklessness."[51]

In addition, an offense that is classed merely as regulatory may become, by virtue of "penalty of stigma," a criminal offense, requiring *mens rea*. In *R v. Weil's Food Processing Ltd.*, Justice Brown cited and followed the distinction between *mens rea* offenses and strict liability offenses. He concurred that regulatory offenses are generally to be regarded as strict liability offenses.[52] Nonetheless, the company argued before the court that given (1) "the quantum of penalty" attached to such offenses and (2) "the stigma attached to these offenses," the offenses ceased to be merely regulatory and were to be equated with criminal offenses requiring *mens rea*.[53]

In *R v. Wigglesworth*, a Supreme Court of Canada case, Madam Justice Wilson said:

> In my opinion, a true penal consequence which would attract the application of s.11 is imprisonment or a fine which by its magnitude would appear to be imposed for the purpose of redressing the wrong done to society at large rather than to the maintenance of internal discipline within the limited sphere of activity.[54]

In the final analysis, to place various environmental offenses beyond the reach criminal law may reduce the difficulties of proving guilt, but it is clear that the corporate bodies that might be found guilty are not often deterred by economic sanctions: these can be and usually are incorporated into business costs and passed on to consumers. In contrast, criminal or quasi-criminal proceedings may be less easy to ignore, particularly if high-ranking corporate officers are targeted or if criminal complicity may be ascribed to both CEOs and shareholders.

In the case of the Zalev Brothers Scrapyard, a company guilty of a number of environmental offenses, the law of Ontario was extremely ambiguous in its application. Barnes traces infractions of environmental regulations in its operations back to 1987. As a consequence, he says:

> [because] of smoke emissions resulting from fire . . . at their scrapyard . . . Zalev Brothers was charged with nine counts under the EPA. A breakdown of the counts is as follows:
> 1) *Four Counts*: "permitting discharge of a material into the environment likely to cause loss of enjoyment of normal use of property"; and
> 2) *Four Counts*: "permitting a discharge likely to cause material discomfort to people"; and
> 3) *One Count*: "failing to promptly notify the Ministry of Environment of a smoke discharge."[55]

In terms of penalties, the EPA provides for a maximum $50,000 fine for the first offense and $100,000 for any additional offense. Charges under the Ontario EPA are normally heard by a justice of the peace. However, in response to a defense motion by Patrick Ducharme, Judge Harry Momotiuk ruled that the EPA charges would be tried by a provincial court judge. Recent changes to the EPA, Judge Momotiuk said, "could give rise to complex legal arguments that should be heard by a judge."[56]

Defense arguments for Zalev included the claims that "Ontario's environmental laws are unconstitutional" and that fines of up to $50,000 a day for polluters are "cruel and unusual punishment."[57] Pat Morand, a lawyer for the Ministry of the Environment's legal branch, described the defense in this way: "What they are saying is . . . we don't have the power to prosecute them."[58] The Zalev trial began March 26, 1990, and was heard before Judge John Menzies.[59] The following are the major points in the defense's constitutional attack on the EPA:

1. The EPA penalties "create the trappings of a criminal offense."
2. Yet, despite (1), the standard of proof to be met by the government under EPA charges is not the same as (it is less onerous than) the standard of proof required in criminal trials.
3. Therefore, because of (1), the province should be required to meet the same burden of proof required in a criminal trial and prove the accused fully intended to break the law.[60]

In short, it would not be sufficient for the government to demonstrate that a spill occurred and that damage ensued as a result. It must also demonstrate that the accused company *intended* to break the law. Additionally, the defense argued:

4. "requiring a company to provide immediate information about a spill after it is discovered can lead to a company incriminating itself, jeopardizing its right to a fair trial."[61]

In light of my proposal to criminalize environmental offenses, it is worthy of note that Barnes's report includes an argument by Susan Ficek, a lawyer for the Ministry of the Environment. She argued that "violations of provincial environmental laws do not become criminal in nature just because the punishment is more severe"; she added, "Increases in penalties do not have the effect of changing regulatory offenses . . . into criminal [federal] legislation."[62] Her rationale appears to be a counterattack on the argument against self-incrimination, clearly taken from criminal law. It appears that environmental crimes or eco-crimes ought to be viewed either as criminal acts, thus requiring appeals to lack of intent as possible mitigation to the charges levied against the offenders, or as noncriminal breaches of regulations. But in the latter case, a simple factual description of the results of their activities ought to be sufficient to convict without the need to prove *mens rea*. In contrast, I have suggested criminalization, which might bring into play many of these additional components of eco-crime. Perhaps one way to avoid some of the complications of criminalization might be to argue that corporate and institutional bodies are only fictitious (although legal) "persons," not vulnerable human accused persons,[63] and thus the legal protection owed to such "nonhuman persons" ought to be modified.

In their *Overview of Environmental Law in Canada*, Roger Cotton and Kelley McKinnon discuss this problem in Section V.C. of "Common Law Principles" and in Section VII.D of "Canadian Environmental Jurisprudence."[64] They cite "an English case from the 1860s," *Rylands v. Fletcher*.

> . . . the defendants had constructed a water reservoir on their land (and to supply water to their mills). The plaintiff operated a coal mine on a property that was separated from the defendants' land by another property.

When the reservoir burst and the plaintiff's mine was flooded, "Lord Cairn refers to the judgment of Blackburn J.":

> We think that the true rule of the law is, that the person who, for his own purposes brings on his land and collects and keeps there anything likely to do mischief if it escapes, must keep it in at his own peril; and if he does not do so, is *prima facie* answerable for all the damage which is the natural consequence of its escape.

This judgment became a fundamental rule of law, and it seems to be exceptionally well suited for all manner of environmental "mischief," from toxins and pollutants to transgenic fish (see chapter 6).

The next point addresses two questions: due diligence as a defense and mandatory self-reporting and the right to silence. The former refers to the review of Justice Dickson at the Supreme Court of Canada. He believed that "there were compelling grounds for the recognition of three categories of offenses, rather than the traditional two." This added the third category, "strict liability," whereby the accused could "prove a defense . . . that he exercised due diligence or reasonable care to prevent the offense." In addition, the other two categories remained "those offenses which are truly criminal and for which the Crown must establish a mental element or *mens rea* and absolute liability offenses which allowed for conviction on the proof that the defendant committed the prohibited act."

In light of this three-part division of offenses, we can reconsider whether mandatory self-reporting, or the right to silence, ought to prevail in cases when the accused is the first to be aware of a grave public danger originating from his own activities or operation, as in *R. V. Weil's Food Processing Ltd.* Hence, it might not be necessary to prove *mens rea* in such cases, if they are considered cases of "strict liability"; the accused might have to prove due diligence in his own defense, but he may not appeal to the presumption of innocence or to the right to silence, as the case is not clearly treated as criminal. It is treated as a case of strict liability, although it remains open to the imposition of criminal penalties.

Because Canada does not have Superfund legislation like the United States, it is particularly important that the wording of judicial orders be used in such cases to protect the public from environmental threats, at least after the fact.

The corporations involved in eco-crimes, spills, and other forms of hazardous pollution have first access to information pertaining to their own operations and their hazards. Often, as in the case of chemical plants and other "risky" manufacturers, their products and processes have been tested in-house before being offered to the public. Because of "trade-secrets" legislation, the information acquired through testing is legitimately withheld from the public, as "risky businesses" disclose only as much as they believe will not harm their public image.[65] In some cases, an irresponsible corporate attitude toward public hazards is not only supported but even dictated by legal counsel.

A recent example is not environmentally related, but it emphasizes some of the difficulties we have discussed. In the case concerning Dow Corning and silicone breast implants,[66] John Swanson argues that when implant recipients discovered the problems arising from their implants, the firm's public relations and legal departments attempted to handle the crisis, rather than allowing the decisions to be made by the company's CEOs. Swanson adds that, despite the mounting evidence to the contrary, Dow Corning consistently used four arguments to try to convince juries, judges, the media, and others that implants were not a problem:

1. There is no valid science that proves silicones cause health problems.
2. Dow Corning would not have survived thirty years in the implant business if implants were not safe.
3. There is always some risk involved in any surgical procedure.
4. Silicone is inert and is not bioreactive in the human body.

With the exception of the third point, these arguments have been and are successfully challenged and refuted.[67]

Moral questions arising from this well-known case parallel the environmental problems/public policy interface examined in this section. The Dow Corning case shows that the scientists involved—surgeons and researchers alike—did not provide the public with enough information to make appropriate choices. Moreover, Dow Corning has "by far the world's most elaborate research capabilities and the best knowledge of silicone chemistry, greater by far than the FDA's or any other organization." Swanson states that Dow Corning's officials and representatives admitted as much; in that case, it is clear that they did not do enough. Their knowledge and the results of their research were not "followed through to completion" on silicone-related health and safety questions, and—even when results were available—Dow Corning "chose not to disclose the results to those who might have benefited."[68] When questioned about some of these issues, Robert T. Rylee, Dow Corning vice president and manager of the company's health care business, replied, "We don't want to be over-educating the plaintiff's attorneys."[69]

Twenty years earlier, Dow Chemical had been involved in an unsavory debate about Napalm B, but the company appears to have learned little from the public revulsion and loss of face that cost it "hundreds of millions of dollars" at that time. It is also disheartening to learn that Dow Corning had an "outstanding business ethics program" and a code of conduct that included such principles as "we will be responsible for the impact of our technology upon the environment" and "we will continuously strive to assure that our products and services are safe, efficacious, and accurately represented in our selling and promotional activities."[70] Dow Corning did not appear to have embraced the ideology recently emerging in the business ethics literature, that is, either the "strategic" or the "fiduciary" "stakeholder theory."[71] This theory starts by positing that all stakeholders (not only shareholders or stockholders in an enterprise) have a legitimate interest in the way the corporation operates. Those affected, whose voices should be heard and whose interests should be considered, include employees, local communities, and suppliers as well as managers and shareholders. Roughly speaking, in the "strategic" formulation of the theory, all of these groups are considered because not to do so would affect the ultimate economic goals of the corporation. In the "fiduciary" model, a Kantian principle of respect for all involved underlies a position that is primarily moral, rather than purely instrumental, as in the "strategic" model.[72]

Although breast implants are not direct environmental threats, they are a hazardous product that has a direct impact on human health, hence on human rights as well. For this reason the case is worthy of study: even in such direct injury cases, it is clear where the balance of power lies between large corporations on one side and a vulnerable public on the other. A final point: women who can afford a breast implant, or who would seek one, are not among the most vulnerable populations. Nevertheless, they were not treated with the respect they deserved, or given the information they required for informed consent, nor were they accorded prompt redress when clear harm befell them.

Thus there is little hope that poorer and perhaps less educated groups, some of whom may have no access to legal redress or even to democratic institutions, would fare any better in the face of powerful corporate interests and of indirect environmental harm.

A New Challenge for Law: Reducing National Security Conflicts

This chapter is about public policy and laws and about humans and their concerns, even though the thesis I support is that the natural systems that support both humans and nonhumans must be viewed as primary. In defense of this thesis, I have argued for the link between the intrinsic value of human and nonhuman life and health and the unimpeded development of individual, specific, and systemic capabilities; I have also emphasized equally the joint interests of individuals and wholes, human and nonhuman. There is another area of great value, however; perhaps it is not as basic as life and health, but it is closely related to it. It is peace. Military operations are, in general, ecologically disastrous and extremely harmful to human health as well. Therefore, if we want to reach any conclusion about what is required to ensure sustainability and reduce our "ecological footprint,"[73] our public policy must take into consideration the close links among ecological degradation, unsustainability, and violent conflict.

For instance, the research of T. Homer-Dixon involves environmental threats to "security" that are additional to those discussed thus far, including "human physical, social and economic well-being."[74] I have discussed the acute and pervasive conflicts, both perceived and real, between economic interests and physical safety and between social development and ecological sustainability. I have also argued for the causal connection among environmental disintegrity, global change, and human health. What remains to be seen, if we are to further strengthen our case for a major change in global public policy, are the *other* effects we can discover on social and national groups and, ultimately, on the individuals that make up these groups.

Homer-Dixon's work is particularly relevant because it examines the causes of violent conflict: "Environmental change may contribute to conflicts as diverse as war, terrorism, or diplomatic and trade disputes," adding, "I bound my analysis by focusing on acute national and international conflict, which I define as conflict involving a substantial probability of violence."[75] We have discussed the emergence of violence over one resource, fish stocks, in an otherwise peaceful and relatively unified country like Canada. We have also noted the multifaceted and acute violence in Nigeria. The former was the result of conflict in support of bioregional interests in the context of a democratic nation; the latter, of diffuse but pressing global demands for Westerners' preference satisfaction, without consideration of how far their "footprint" ought to have been allowed to extend. In the case of the Ogoni in Nigeria, the problem was rendered acute by the political context: a violent military regime allied to Western economic interests.

As was noted earlier, poorer, developing countries will be less protected from immediate threats, and it may become increasingly difficult for policymakers in those areas to mitigate environmental impact and minimize damage. In addition, it should be noted that, as the threats of global nuclear war have decreased, fears regarding unpredictable, complex, and chaotic developments in our environment have been increasing. They are no longer viewed as tolerable, even if they once were, because "we now realize that we do not know where and when we might cross a threshold and move to a radically different and perhaps highly undesirable system."[76] Both of these emerging realities mandate serious revisions in global public policy.

The literature on the connection between environmental hazards and violent conflicts represents an important addition to environmental ethics scholarship. Nevertheless, as Homer-Dixon emphasizes, it has many unresolved problems. Two of these are particularly relevant from the standpoint of integrity. The first is also a problem present in all holistic ethics: the connection, if any, between social and natural systems, often taken for granted by the complex-systems theorists on whose work the definition of integrity has for the most part relied.[77] Homer-Dixon says:

> the prevailing, "naturalistic" epistemology and ontology of social science may hinder accurate understanding of the links between physical and social variables within environmental and social systems. In particular it may be a mistake to conjoin in causal generalizations, types of physical events with types of intentional social action.[78]

Although Homer-Dixon treats this conjunction as unproblematic "for the purposes of [his] article," holistic theories in ethics or public governance do not fare well and are often taken to be unacceptable. Thus, from the standpoint of integrity, this position cannot be accepted: for our ethics, we *cannot* conjoin the holism of our environmental position with a similar approach to social systems on pain of being accused of fascism, totalitarianism, and the like.

Another problem Homer-Dixon outlines that is particularly relevant is the "modern realist perspective that is often used to understand security problems," as "realism focuses on states as rational maximizers of power in an anarchic system." But we have already disputed this assumption in chapters 3 and 7, as we argued for the impotence of present national democracies in the face of environmental threats. The emphasis on nations as discrete entities reduces or eliminates the necessary emphasis on transboundary environmental problems. Yet the latter are, for the most part, the source of both acute physical threats and anticipated and emerging violent conflicts,[79] as an international version of the "problem of the commons"[80] emerges from the nation-states, which comprise "the last remaining Hobbesian 'state of nature.' "[81]

In contrast, if my argument is accepted, the existence of national states supporting their own citizens' preferences through their policy and institutions is a major obstacle to the implementation of global regulations. Nevertheless, because nations and states are all too real in the world at present, we need to understand the causal relations between environmental conditions and conflicts.

Figure 1 helps to clarify the reasons for the conflicts Homer-Dixon anticipates, as well as the reasons for the two types of interventions he envisions: (1) from "those that seek to prevent negative social effects,"

Figure 1. Environmental Change and Acute Conflict

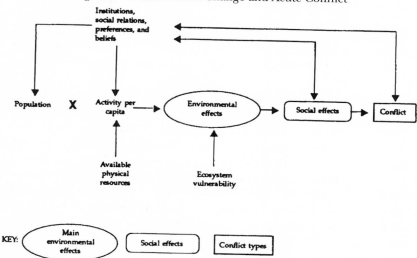

Source: Thomas Homer-Dixon, "On the Threshold: Environmental Changes as Causes of Acute Conflict," *International Security* 16, 2 (Fall 1991):76–116.

and (2) from "those that seek to prevent the conflict that could result from these social effects."[82] Although the author views these as appropriate "first-stage" and "second-stage" interventions, I argue that the preventive, proactive "intervention" dictated by the principle of integrity, if implemented even now through strong regulations, might serve to mitigate or even halt many global environmental problems before they become too widespread to be contained. The effort and the expenditures required by the first- and second-stage interventions ought to be devoted to the major reevaluation of current practices and policies required by the ethics of integrity.

In sum, the examples of regulations and policies we have examined have not accomplished the goals for which they were intended. The results of the lack of coherence, lack of definition, over- and underinclusiveness, and absence of enforceability in present regulations (both local and global) have permitted direct attacks on individual life and health, through global change and environmental degradation leading to indirect attacks on all life. Further hazards are due to the emergence of violent conflicts. Hence, public policy will have to enforce a reduced ecological footprint through a global ethic that transcends fragmented national interests when environmental issues are at stake.

Restraints and Reductions for a Smaller Eco-Footprint: The "Golden Mean" in Public Policy

> If we are to live sustainably, we must ensure that we use the essential products and processes of nature no more quickly than they can be renewed and that we discharge wastes no more quickly than they can be absorbed.[83]
>
> William Rees and Mathis Wackernagel

As we saw earlier, the Ontario Environmental Protection Act includes man-made things and processes as part of its definition of *environment*. This may be useful for those using the act to seek redress for some injury sustained, especially in the workplace. But the "products and processes of nature" are different in kind from the products and processes engendered by humans. In fact, the proliferation of the latter puts a serious strain on the functioning and even the existence of the former. Moreover, the "city" that is often taken to be "the pinnacle of human achievement" is not natural but a "built environment."[84] Although the city represents the most visible example of cultural, social, educational, and economic human endeavor, William Rees argues that the most important and basic aspect of the city's flourishing" has been forgotten; namely, the natural ecological basis on which it depends.

When this forgotten component has been recognized, it is clear that what the city is and what it does extend far beyond its political boundaries. As Rees shows, because the city's growth depends on natural life-support systems that extend well beyond its borders, the city as it functions now is basically unsustainable. The proliferation of urban centers over most of the inhabited parts of the world only adds to this problem. In order to understand what is happening, Rees suggests a mental exercise: to think of a modern metropolis

> if it were enclosed in a plastic hemisphere that let in light but prevented material things of any kind from entering or leaving—like the "Biosphere II" project in Arizona. The health and integrity of the entire human system so contained would depend entirely on what was initially trapped within the hemisphere. It is obvious to most people that such a city would cease to function and its inhabitants would perish within a few days.[85]

No city is entirely self-sufficient, and even Biosphere II admitted sunlight, that is, something coming from outside. For most of us much more is required for our centers to function and support us in the style we prefer.

For instance, the flat valley bottom of the lower Fraser Valley (east of Vancouver, British Columbia, Canada) is in a fertile geographical area with a good climate, yet it "depends on an area 19 times larger than that contained within its boundaries, for food, forestry products, carbon dioxide assimilation and energy."[86] Rees's methods were also applied to a study in a much less productive area in Latvia,[87] and the area on which these northern cities depended was much greater. The amount of "resources consumed by the twenty-nine cities in the region (Baltic Sea area)" covered an "area of ecosystems that is 200 times the total area of the cities themselves."[88] In addition, Rees shows that

> the present Ecological Footprint of a typical North American (4–5 ha) represents three times his/her fair share of the Earth's bounty. Indeed, if everyone on earth lived like an average Canadian or American, we would need at least three such planets to live sustainably.[89]

Thus we can add yet another argument in support of a changed morality and public policy: not only are many northwestern practices unsafe and unfair to those who bear the burdens of our affluent lifestyle, but, based on Rees's analysis, when the "accounting tool" of the "Ecological Footprint" is used, our practices and lifestyle are shown to be completely unsustainable. Because we do not have an additional "three planets" available to provide resources and sinks, we can only extend our unreasonable expectations for a very limited time. Even so, this brief time gain is taken at the expense of future generations and the poor in developing countries. We must resign ourselves to substantially reducing our footprint: "the Ecological Footprint of humanity as a whole must be smaller than the ecologically productive portion of the planet's surface."[90]

A further question arises: how do we also limit the part of the planet we are prepared to consider "productive"? The integrity argument is based on the necessity of allowing a substantial percentage of the planet to pursue its own evolutionary path, that is, not to be used for human interests or treated only as instrumentally valuable. Reed Noss suggests at least 25 percent of the earth's surface for that purpose, and in some areas and for some specific cases, as much as 50 percent of the earth to be treated as "core areas," left wild and unmanaged.[91]

Noss's concern is for the restoration of the habitat necessary to support the large carnivores who need vast areas for their survival. I have argued that the same wild areas also provide the life-support services that are necessary for all life, including humans. In that case, Rees's argument is even more foundational than he envisions for both ethics and public policy. Not only can we not use more of the planet than is available for our various interests and productions, but we must also separate what is truly available for our use (for food, shelter, energy) from what is not. The latter must be respected and left unmanaged, so that it may provide the support systems necessary for all life (and to maintain the instrumental capabilities of the rest).

Our ecological footprint must not exceed our available fair share, but it must also stop short of extending even that far, if the wild, protected areas of true integrity have already been excluded from the common pie to be shared. To achieve this goal requires individual and aggregate restraints the like of which have not been seen in most of the northwestern world. For this reason, it is doubtful that persons will freely embrace the choices that would severely curtail their usual freedoms and rights, not to mention their conveniences and comforts, even in the interest of long-term health and self-preservation. The flourishing of their progeny and equity for their fellow humans appears even less likely to ensure the adoption of the required restraints.

The only hope for real change now lies in the emergence of global regulatory institutions willing to act paternalistically on our behalf, on the basis of collaboratively designed conventions and charters, similar to the *Earth Charter* discussed earlier. For the "bottom-up" dimension of the problem, individual moral convictions and the return to a global/communitarian respect for the common good will be required. The "top-down" regulatory and public policy aspect will have to be prescribed by an interdisciplinary team of biologists, ecologists, political scientists, medical specialists, and philosophers with a strong traditional moral basis. Such a team would take the role of the "wise man" of Aristotelian doctrine. For major decisions, the team would work to reach equitable decisions. For lesser cases, perhaps others might work with the common charters and ultimately decide as the team would.

From the practical standpoint, only such a team should possibly be entrusted with environmental decisions having a direct impact on the future of life on earth. In our quest for an ethic compatible with the principle of integrity, and with the ethics of integrity in general, the Aristotelian "golden mean" provides a useful model, not only for individual morality but also for public policy. In chapter 7, the importance of "limit" was stressed. The "mean" between excess and defect is equally appropriate as the goal of public policy, and the "wise" choice is intended to be universally valid; hence it could not be a choice for short-term advantage for the agent or his peers at the expense of the balance of justice for all. The "mean" should now be understood as the universally fair choice, embodying justice for all humans (and all life) and including access to those goods (ecological, life-supporting goods) without which even the actualization of the human character and the fulfillment of our individual and specific end cannot succeed.

In sum, neither international nor national laws concerning the environment appear sufficient to bring about the changes required by the present acute environmental problems. These regulations fail to protect the majority of humans from physical harm, from the infringement of their personal integrity, and from the effects of present and future environmentally engendered violence. In contrast, legislative help can be found in the holistic formulations of the principles of the *Earth Charter* and of some other recent conventions, whereas changed individual moral consciousness can be based on the ethics of integrity.

For both individual and public decision making, strong philosophical support is present in the thought of Aristotle and Kant. The concept of "limit" is clearly emerging from the research of Rees. For Aristotle, it is an integral component of the standard of moral action, as excess is seen to be as far from the true "good," as lack (or defect). The "mean," relative to the specifics of the case, is what the wise one would choose. In the political arena this would translate into the common good, according to criteria of universal justice.

Sadly, these guidelines are still much more suggestive (and even in that regard, extremely controversial) than they are practical. Still, the *Earth Charter* also provides general *holistic* guidelines, albeit without specific details of either the *reasons* behind its norms or precise second-order principles needed to make the charter truly operational.

The Ethics of Integrity and the New Earth Charter:
A Joint Basis for Public Policy?

Following the 1992 meeting at Rio de Janeiro and the articulation of the Rio declaration, *Agenda 21* (including the conventions therein on biological diversity and climate change), the members of the Earth Charter Council recognized a need to follow up on the mandates of these documents. Their collaboration, "Making Sustainability Work," starts by recognizing the need to seek values and principles necessary to realize sustainability: it is therefore very close to the aims of this volume, that is, the exploration of what it means to "live in integrity" or to live in a truly sustainable manner.

It is encouraging to note that, like my earlier work on integrity, this document also aims to seek out and integrate into a coherent whole various environmental regulatory documents. Nicholas Robinson says, "What is needed is a *real* partnership among each body of law. They must be integrated and linked."[92] In his introduction to the "Principles of Environmental Conservation and Sustainable Development," he adds:

> This summary and survey may be used as a reference for those who, in the future, will draft national legislation or treaties, or "soft law" declarations. Its norms are those to which all people can subscribe. . . . These environmental laws are not therefore, simply a legislative policy choice. To the contrary, they reflect the same sort of fundamental values as do Human Rights."[93]

In giving parity to environmental values with respect to human rights, Robinson reaffirms the position supported by the ethics of integrity. But, it bears repeating, the parity between the two areas is good insofar as it eliminates a useless and unrealistic dichotomy between human and nonhuman life, at least at the level of life, health, and survival. Yet it retains its value only if it does not degenerate into the support for any and all human "rights" (as preferences). The primacy of the ecological component, that is, of general sustainability (S-1) as defined earlier (see pages 175–76), must be understood as underlying the applied, or secondary, sustainability of human interests (S-2). No other document examined comes as close to our position as the *Earth Charter.*

For instance, its "Summary of Principles" starts with "1. The Goal: a Global Partnership." This paragraph refers to "shared ethical principles and practical guidelines" and states that the "objective of international environmental and sustainable development" is to "ensure [sustainability] for present and future generations" (including the "community of life"), by "promoting equitable and sustainable development and by protecting and restoring *the health and integrity of the Earth's Biosphere.*"[94]

This first principle sets the stage for the second and third principles, a "Preamble on the Human Situation" and a "World View." In both, but particularly in the latter, many of the facts that support the principle of integrity are stated, although they are not defended by argument. The critical moment now confronting humanity is taken as a given, and the remedy appears to be a new foundation for ethics and public policy beyond the present reliance on the "Declaration of Human Rights." Principles III and IV are cited here in their entirety:

III. World View
  1. The biosphere is a unity, a unique and indivisible ecosystem, and all of its diverse constituent parts are interdependent.
  2. Humanity is a part of nature and the community of life, and all life depends for survival and well-being on the functioning of natural systems.
  3. Every life form is unique and possesses intrinsic value independent of its worth to humanity. Nature as a whole and the community of life warrant respect.

IV. A Common Concern and Universal Responsibility
  1. The well-being of the community of life and the protection of the environment are a common concern of humanity.
  2. Nature as a whole, the Earth, and all life forms should be respected. All persons have a fundamental responsibility to respect and care for the community of life.
  3. Protect, preserve, and, insofar as possible, restore the health and integrity of ecosystems, ensuring the functioning of essential ecological processes and life-support systems throughout the Earth.
     a) Provide special protection to fragile ecosystems such as are found in deserts, semi-arid lands, mountains, wetlands and certain coastal areas and on small islands.
  4. Conserve biodiversity including the diversity of species, the range of genetic stocks within each species, and the variety of ecosystems.
     a) Provide special protection to endangered species and their habitats.[95]

In contrast with much of mainstream environmental ethics, with their emphasis on enlightened anthropocentrism (see discussion in chapter 4), the principles of the *Earth Charter* are uncompromisingly nonanthropocentric and holistic. Bryan Norton argued that holistic supporters of intrinsic value are characterized by their refusal to engage in "real issues," as they maintain their position from an "ivory tower." The *Earth Charter*, in contrast, presents the only set of principles capable of responding to the critical problems we encounter. Yet it includes radical statements at great variance with the cautious pronouncements of local or national laws, such as the Canadian Environmental Protection Act. For example, it states that every form of life is "unique" and that it has intrinsic value "independent of its worth to humanity"; also, "the biosphere is a unity, a unique and indivisible ecosystem" and "the well-being of the community of life and the protection of the environment are a common concern of humanity." These statements are not tempered by references to human development issues. To be fair, human development concerns are *also* taken up in later principles, but the relation between the two, in cases of conflicts, is not discussed. To speak of a "common concern and universal responsibility" is to exceed by far the spirit and the letter of regulations that usually place environmental concerns *second* to the economic "freedoms" of the marketplace (at least implicitly).

In chapter 1 we saw that reviews of my earlier work considered the principle of integrity to be too radical for general acceptance. The *Earth Charter* in its present form appears to be at least as radical. Although it does not offer philosophical argument in support of its "principles," and it does not debate possible contrasting positions, it states as facts that all nature is "an indivisible ecosystem," that "humanity is a part of nature," and that "all forms of life have intrinsic value." Moreover, not only are the aims of the charter practical actions and public policy, but these are sought and listed as required to move humanity away from a path destructive to all life.

Under "A Common Concern and Universal Responsibility" (VI.3), "the health and integrity of ecosystems ensuring the functioning of essential ecological processes and life-support systems throughout the Earth" are listed and advocated much as they are in the ethics of integrity. In addition, although there is no explicit mention of zoning or of cores or buffers as means to protect and restore integrity, under "Sustainable Development" (VI.3 and 3a) the charter states:

3. Protection of the environment is best achieved by preventing environmental harm rather than by attempting to remedy or compensate for such harms.
3a. Activities which are likely to cause irreversible environmental change or damage should be avoided altogether.

In conjunction with the precautionary principle (VI.5), the principles of the *Earth Charter* are just as biocentric, holistic, and radical as the principle of integrity. The public policy aspect of both is new as well as radical. If points VI.3 and VI.3a are to be enforced globally, then the sort of reduction in our activities advocated on Aristotelian grounds in chapter 7 appears to be unavoidable. It should be our personal and joint responsibility and our moral obligation.

For the first time, I believe, there is an environmental act, the *Earth Charter*, that demands true environmental protection and that clearly attributes intrinsic value to nonhuman nature. In addition, it clearly and repeatedly supports the necessity for ecological integrity ("ecological function," "health and integrity of the Earth," "the function of natural systems") for the survival of humanity, as well as for all life. This is also the main contention supported by the ethics of integrity.

As long as human economic interests are pitted against ecological sustainability, without the recognition that the former are absolutely dependent upon the latter, there is no possibility of moving forward to a saner and safer future. It is equally impossible to support the international and intergenerational equity that all regulatory acts demand, without recognizing the limits and constraints imposed by their demand and by ecological sustainability. The work of Noss[96] appears to have been incorporated (albeit not explicitly), and his conclusions are part of the *Earth Charter*. Although Noss's position emphasizes the public policy requirements of conservation biology goals rather than an ethic of human concern, the *Earth Charter* recognizes the intimate connection between the two. Hence, many of the principles cited in this section could find support in the *Wildlands Project*,[97] as they acknowledge the necessity for habitat protection, respect for natural systems, curtailed human activities, and the intrinsic value of nature beyond human use.

The unimpeded development of individual, specific, and system capabilities, always emphasizing the joint interests of individuals and wholes, humans and nonhumans, is supported in the *Earth Charter*, as it is in the ethics of integrity.

It is disheartening to learn that the Rio + Five meeting of the United Nations in New York in June 1997 not only did not move forward from the point reached by the documents of the 1992 Earth Summit in Rio, but that the support for the principles emphasized in the *Earth Charter* actually lost ground. On the other hand, the lack of popular appeal for environmental principles, universally demonstrated at the meetings of Rio + Five, indicates the failure of popular appeals to moderate anthropocentrism, and the incapacity of the latter to provide a solid basis for ecologically sound policies. The main problem that held back environmentalism as defense of the wild was interhuman conflict, mainly on issues of justice between the Northwest and the Southeast. The urgency of famine and other disasters faced by developing nations took precedence over long-term environmental concerns.

It is more urgent to make food available to starving or malnourished people today than to take steps to ensure food sustainability for their future and their children's. The immediate agonizing problem takes precedence. But if the "solution" offered to the hungry eventually aggravates the very conditions that caused their hunger, then it is not a solution at all. The ethics of integrity and the principles and the vision of the *Earth Charter*, if implemented, would not have permitted (or presently permit) the practices that cause or worsen the environmental problems that are at the root of hunger itself.

In simplified form, the sequence is as follows: industrial practices and affluent northwestern lifestyles introduce anthropogenic stress into various systems at many locations simultaneously. This causes the biotic impoverishment of several systems and the collapse of many. In turn, this results in the loss of "nature's services" that could have been provided by the affected systems. Hence, the loss of integrity is indirectly responsible for floods, loss of soil productivity, UV damage, harm to the ozone layer, and the presence of hazardous food (see chapters 2, 6, and 9). All these contribute significantly to the loss of food productivity globally, as does the "cattle culture"[98] prevalent in the West. In this sense, the insistence on a quick fix for environmentally based problems may well end up being harmful to the very people on whose behalf the fix was initiated. The short-term food supply in that case will not last, or it will not be healthy and nourishing, or both. A vicious circle is present: when there are no strong laws for environmental protection, catastrophes and acute crises occur, demanding priority. When the response to these crises is not governed by the ethics of integrity, the problems are at best only temporarily alleviated, while the root causes maybe further exacerbated.

This is why even problems that are routinely viewed as pertaining only to the human species, such as famine, are entirely dependent on ecological sustainability and an uncompromising position on respect for nature. Whether the *Earth Charter* and its many nonanthropocentric principles are generally viewed as presently desirable by those who are under immediate threats in the Southeast and those who are not prepared to relinquish their unjust overconsumption in the Northwest ought not to deter desperately needed environmental legislation. The latter must be based on the real public good, as that cannot be promoted apart from respect for nature. Both the ethics of integrity and the *Earth Charter* clearly acknowledge and support the mutuality between the two causes, and resist all misguided attempts to separate and dichotomize the two issues, as they ultimately need to be understood as one.

The problems of accepting and implementing this position are grave, and the final short chapter of this work will indicate what might be required to accomplish those feats. In essence, we will need more research and another interdisciplinary study to suggest ways of rendering operational the radical changes at all levels of life that the *Earth Charter* recommends and the ethics of integrity support and defend.

The next chapter returns to the ethics of integrity and the second-order principles listed in chapter 2. I attempt to provide the details specifically required to apply the ethics of integrity.

Notes

1. A. J. McMichael, "The Health of Persons, Populations, and Planets: Epidemiology Comes Full Circle," *Epidemiology and Society* (Oxford, England: Epidemiology Resources, 1995).

2. Gunnar, Skirbekk, ed., *The Notion of Sustainability* (Oslo, Norway: Scandinavian University Press, 1994); see also W. E. Rees, "Defining Sustainable Development," CHS Occasional Paper Series (Vancouver: University of British Columbia Centre for Human Settlements, 1989).

3. L. Westra, *An Environmental Proposal for Ethics: The Principle of Integrity* (Lanham, MD: Rowman & Littlefield, 1994), especially chapter 2.

4. James Karr, personal communication, August 1996.

5. L. Westra and P. Wenz, *The Faces of Environmental Racism: The Global Equity Issues* (Lanham, MD: Rowman & Littlefield, 1995).

6. Theo, Colborn, Dianne, Dumanoski, and John Peterson Myers, *Our Stolen Future* (New York: Dutton, 1996).

7. Colborn, et al., *Our Stolen Future*; see also Valery Forbes and Peter Calow, "Costs of Living with Contaminants: Implications for Assessing Low-Level Exposures," *Belle Newsletter* 4, 3 (March 1996): 1–8.

8. Forbes and Calow, "Costs of Living with Contaminants."

9. R. Ulanowicz, *Ecology, The Ascendent Perspective* (New York: Columbia University Press, in press); see also Colborn, et al., *Our Stolen Future*.

10. Forbes and Calow, "Costs of Living with Contaminants," p. 3.

11. A. J. McMichael, *Science* 267 (February 17, 1995): 957; see also A. J. McMichael, "The Health of Persons, Populations, and Planets: Epidemiology Comes Full Circle"; Jonathan Patz, Paul Epstein, T. H. Burke, and John Balbus, "Global Climate Change and Emerging Infectious Diseases," *Journal of the American Medical Association* 275, 3 (January 17, 1996): 217–23; Rita Colwell, "Global Climate and Infectious Disease: The Cholera Paradigm," President's Lecture, February 10, 1996, American Association for the Advancement of Science, *Science* 274 (December 20, 1996): 2025–31.

12. Robert E. McGinn, "Technology, Demography, and the Anachronism of Traditional Rights," *Journal of Applied Philosophy* 11, 1 (1994): 57–70.

13. Westra and Wenz, *The Faces of Environmental Racism*.

14. L. Westra, "Terrorism, Self-Defense and Whistleblowing," *Journal of Social Philosophy* 20, 3 (Spring 1990): 46–58.

15. Peter Taylor, "Environmental Capacity and the Limits of Predictive Sci-

ence—The Precautionary Principle in Control of Hazardous Substances," *Joint International Symposium on Consequences of Hazardous Waste Disposals* 1 (1991): 32.

16. J. Bodin, *Six Books of a Commonwealth* (London 1606), trans. R. Knolles, ed. Kenneth D. McRea (Cambridge, MA: Harvard University Press, 1962), bk. 1, ch. 8, p. 92. "Nature" and "natural laws" are here understood in the sense of the language of the U.S. Clean Water Act (Public Law 92-500, 92d Congress, S. 2770, October 18, 1972; "Declarations of goals and policy" Sec. 101).

17. Ibid.; see also Charles Beitz, "Political Theory and International Relations," in *Political Theory Today*, ed. R. Held (Stanford, CA: Stanford University Press, 1991).

18. Bodin, *Six Books of a Commonwealth*, p. 98.

19. David Ehrenfeld, *The Arrogance of Humanism* (New York: Oxford University Press, 1978).

20. Beitz, "Political Theory and International Relations," p. 240.

21. Beitz, "Political Theory and International Relations," p. 243.

22. H. Shue, "Priority for Compatriots: What Would It Mean?" in *Basic Rights: Subsistence, Affluence and American Foreign Policy* (Princeton: Princeton University Press, 1982), p. 132; see also H. Sidgwick, *The Elements of Politics*, 4th ed. (London: Macmillan, 1980), p. 309.

23. O. O'Neill, "Transnational Justice," in *Political Theory Today*, ed. R. Held (Stanford, CA: Stanford University Press, 1991), pp. 278–79.

24. O'Neill, "Transnational Justice," p. 294.

25. O'Neill, "Transnational Justice," p. 298.

26. O'Neill, "Transnational Justice," p. 299.

27. S. Funtowicz and Jerome Ravetz, "Science for the Post-Normal Age," in *Perspectives on Ecological Integrity*, ed. L. Westra and J. Lemons (Dordrecht, The Netherlands: Kluwer, 1995), pp. 146–61.

28. K. Shrader-Frechette, *Risk and Rationality* (Berkeley: University of California Press, 1991).

29. K. Shrader-Frechette *Nuclear Power and Public Policy* (Dordrecht, The Netherlands: Kluwer, 1982); see also K. Shrader-Frechette and E. D. McCoy, *Method in Ecology* (New York: Cambridge University Press, 1993).

30. Bryan Norton, "Why I Am Not a Nonanthropocentrist: Callicott and the Failure of Monistic Inherentism," *Environmental Ethics* 17, 4 (Winter 1995): 341–58.

31. D. A. Brown, "The Role of Law in Sustainable Development and Environmental Protection Decision Making," in *Sustainable Development: Science, Ethics and Public Policy* (Dordrecht, The Netherlands: Kluwer, 1995), pp. 64–76.

32. Brown, "The Role of Law in Sustainable Development and Environmental Protection Decision Making," p. 64; see also P. W. Birnie and A. E. Boyle, *International Law and the Environment* (Oxford, England: Clarendon Press, 1992); P. Sands, *Greening International Law* (New York: New Press, 1994).

33. Brown, "The Role of Law in Sustainable Development and Environmental Protection Decision Making."

34. Brown, "The Role of Law in Sustainable Development and Environmental Protection Decision Making"; see also Shrader-Frechette, *Risk and Rationality*; Shrader-Frechette and McCoy, *Method in Ecology*.

35. Canadian Environmental Assessment Act, S.C. 1992, c. C-37, s.2 (1).

36. Brown, "The Role of Law in Sustainable Development and Environmental Protection Decision-Making."

37. *Environmental Assessment Act*, S.O. 1990, C.E-18, s.l.

38. Elizabeth Skakoon, "Reports on the *Ontario Environmental Protection Act* and the *Ontario Environmental Assessment Act*" (1996), research supported by SSHRC grant No. 86000.

39. Westra, *An Environmental Proposal for Ethics*, see chapter 1.

40. K. Shrader-Frechette, "Hard Ecology, Soft Ecology, and Ecosystem Integrity," in *Perspectives on Ecological Integrity*, ed. L. Westra and J. Lemons, pp. 125–45; see also K. Shrader-Frechette, review of *"An Environmental Proposal for Ethics: The Principle of Integrity*, by L. Westra, *Environmental Ethics* 17, 4, (Winter 1995): 433–35.

41. C. Barnes, "The Zalev Brothers Scrapyard," case research with the support of SSHRC grant No. 86000.

42. *The Windsor Star* (Ontario), April 20, 1990.

43. *The Windsor Star*, April 20, 1990.

44. *The Windsor Star*, April 20, 1990.

45. *The Windsor Star*, April 20, 1990.

46. *The Windsor Star*, April 20, 1990.

47. *The Windsor Star*, April 20, 1990; see Roger Cotton and Kelley McKinnon, "An Overview of Environmental Law in Canada," in *Environmental Law and Business in Canada*, ed. Geoffrey Thompson, Moira L. McConnel, Lynne B. Huestis (Aurora, Ont., Canada: Canada Law Books, 1993), pp. 3–30.

48. *R.v. Sault Ste. Marie* (1978), p. 374.

49. *Sault Ste. Marie*, p. 374, emphasis in original.

50. *Sault Ste. Marie*.

51. *Sault Ste. Marie*.

52. *R v. Weil's Food Processing Ltd.* (1987), p. 255.

53. *Weil's Food Processing*, pp. 255, 256–257; see Barnes, "The Zalev Brothers Scrapyard."

54. *R v. Wigglesworth* (1987), p. 402.

55. *The Windsor Star* (Ontario), August 13, 1988; see Barnes, "The Zalev Brothers Scrapyard."

56. *The Windsor Star*, August 13, 1988; see Barnes, "The Zalev Brothers Scrapyard."

57. *The Windsor Star* (Ontario), February 9, 1990.

58. *The Windsor Star*, February 9, 1990.

59. *The Windsor Star* (Ontario), March 27, 1990.

60. Barnes, "The Zalev Brothers Scrapyard."

61. *The Windsor Star*, March 27, 1990.

62. Barnes, "The Zalev Brothers Scrapyard."

63. P. A. French, *Collective and Corporate Responsibility* (New York: Columbia University Press, 1984).

64. Roger Cotton and Kelley McKinnon, *Overview of Environmental Law in Canada*, Sec. V.C. of "Common Law Principles" and Sec. VII.D.; see also "An English Case from the 1860s," *Rylands v. Fletcher*, pp. 13–14, 19–20.

65. L. Westra, "On Risky Business," *Business Ethics Quarterly* 4, 1 (January 1994): 97–110; see also E. Draper, *Risky Business* (Cambridge, England: Cambridge University Press, 1991); Colborn, et al., *Our Stolen Future.*

66. John Swanson, "Dow-Corning and the Breast Silicone Implants," paper presented at the Business Ethics Society Meeting, August 10, 1996, Québec City, Canada.

67. Swanson, "Dow-Corning and the Breast Silicone Implants."

68. Swanson, "Dow-Corning and the Breast Silicone Implants."

69. Swanson, "Dow-Corning and the Breast Silicone Implants."

70. Swanson, "Dow-Corning and the Breast Silicone Implants."

71. W. Evan and E. Freeman, "A Stakeholder Theory of the Modern Corporation: Kantian Capitalism," in *Ethical Theory and Business*, 3d ed., ed. T. Beauchamp and N. Bowie (Englewood Cliffs, NJ: Prentice-Hall, 1988), pp. 97, 101–5; see also Kenneth Goodpaster, "Business Ethics and Stakeholder Analysis," *Business Ethics Quarterly* 1, 1 (January 1991).

72. Goodpaster, "Business Ethics and Stakeholder Analysis."

73. W. E. Rees and M. Wackernagel, *Our Ecological Footprint* (Gabriola Island, BC: New Society, 1996); see also W. E. Rees, "Revisiting Carrying Capacity: Area-Based Indicators of Sustainability," *Population and Environment* 17, 3 (1996): 195–215; W. E. Rees and M. Wackernagel, "Urban Ecological Footprints: Why Cities Cannot Be Sustainable and Why They Are a Key to Sustainability," *Environmental Impact Assessment Review* 16 (1996): 223–48.

74. Thomas Homer-Dixon, "On he Threshold: Environmental Changes as Causes of Acute Conflict," *International Security* 16, 2 (Fall 1991): 76–116.

75. Homer-Dixon, "On the Threshold."

76. Homer-Dixon, "On the Threshold."

77. Westra, *An Environmental Proposal for Ethics.*

78. Homer-Dixon, "On The Threshold."

79. E. Ayres, "The Expanding Shadow Economy," *World Watch* (July/August 1996): 11–23.

80. G. Hardin, "The Tragedy of the Commons," *Science* 162 (1968): 1243–48.

81. E. Partridge, personal communication, 1996.

82. Homer-Dixon, "On The Threshold."

83. Rees and Wackernagel, *Our Ecological Footprint*, p. 9; see also Rees, "Revisiting Carrying Capacity: Area-Based Indicators of Sustainability," and Rees and Wackernagel, "Urban Ecological Footprints."

84. Rees and Wackernagel, *Our Ecological Footprint*, p. 9.

85. Rees and Wackernagel, *Our Ecological Footprint*, pp. 14–15.

86. Rees and Wackernagel, *Our Ecological Footprint*, pp. 14–15.

87. E. Cilinskis, and J. Zaloksnis, "Solid-waste Management in the City of Riga, Latvia: Objectives and Strategy," *Ambio* 25, 2 (1996): 103–7.

88. C. Folke, J. Larsson, and J. Sweitzer, "Renewable Resource Appropriation," in *Getting Down to Earth*, ed. R. Costanza and O. Segura, (Washington, DC: Island Press, 1996).

89. Rees and Wackernagel, *Our Ecological Footprint*, p. 13.

90. Rees and Wackernagel, *Our Ecological Footprint*, p. 13.

91. Reed F. Noss, and A. Y. Cooperrider, *Saving Nature's Legacy* (Washington, DC: Island Press, 1994).

92. Nicholas Robinson, "Evolving Legal Principles for Sustainable Development," in *Earth Charter*, pp. xi–xv.

93. Robinson, "Evolving Legal Principles."

94. Steven C. Rockefeller, *Principles of Environmental Conservation Summary and Survey*, *Earth Charter* (April 1996); *Summary of Principles*, *Earth Charter* (1996).

95. Rockefeller, *Principles of Environmental Conservation Summary and Survey*.

96. Reed F. Noss, "The Wildlands Project: Land Conservation Strategy," *Wild Earth*, Special Issue (1992): 10–25; see also Noss and Cooperrider, *Saving Nature's Legacy*, and Reed F. Noss, "What Should Endangered Ecosystems Mean to the Wildlands Project?" *Wild Earth* 5, 4 (Winter 1995/96): 20–29.

97. Noss, "The Wildlands Project: Land Conservation Strategy."

98. Jeremy Rifkin, "The Cattle Culture" in *People, Penguins and Plastic Trees*, ed. C. Pierce and D. VanDeVeer 2d ed. (Belmont, CA: Wadsworth, 1995), pp. 445–51; from Rifkin, *Beyond Beef* (New York: Penguin, 1992).

From Living with Integrity to Living in Integrity: Second-Order Principles for a Global Ethic

Perhaps it is easier to reconcile environmental ethics with social and political philosophy than to clarify the connection between the former and theories of intrahuman morality. Ancient and Kantian virtue ethics were shown in chapter 7 to be compatible with the ethics of integrity. But the original discussion of integrity[1] advanced a much stronger claim: it argued that the principle of integrity was to provide the ground for an environmental proposal for *ethics*, not just for an environmental ethic. That claim demands more than compatibility with other traditional moral theories: compatibility is necessary, but it is not sufficient to make good on the original claim that the principle of integrity must be understood to support a new ethic.

In order to fulfill that promise, the connection between human individuals and communities and the ecological system that supports them, and the connection between individual biological function and the latter, must be clarified. In chapter 7 we argued that the good must be treated as primary, and it must be understood to refer to the biological integrity of the individual and the species, ours and others', within the integrity of habitats most appropriate to each. Hence the "integrity" of the individual, even the individual human, is not taken to mean moral or character integrity: it is intended as our optimum capacity (c). Thus we acknowledge the intimate and necessary causal connection between c (optimum individual biological capacity), and C (optimum capacity of the whole or ecological integrity) of the habitat any species requires for the fulfillment of that capacity. The principle of integrity is holistic. But integrity itself is understood as encompassing both structure and function: these two aspects can be completely separated only in the abstract.[2]

That argument supported the necessary connection between individuals and wholes. We must respect and protect the earthworm not only for itself (its intrinsic value) but for ourselves and for other species (its instrumental value as decomposer and as part of the biomes of soils). The idea is not to keep reserves or zoos housing worms taken out of their natural habitats in order to protect those individual worms or even the species, in isolation. The goal is to preserve and respect the worm community and its capacities, within its habitat and ours.

To be sure, the relation between the individuals (of most species other than humans) and the whole ecosystem is reciprocal to some extent. For instance, speaking of trees and frogs, Charles Little says:

> The death of forest-associated correlative species strongly suggests extreme ecosystem imbalance. UV-B harms not only trees; now researchers at Oregon State University have found that the frogs living in forest pools and stream sides of the Cascade Mountains are failing to regenerate: The increased UV-Bs have scrambled the cells of the frog roe, which are laid in uncovered shallow water.[3]

This sequence of events uncovers the reciprocity between species and an ecosystem. If the trees are "hit" by acid rain or global warming or UVB, declines and extinction of other species dependent upon them are sure to follow:

> In England mycologists report that twenty species are in decline. In general European researchers believe that the mushroom decline is bound up with the decline of forests from acid rain, excess nitrogen, ozone and related causes.[4]

Ecologist Orie Loucks studied "soil invertebrates in parts of Ohio and Indiana" and noted that, because of "air pollution deposition," they show a "50 percent decline in the density of earthworms."[5]

Scientific research discloses the mutual support prevalent between shared habitats; speaking once again of frogs, Colorado biologist Jeffrey Minton says: "Very clearly, here is a support group for the tree."[6] In this sense, any attack on an individual animal or plant is at the same time an attack on its habitat, and vice versa. Similarly, if the organic integrity of any individual in any of these species were under attack, the system would suffer as well. For example, an attack on the frog's reproductive system would eventually have the same effect as one on the frog's life, as far as both its ecosystem and its species are concerned.

These facts support the argument of the principle of integrity, stating that there is no conflict between holism and respect for individuals at the basic level of life and life support. But the same cannot be said for the relation between individuals and wholes in *one* sense, where our own species is concerned. Frog, tree, and earthworm each have a specific niche and function within the ecosystem, but the human's role is not so clearly determined. The human species has no clear function within a system: it is affected by any serious alteration in the collective functions and processes within the system it inhabits, but their possible alteration or extinction is not equally hazardous to other species or to the evolution of the system as a whole.

In addition, conflicts may remain "between individual humans who are seeking to survive now, with other forms of life (even species) and acting in ways which create long-term damage to support systems."[7] This can be acknowledged for both human and nonhuman species, within the integrity paradigm. Both survival and self-defense are basic to the ethics of integrity, as is argued in my earlier work. Combined with the principle of proportionality (see chapter 10), these two principles should ensure that no conflict remains with the principle of integrity itself. To inflict long-term damage might diminish integrity somewhat, but if the second-order principles proposed here and in chapter 2 are actually *lived* by our species, then the conflict among species will not permanently alter the system's capacities. This ought to follow because our species is the only one capable of inflicting irreversible damage to the capacities of the system, hence to its integrity (C).

For instance, beaver communities also alter their habitats and may cause damage to several species; flora may perish under water as beavers flood the area when they establish their "lodges." But the system's basic capacity to recover and continue with its evolutionary trajectory is not affected as it would be if humans were to pursue activities involving toxic and chemical substances. There is a difference in kind between these two sorts of disturbances, and only the latter are proscribed by the ethics of integrity.

However, humans are currently under attack from the various altered functions of component parts of their habitat, as are the parts themselves and the system as a whole.

This is one point where the part/whole (ecosystem) and the component/organism (individual human) analogy breaks down. The similarity remains clear insofar as anthropogenic habitat alteration and degradation are clearly as harmful to the human being as they are to the nonhuman animal or plant. As miners discovered long ago, a canary is the first to die when miners and canaries are equally exposed to poisonous gases. Nevertheless the canary is not the only one affected; in fact, it is precisely because *both* are, albeit in different measures, that a canary is used at all. The same is true of other life-forms and their habitats: we first become

aware of the grave hazards we face when we note tumors in fish, her-
maphrodite whales, and other affected wildlife in the habitats we share.[8]

In this sense we are just as affected as nonhumans are, although it
takes us much longer to know the consequences of hazards that act
more quickly, perhaps even lethally, on smaller creatures. In contrast,
the reciprocity that is so clearly a part of the interactive processes of
parts and ecosystemic wholes is absent in our case. As William Aiken
remarked to me in June 1997, one might argue that humans have co-
evolved with some species. However, human existence, even in those
cases, is not crucial to the maintenance of "nature's services." The disappearance of any species affects the function and processes of the
whole. Even reproductive harms to individuals in any species disrupt the
whole system: when the structural basis of the ecosystem is affected, all
its functions may be at risk. Yet, even as we must acknowledge that we
lack a role like that of the earthworm or the honeybee, we can still feel
both solidarity and "connaturality"[9] with all other life as we join with
them for the purpose of self-defense.

This chapter first addresses the relation between science and the second-order principles (SOPs). The first three of these principles deal
with methodological and epistemological issues in relation to personal
decision making from the moral point of view as well as in relation to
public policy. The following sections discuss the "sustainability" second-
order principles (4 and 5) and review the argument leading from the
principle of integrity to the ethics of integrity before turning to principles 6, 7, and 8, the "living in integrity" principles. Number 6, "accepting the limitations of strict zoning," represents the essential meaning of
the ethics of integrity. When we conduct ourselves and design and accept public policy as though we were living in a buffer zone—when we
recognize the primacy of respecting core/wild areas for their intrinsic
as well as their instrumental value—we have accepted the basic tenet of
the principle of integrity. This acceptance in principle should ensure
that we are prepared to tailor all our activities and projects in accordance with that tenet.

Principles 7 and 8 elaborate further on the implications of living in
integrity, by exploring the relation between micro- and macrointegrity
(that is, the connection between individuals and wholes) and the relation between environmental causes and possible effects.

The Relation between Science and the Second-Order Principles: Following the Principle of Integrity (Methodological and Epistemological Principles, SOPs 1–3)

The conceptual, theoretical and evaluative problems associated with
developing a precise, quantitative, and explanatory ecological sci-

ence have suggested to some experts that ecology can play virtually no role in grounding environmental policy.[10]

Kristin Shrader-Frechette and Earl McCoy

In the first chapter of their important book *Method in Ecology,* Kristin Shrader-Frechette and Earl McCoy explicitly define "What Ecology Can't Do." To be sure, ecology's case studies can give appropriate scientific answers to limited, localized questions, but "general ecological theory was and is not precise enough to help adjudicate courtroom conflicts over environmental welfare."[11] Further, the authors argue,

> insofar as ecology is required for solving practical enviromental problems, it is more a science of case studies and statistical regularities, than a science of exceptionless general laws.[12]

This wholesale condemnation needs to be clarified. After all, in the limited sense the authors propose—that is, to provide some degree of precision and specificity for particular cases, where ecological imperatives are contrasted with exploitive corporate requirements—ecology *can* do and in fact *does* the job it is required to do, by the authors' own admission. Where is the problem with ecology then? We are told that it is "more a science of case studies and statistical regularities," than "a science of exceptionless general laws," and perhaps this *expectation* is at the root of the difficulty, rather than the science of ecology as such.

From the perspective of complex-systems theory we have adopted, this *expectation* itself is flawed. In chapter 1, I argued that post-normal science involves more than the acceptance of "values" as integral components of environmental policy. It also demands the acceptance of the rest of the post-normal science paradigm, that is, the acceptance of uncertainty and complexity as expected components of most scientific discourse (at least in the life sciences), together with the actual unpredictability that reflects the constant element of surprise present in nature. In that case, perhaps the expectations of both policymakers and lay persons are unrealistic, and the national and international laws that demand an unavailable precision are flawed.

Hence, decisions must be made in the context of surprises and uncertainties, as these are not problems to be ironed out through "better" (more precise or more rigorous) methodology; the indeterminacy that gives rise to these uncertainties must be viewed as the appropriate reflection of what happens and what will happen in actuality. If reality checks show that unpredictability and surprise are the natural way events happen even without deliberate human intervention, we must not continue to design public policy and adjudicate global environmental disputes on the basis of standards of nonexistent precision.

What is wrong with ecology? It could seem that a major component of what is "wrong" is an outdated and insupportable societal and scientific worldview, a gestalt of assumptions and expectations that cannot be realized within a newer scientific paradigm. In order to suggest some helpful guidelines for translating this paradigm into public policy guidelines, I have proposed some second-order principles, following upon the admittedly vague and general principle of integrity. In chapter 2 I proposed six second-order principles and added another two in conclusion. In the light of the arguments of the previous chapters it seems clear that the first six principles were not sufficient, and that is why I proposed an additional two principles. Second-order principle number 7 requires respect for microintegrity, that is, the integrity of individuals within a whole; number 8 demands the introduction and acceptance of the risk thesis (see chapter 3), as well as the potency thesis, demanding a respect not only for future generations but also for future capacities of *individuals*, thus extending the respect for the capacities of wholes (*C*) that is the hallmark of the principle of integrity.

The first three second-order principles are primarily concerned with method and with epistemology, although neither is discussed in an abstract way. In this once again our position is somewhat different from that found in *Method in Ecology*. For instance, in that work, "complexity," an ontological category, is discussed only once, according to the index, in relation to the "complexity-stability" hypothesis that is viewed now as scientifically indefensible. In contrast, "uncertainty," an epistemological category, is discussed repeatedly, and I count nineteen instances of discussion in the index, many covering several pages of text.

Our position gives primacy to actual existent processes, as well as to individuals and wholes; hence, I use either *complexity*, with its clear ontological connotations, or *indeterminacy*, for the same reason. In essence, even when we are concerned with methodology in science and the ensuing knowledge, we give primacy to the existing reality with *its own* characteristics, even if these characteristics should result in a less precise and less defensible scientific understanding of reality than we might have expected in the past. The idea is not to seek total clarity about the functioning of natural systems in order to grasp their "laws" completely. The main point is that we *can* admit that our research will not yield complete, accurate knowledge, no matter how well funded and well done it is. Hence we will have to abandon the "arrogance of humanism"[13] in favor of a position more compatible with our limitations.

Particular cases and issues may yield precision in scientific research, but the integrity approach aims at general, universal principles and theories, and thus it cannot be content with those "successes." It must strive beyond them, even if that entails acknowledging that precision and predictability cannot be found in a chaotic, biotically indeterminate, and complex nature, and that our knowledge must then be correspondingly finite and imprecise. The question will remain, however: How do we design and implement policy and regulations for the public good under these unavoidable conditions?

In an effort to answer this question, I have suggested the six second-order principles proposed in chapter 2. I now return to those principles and add another two in order to flesh out what was left unclear in the earlier discussion. These principles can be divided into three groups: (1) epistemological and methodological principles (SOPs 1–3); (2) principles for sustainability (SOPs 4–5); and "living in integrity" principles (SOPs 6–8). The last set incorporates the two new principles, which as we shall see could also be termed elaborations of SOP 6. To be sure, this grouping is somewhat arbitrary, as all eight SOPs may and *do* contribute to "living in integrity," say, or to sustainability. Nevertheless, this grouping teases out common threads as well as separate emphases and may help to clarify the deep, holistic meaning of living in integrity.

Second-Order Principle 1: Embracing Complexity

SOP 1   In order to protect and defend ecological integrity, we must start by designing policies that embrace complexity.

The first second-order principle proposed in chapter 2 was "We must embrace complexity." This requires a paradigm shift from the assumptions of mainstream science. The present scientific paradigm accepts the presence of *uncertainties*, thus requiring stakeholders' input and the addition of human rights and justice considerations to public policy. Shrader-Frechette and McCoy argue that "ecology is permeated by a misguided and naive positivism and by the belief that science can avoid value judgments."[14] The remedy they suggest, as we saw, is to argue for a "logic of case studies" in order to supplement "the shortcomings of positivistic, hypothetico-deductive science."[15] But neither "procedural rationality" nor "democratic process"[16] is sufficient to render ecology more rigorous, as anticipated by these authors, because they say democratic process is not part of biological science as such.

To be sure, rigor and precision will be available in statistical regularities and specific cases, and this supports the argument of *Method in Ecology* as a whole. In contrast, "embracing complexity" means accepting that "uncertainties are not open to methodological corrections." The acceptance of complexity demands the recognition of *limits*, not only to our activities, but also to our rationality, our investigative ability, and our scientific research. This does not affect specific cases as gravely as it does our overall regulations and policies. Therefore the acknowledged limits of our understanding and our predictive capacities ought to support the drastic alterations required for both public policies and laws, according to the ethics of integrity.

Complexity, when accepted, is the appropriate corrective to the arrogance that prompts us to espouse "ecosystem management" instead of the rigorous management of our own aggressive individualism. If natural systems are too complex to be "managed" with any assurance that we *do* know (or *can* know) precisely how far we can go when our preferences come in conflict with the necessary requirements of nonhuman life and its habitats, this goes well beyond the need to incorporate uncertainties into our otherwise rigorous scientific assessments. Hence, in his discussion of the precautionary principle, Peter Taylor argues, "It would be rational and scientific to argue that the *assumption of the possibility of management* may ultimately prove the greatest environmental risk."[17] Embracing the precautionary principle, like embracing complexity, which I believe is perhaps the major cause of the introduction of the PP, is more than designing a different political move. Taylor adds:

> It has profound philosophical, scientific and cultural implications. It is a major paradigm shift. It moves from an "effects-based" science of the environment, to a "source based" science of production and consumption. It is pro-active, not reactive. It is scientific, but it does not require science to be predictive, nor does it rely on proof of cause and effect."[18]

We can now restate the first of the second-order principles. This "complex" imperative includes the following argument:

1a. It is necessary to reject linear, purely deductive science;
1b. It is also necessary to acknowledge the synergistic and cumulative effects of all our activities; therefore
1c. We must recognize that not all natural systems can and should be managed.

Therefore the principle of "complexity" indicates that many areas of the earth should be left unmanaged and that many areas and landscapes of sizes appropriate to their geographical locations ought to be left unused and unmanaged. The size of these areas must be determined in consultation with conservation biologists, ecologists, and other scientists, and we ought to accept fully that the proposed "managers" (humans) are, at the same time, "within the ecosystem they propose to manage."[19]

As mentioned earlier, current scientific paradigms accept the presence of uncertainty in ecology. But "uncertainty" is an epistemological category, whereas the complexity that gives rise to uncertainty is an *objective* state of natural systems and their processes. This indeterminacy indicates the limits of our capacity to understand, hence the necessity for constraints on our actions. When we "learn all that can be learned" about the functioning of ecosystems, at the same time we recognize what *cannot* be learned. We are then in a better position to draw our own conclusions about our activities, viewed from the standpoint of our cognitive limitations.

Second-Order Principle 2: Accepting the Paradigm Change of Post-Normal Science for Public Policy

> SOP 2   We should not engage in activities that are potentially harmful to natural systems and to life in general. Judgments about potential harms should be based on the approach of post-normal science; see (1a) above in SOP 1.

SOP 2 uses this conclusion to prescribe in a general way that we should not engage in potentially harmful activities. In support of this rather vague norm, it asks us to rely on "post-normal science," narrowly defined as the "inversion of hard facts and soft values."[20] But, as we noted in chapter 1, the post-normal science paradigm is far richer than that. Beyond the increased relevance of values (1), we need to add the switch from Newtonian science to complex-systems theory (2) and to the recognition that the biological/ecological point of view may foster several possible developmental paths, which may result in different ecosystem configurations. S. O. Funtowicz and Jerome Ravetz outline the "elements of a post-normal science," as follows:

1. The appropriate management of uncertainty
2. The appropriate management of quality
3. Plurality of commitments and perspectives
4. Intellectual structures
5. Social structures[21]

A brief discussion of these points is in order. In almost all environmental issues, from climate change effects to the impact of biotic impoverishment and the consequences of adopting agricultural transgenics, we are faced with severe epistemological uncertainties. Funtowicz and Ravetz argue:

> In new fields, particularly those relating to the environment, where the characteristic uncertainties are large, complex, and less well-understood, it is necessary to have explicit guidelines for their management.[22]

But the required "management" should include accepting that

> to wait until the relevant high-precision natural sciences were available before doing anything about global warming or species preservation, would be a counsel of perfection indistinguishable from a counsel of despair.[23]

Hence, mainstream science's requirements for ecological precision must be modified, in line with what is possible and appropriate, without fostering expectations of an unavailable standard. The second point adds that the "quality" of the results of our research can be judged only when it is clearly acknowledged that

> uncertainty in input information produces irreducible uncertainty in conclusions; the relevant question of quality is the degree to which the recommended policy choices are robust against those underlying uncertainties.[24]

What is required is that policymakers "not claim ethical neutrality" and that uncertainties be acknowledged, rather than being hidden by "unsupported hunches and loaded rhetoric." It is also important to use the precautionary principle in a manner appropriate to the issue, because to require *proof* of harmlessness for each substance, process, or activity under consideration "would amount to a uniform ban of almost all human activities." In contrast with the quest for legal standards of proof or for some pure scientific "truth," dialogue will inform the quality of public policy; then "(ethical) principles will be explicit and become part of the dialogue."[25]

The next point is more difficult to reconcile with the ethics of integrity. Funtowicz and Ravetz define quality as "replacing the old ideal of scientific truth" with a dialogue comprising "ethics and morality." This leads to point three, a "plurality of commitments and perspectives." But ethical principles cannot produce a "plurality" without a framework intended to establish priorities among "commitments and perspectives." It is one thing to agree that it is wrong to exclude the public from participating in public policy determinations. It is quite another to judge all stakeholders' input to be equally relevant from the moral point of view. Some stakeholders may have vested interests in a certain outcome, whether or not this outcome leads to the public good. It is morally right to respect a plurality of perspectives or positions, but *not* to give them all equal weight.

If the first principle is the principle of integrity, and if this primacy is justified in the light of universal life protection, then *all* "commitments and perspectives" ought to be ranked according to it. From a logical point of view it is not possible to "respect" equally all perspectives, because every choice we make corresponds to downgrading or eliminating another choice. That is why I have argued that a democracy, even one that attempts to protect citizens' rights, is insufficient to ensure environmentally sound choices, without additional provisions designed to implement the ethics of integrity, whenever those rights come in conflict with majoritarian choices.

The "social structures," "intellectual structures," and "plurality" aspects of post-normal science may come in conflict with the PI. Without expecting "definitive scientific knowledge" or "enforced uniformity of opinions," the ethics of integrity demand certain priorities. Hence commonality with post-normal science is possible only if the inconsistency between pluralities and quality assurance can be resolved. The authors acknowledge that, "in the absence of *ethical commitment of a particular sort*, the whole process of quality assurance would collapse"[26] [emphasis added]. The presence of a smorgasbord of "commitments" and "opinions" will not yield or even permit ethical principles, nor will it ensure "quality."

Second-Order Principle 3: Accepting the Precautionary Principle to Limit Human Activities

> SOP 3   Human activities ought to be limited by the requirements
> of the precautionary principle.

SOP 3 requires the acceptance that the precautionary principle, in conjunction with "an interactive dialogue between science, law and stakeholders," clearly brings out values and principles.[27] Without repeating here the discussion of the precautionary principle in chapter 1, we need to keep in mind that the threat of relativism just alluded to persists. We saw the components of post-normal science according to Funtowicz and Ravetz. I now propose a different but complementary analysis. I believe that post-normal science comprises at least three compatible aspects, only one of which is increasingly viewed as acceptable by the scientific community's mainstream representatives, especially in North America. These aspects are (1) the increased relevance of ethical and social values, thus introducing the need for public discourse and debate; (2) the switch from the expectations of Newtonian scientific paradigms to complex-systems theory, in which post-normal science found its true home; and finally (3) the recognition that the ecological/biological point of view may foster several possible developmental paths, which may result in different configurations for ecosystems.

The problem, I believe, is that while aspect (1) is finding increasing favor, particularly as it appears to move apace with the "political correctness" demands of modern liberal democracy, aspects (2) and (3) are tacitly ignored, or taken to represent a "fringe" view, hardly worth refuting, at least in North American "mainstream science." At worst, this partial acceptance combines science as usual with a smorgasbord of unprioritized "values," all of which are viewed as worthy of consideration, yet without a principled framework within which to assess their importance. This results in a plethora of competing preferences and thus policies based on compromise and on relativism and ultimately on the perpetuation of business as usual.

Although some may argue that compromise among competing political positions, which gives rise to democratic choices, is an acceptable means to legitimate policy, I argue instead that in questions affecting our habitat—hence our survival and that of other life on Earth—this approach is both insufficient and morally incorrect. At best, the acceptance of the legitimacy of stakeholders' values may mitigate local hazards and protect some from gross inequities.[28]

These two possible responses to the acceptance of public debate and value-based discourse in public policy partially parallel two possible applications of the "stakeholders' ideology" in business ethics.[29] Kenneth Goodpaster argues that stakeholders' theory represents a drastic ideological switch in corporate culture. The corporation is no longer viewed as a "top-down" enterprise based only upon shareholders' interests constrained only by laws and professional ethics. According to this new theory, the corporate body is viewed as both responsible and responsive to local communities, employees, suppliers, and the public at large.[30]

Unfortunately, this improved scenario may be seen by the corporation primarily as a "strategic" move, or as a public relations ploy to gain the trust and acceptance that many business enterprises have lost because of their risky practices, and because of several well-publicized disasters (Bhopal, Chernobyl, *Exxon Valdez*). In that case, what happens is simply public manipulation, perhaps with some minor concessions, but no basic acceptance of the primary importance of morality in the interaction with newly recognized stakeholders' groups.

In contrast, if the stakeholders' ideology is applied in the spirit of a true moral commitment, then better results may follow for the protection of the public interest. Many argue, however, that the corporation's composition and definition are radically altered in the process.[31] In that case, it is easy to see why the first alternative is often chosen, with less than favorable outcomes for the public good, even when our good includes the protection of our life-support systems. In either case, although in quite different measures, the emphasis on values is a welcome addition to the earlier "experts only" science.

Nevertheless, returning to the interface between science and public policy, when only one aspect of post-normal science is viewed as meaningful and legitimate, then those who perform such a selective adoption of one aspect of a new paradigm have not grasped the full meaning of post-normal science. The point is not that because of morality or democracy or other nonscientific ideals we must introduce "values" to mediate between expert opinion and public policy decisions. In contrast, the point that flows from the acceptance of post-normal science is that moral values must have primacy because they are an *integral* part of the practice of science itself; in fact, Brian Wynne and Sue Mayer say, "Where the environment is at risk, there is no clear-cut boundary between science and policy."[32] This can be applied in three different senses: (1) with respect to the inherent complexity of the natural world, which science attempts to portray and explain; (2) with respect to the *limits* required in order to manage ourselves while trying to manage ecosystems; and finally (3) although several evolutionary trajectories may be possible for each specific ecosystem at a certain time and geographical location, these possibilities can (and must) be ranked from the standpoint of the primary value of life, and thus of life support.

For this reason, I have argued that it is not appropriate to draw a line between moral/philosophical concepts on one side and "real science" on the other, when we attempt to design ecologically based environmental ethics. This results in relegating concepts like ecological integrity to the status of purely philosophical notions.[33] But this approach is inaccurate, as the concept of ecological integrity is understood and used as a scientific term by many scientists.[34] Neither these scientists nor I[35] intend "integrity" as a purely philosophical or heuristic notion. Further, Aldo Leopold's "land ethic"[36] also treats integrity as an objective state.

Yet to make these claims on behalf of post-normal science and complex-systems theory is not to ignore or to paper over the scientific differences between ecosystem ecology and evolutionary ecology and their adversarial history.[37] In his chapter on "Evolutionary Heresies," Joel Hagen is correct in terming ecosystem ecology "a form of functional biology" and stating that "function was at the very heart of the ecosystem concept."[38] Although Hagen's chapter as well as much of his book appear to emphasize the conflict among different approaches to ecology,[39] that chapter helps to clarify the current hostility between the different schools, and in turn, to emphasize the reasons many environmental philosophers despair of using ecology fruitfully for public policy. Nevertheless, it is also true that the approach I defend is based on the fact that "species play functional roles within the community or ecosystem," as the Odum brothers had it, and that the "integrity of the ecosystem depends upon the activities" of all organisms within it, whose roles and functions appear to be interdependent.[40]

Despite the controversies and the occasional lack of collegiality and scientific cooperation among the different schools of ecology, the collaborative definition of integrity I have proposed and defended[41] demonstrates respect for possible future evolutionary paths of ecosystems (and for their historical past as well) and demonstrates that complex-systems theorists and others who embrace the ecosystem approach may be keen to integrate evolutionary considerations in their theories. Hence, without doubting the historical accuracy of Hagen's work, I find somewhat problematic his statement that "ecosystem ecology, a form of functional biology, became by implication non-evolutionary."[42] It may not be necessary to drive a deep wedge between the two approaches or to discard one in order to adopt the other. In contrast, I have suggested that reductionism and deterministic science must be rejected, as they are totally incompatible with post-normal science, as the latter tends to both represent and explain reality, while also providing a sound reason for the limits of our own understanding. In sum, for appropriate public policy, we need to accept the import of post-normal science and to consider the limits imposed by the precautionary principle.

The Sustainability Principles: Second-Order Principles 4 and 5

Sustainability was defined from the perspective of integrity in chapter 8. The main difficulty present in the abundant literature on the topic is that sustainability is used as a catchall term to refer to a variety of enterprises, activities, and situations, including "sustainable society" as a whole.[43] In some sense this is a useful step, as it is not only this or that practice but the whole of "contemporary industrialized society" that is unsustainable.[44] I have argued, following Karr, Goodland, and others, that "ecological sustainability" is primary and that both social (or societal) sustainability and economic sustainability clearly depend upon it. As Jorgen Randers explains it, "Man's physical activity on earth will temporarily reach high levels before a forced reduction takes place."[45] In fact, "unless something significant is done, physical growth will come to an end through a process of 'overshoot and collapse.' "[46] Hence all discussions of "sustainability" that collapse the several meanings of the term into one are basically flawed, because they do not recognize the basic dependence of all life and life-forms on nature's services. It is useful to cite a recently published list of these services. Gretchen Daily writes that they include:

- Purification of air and water
- Mitigation of floods and droughts
- Detoxification and decomposition of wastes
- Generation and renewal of soil and soil fertility
- Pollination of crops and natural vegetation
- Control of the vast majority of potential agricultural pests
- Dispersal of seeds and translocation of nutrients
- Maintenance of biodiversity, from which humanity has key elements of its agricultural, medicinal, and industrial enterprise
- Protection from the sun's harmful ultraviolet rays
- Partial stabilization of climate
- Moderation of temperature extremes and the force of winds and waves
- Support of diverse human cultures
- Providing of aesthetic beauty and intellectual stimulation for the life of the human spirit.[47]

She adds, "In general human beings lack both the knowledge and the ability to substitute for the functions performed by these and other cycles."[48] Not all of these "services" refer purely to ecological sustainability, and more is said about this in chapter 10.

The two-part definition of sustainability proposed in the previous chapter emphasizes the foundational value of unmanipulated systems (or "intact systems," as Anne Ehrlich termed them) to provide for services for which we cannot substitute. The goal of protecting and restoring ecosystem integrity is precisely the same as the goal of protecting sustainability (as S-1); in turn, the protection and restoration of ecosystem health (I_b, or the restoration and sustainability of specific human activities and enterprises abiding by certain limits) corresponds to the secondary and dependent sense of sustainability (S-2).

It is the dependence of the latter on the former that is emphasized in the two second-order principles that pertain primarily to sustainability (SOPs 4 and 5).

Second-Order Principle 4: Reducing Our Ecological Footprint

SOP 4 We must accept an "ecological worldview," and thus reject our present "expansionist worldview" and reduce our ecological footprint.[49]

Recognizing the value and the extent of the services provided by nature and the complexities inherent in our natural systems means accepting the requirement to moderate consumer choices and our affluent Western lifestyle. In chapter 8 we considered the practical and scientific implications of our present ecological footprint, as argued by William Rees. At this time we need to argue for the moral difficulties arising from our present lifestyle and attitudes.

Respect for all life leads to understanding sustainability as ecological sustainability (S-1) not as the sort of sustainablity that applies to the continued existence of specific resource uses we want to enjoy (S-2, or the derivative aspect of sustainability). From the moral point of view, it is not acceptable to simply follow our preferences wherever they might lead. The ethics of integrity, understood as living according to the SOPs that follow upon the principle of integrity, demand that we consider the implications and the consequences of all our actions, even when the actions themselves appear harmless.

Our present ecological footprint is not only ecologically inappropriate and imprudent from the human point of view; it is also a tool of oppression for too many others now and in the future. When the full consequences of our actions are appreciated, we discover that our ecological footprint extends far beyond the location of our own "habitat" and that we are taking away the present and future life support of those whose habitat is elsewhere. Those individuals may be only vaguely aware of what is taking place, or they may not have any access to the information they need in order to make informed and aware decisions about their lives and their future.

Many of the transactions that transfer resources from a cash-poor area to an affluent one are viewed merely as "trade," and it is assumed that both sellers and purchasers benefit. But in order to classify those exchanges as business transactions involving simple trade-offs, we ought to be sure that the moral and legal conditions governing contracts are in fact present. Contractual rights are correlative with contractual duties and attach to specific individuals, who thereby acquire specific obligations. In general, the rules of contracts are governed by moral constraints:

1. Both parties to a contract must have full knowledge of the nature of the agreement they are entering.
2. Neither party must intentionally misrepresent the facts of the contracted situation to the other party.
3. Neither party must be forced to enter into the contract under duress or coercion.
4. The contract must not bind the parties to an immoral act.[50]

An analysis of these four conditions will show that all rules are violated by most of the business transactions occurring between North and South, as well as by some of the commerce that takes place between more and less affluent populations in developed countries. The first condition of a morally and legally binding contract addresses the question of full information and knowledge of the circumstances of the contract. In order to fulfill this provision and those of Kantian morality, for instance, respect for autonomous individuals requires providing those with whom we enter into a contractual relation with full information about the nature of the transaction. This must include not only the specifics of the products that are being sold (for example, the fact that some chemicals sold to developing countries may have been banned in the seller's country) but also both the known implications of the product's use and the scientific uncertainties involved.

Some have argued that the possible lack of information governing such transactions may render meaningless the "consent" required.[51] Additionally, I suggest that the lack of disclosure guaranteed by the trade secrets act renders the contract both immoral and illegal. The same holds true in a situation where a disposal site is sought. Once again, all the implications regarding the consequences for both the environment and the stakeholder's health must be disclosed, as well as the possible uncertainties about risks. Where neither complete disclosure nor detailed discussion of consequences is available, once again the contract ought to be void.

The second condition for the presence of a valid moral and legal contract renders this point even more explicit. When a corporation or institution does not disclose all information pertaining to a transaction, that is, the import of resource trading and the export of wastes implicit in the present size of our "ecological footprint," then deliberate misrepresentation occurs. At the very least, those initiating the trade are aware of most of the implications of their activities. To hold back any available information amounts to misinforming those with whom a contract is sought.

The third clause requires "no duress or coercion." Many have argued convincingly that the circumstances prevailing, for instance, in a one-industry town or an impoverished nation cannot support free choice, but render all decisions to buy or sell or accept some condition in exchange for money equal to "choices" made under duress. In addition, one could argue that because business has an implicit contract with society,[52] the way a business operation affects *all* stakeholders—not only those with whom business has specific dealings—must be considered from the same standpoint. In that case, a conflict exists between the imposition of hazards without full disclosure and the existence of trade

secrecy regulations or any laws protecting corporate privacy or proprie-
tary information.[53]

Trade secrets are defined in part as

> non-public information . . . that concerns a company's own activities, tech-
> nologies, future plans, policies or records and which, if known by competi-
> tors, would materially affect the company's ability to compete
> commercially.[54]

The existence of trade secrets, it can be argued, precludes in principle
the possibility of a fair contract between society and the corporate institutions that invoke those regulations in order to protect their operations
from scrutiny.

Finally, the fourth rule requires that a contract not "bind the parties
to an immoral act." The vulnerability of stakeholders due to the risk of
physical harms caused by nondisclosure indicates that immoral acts may
well be part of the implicit and explicit contracts that are in force even
now. And if the contract is rendered null and void by the circumstances
of its implementation, those circumstances render the very existence
of a "contract" impossible; this conclusion appears unavoidable if one
accepts Thomas Donaldson's argument that there is (and ought to be)
a "contract" between business and society. In that case then, the present
form of interaction between business and society needs a complete over-
haul and a reexamination from the standpoint of morality. We can conclude that not only is the present affluent northwestern society
unsustainable on practical and scientific grounds, as William Rees
shows, but it is also unacceptable on moral grounds.

Second-Order Principle 5: Rejecting Technical Maximality

SOP 5   It is imperative to eliminate many of our present practices
        and choices, as well as the current emphasis on "technolog-
        ical maximality" and on environmentally hazardous or
        wasteful individual rights.[55]

This "imperative" captures the normative essence of the ethics of integrity. It also represents its most controversial aspect. Those who criti-
cize deep ecology and eco-holism, by claiming that these positions
would return humankind to "shivering in the dark in caves" to bolster
their argument, use precisely this emphasis on the biotic community at
the expense of *some* rights. Paul and Anne Ehrlich indict this reactionary
response to environmentalism in their recent work on the widespread
"brownlash" we are facing. Those who are part of this movement include "wise-use" representatives, in turn, "including . . . extractive and

polluting industries, who are motivated by corporate interests as well as property rights activists and right-wing ideologues."[56]

As we saw in chapter 1, David Korten's work demonstrated the media's intimate connection with the corporate interests that support much of the "independent" groups and their reports. The Ehrlichs argue that many of these groups choose names that sound like genuine environmental or scientific associations: "they adapt a strategy biologists call 'aggressive mimicry.' "[57] These groups' work, however, is in direct conflict with the aims their names imply.

Changes of any kind are perceived as threatening to affluent northwestern societies, particularly when the changes advocated imply restrictions on what we tend to believe strongly are our *rights* to our *choices* and the *preferences* whose implementation we have earned. In that context, changes that appear to move toward a "back-to-nature" lifestyle are viewed as less than desirable. In contrast, the drive to acquire state-of-the-art possessions and to use and support a host of complex technical enterprises is so deeply embedded in our lifestyle as to go unquestioned. What is "technological maximality"? Robert McGinn defines it as follows:

> in speaking of an item of technology or a technology-related phenomenon as exhibiting "technological maximality" (TM), I mean the quality of embodying in one or more of its aspects or dimensions the greatest scale or highest degree previously attained or currently possible, in that aspect or dimension.[58]

According to McGinn, present-day society approaches technology in a way that follows a pattern that "involves the interplay of technology, rights and numbers"; as such, it is foundationally flawed.

> Technological maximality, unfolding under the auspices of traditional rights supposedly held and exercised by a large and increasing number of parties, is apt to dilute or diminish contemporary societal quality of life.[59]

It is not only the size and the wide dissemination of a product or practice that is at issue, but also the "speed of production of a technic or system," the "intensity of use or operation of a technic or system," and many aspects of a "technic" diffusion, the volume of production, and the domain and duration of its use.

From the standpoint of the ethics of integrity, in relation to environmental hazards, both the *speed* with which a technology is produced and the *intensity* of its use are particularly relevant. The speed of production guarantees that the social contract between producers and stakeholders cannot be fulfilled, as was argued in the previous section. All possible

testing cannot be completed on synergistic and cumulative effects arising from the technic, and consensus cannot be sought from all possible
stakeholders. The move from scientific discovery to technological application, and from there to rapid dissemination, all too often serves the
logic of the marketplace, not the logic of morality or safety.

Hence the obstacles to sustainability include more than inappropriate
trading activities leading to circumstances that leave morality out of the
contractual conditions of the transaction. They include unfair and immoral transfers of ecological capacities, as well as the circumstances of
the production and distribution of technologies. Each new and existing
technological activity should be questioned from the standpoint of its
maximality, in two senses additional to the ones addressed so far: the
"traditional Western conception [of] individual rights," including
"property and procreative rights," and the "large and increasing number of parties," mostly human, who engage in maximalist behavior and
who affirm and demand those rights. McGinn's examples include our
supposed "mobility rights" (leading to the nonessential use of all-terrain vehicles in fragile environments) and abuses arising from develop-
ers' "property rights."

There is a clear conflict between striving for the "greatest," the "tall-
est," or the technologically "most complex" innovation and accepting
the primacy of ecological integrity, with its thrust to protect the "work of
nature"[60] for all life. The "tragic hero" mentality advocated by Samuel
Florman[61] supports the untrammeled expression of the "human spirit"
through technological projects, but it is incompatible with the holistic
and biocommunitarian thrust of the ethics of integrity. The human "adventure" cannot forge ahead without first considering the humans (and
nonhumans) who are not respected or fairly treated, because of the size
and weight of the "eco-footprint" that the adventure generates. Further,
that oppressive lifestyle cannot continue to trample underfoot the natural systems on which all life depends.[62]

To question human rights is particularly difficult today, and many
view this sort of problem as a decisive negative factor against ecocentrism. How can we, in the enlightened nineties and close to the turn of
the century, even consider seriously a moral principle that does not respect *all* individual rights? Shrader-Frechette suggests a way to avoid
both an untenable individualism and the "environmental fascism" that,
she argues, Tom Regan and others identify with a holistic approach to
sustainability.[63] She terms her position "hierarchical holism":

> Several of the most prominent characteristics of this hierarchical holism
> are: (1) that it is based on a metaphysical rather than merely a scientific
> notion of the biotic community; (2) that it relies on an anthropocentric

rather than a purely biocentric ethic; and (3) that it includes some second-order ethical principles capable of adjudicating conflicts among human versus non-human interests.[64]

In contrast, the ethics of integrity are compatible only with (3) in this list, as that "characteristic" includes second-order principles intended to perform the same task as our second-order principles in conjunction with the principle of integrity. However, the either/or positions outlined in her (1) and (2) have no place in the integrity paradigm (although her "hierarchical holism" modifies the contrast to some extent). With regard to her first characteristic, she views the biotic community as both scientific and metaphysical, but primarily metaphysical. According to my view, the biotic community, as integrity itself, is viewed primarily in scientific terms, and the philosophical/metaphysical aspects are interdependent with the scientific understanding and follow upon it. Our scientific understanding is moderated by our realistic expectations of the precision we can expect, through second-order principles 1 (embracing complexity), 2 (accepting the post-normal science paradigm), and 3 (adopting the precautionary principle).

Shrader-Frechette's second characteristic contrasts an anthropocentric and biocentric ("integrated") ethic with a purely biocentric one. I have argued that this opposition is no longer present at the life-support level defended by the ethics of integrity. From that perspective, Shrader-Frechette's "second-order principles" alluded to in (3) may prescribe action and policy that are not too different from those dictated by the second-order principles that are the subject of this chapter. Shrader-Frechette's principles also support a strong rights/weak rights framework.[65] Although we also argue with McGinn for the reduction of rights that could be termed weak, in conjunction with the unconditional support of "strong" rights (to life and to individual physical integrity), the reintroduction of anthropocentrism as in Shrader-Frechette's (2) is worrisome and needs further clarification to ensure that one does not simply return to a "weakened anthropocentrism," Norton-style (see the discussion of that problem in chapter 4). The "rights" question is a particularly difficult one. Citing Dworkin, Shrader-Frechette says, "strong rights . . . are essential to human dignity and personhood; they are rights that can never be overridden."[66] But Western democracies, for instance, enshrine rights that must be questioned, from the standpoint of integrity. Two examples come to mind: (1) Native American and Inuit rights to self-determination, including economic advancement; and (2) equal rights to reproductive technologies. For the former, a common occurrence is the emergence of demands for increased hunting and fishing quotas that promote short-term economic advancement, while depleting natural systems in the long term. This apparent conflict, however, is only temporary: any decision supportive of native rights, in these cases, results in the long-term *denial* of the same rights, because of the collapse of the ecological basis of the native enterprises.

Reproductive rights are even more problematic: the "right" to a safe environment may be in direct conflict with the right of all persons to use reproductive technologies. Overpopulation is a direct threat to ecological systems.[67] Yet in northwestern democracies, the trend is toward legitimating fertility treatment for anyone who wants and can afford it, while supporting birth control practices for those in less-developed countries. In some cases, birth control practices are coercive and disrespectful;[68] additionally, the social needs of different cultures are not respected and the real impact of additional births in northwestern countries is not calculated fairly in relation to those in the Southeast. It is common knowledge that affluent countries' citizens consume over forty times the resources of those in developing countries, on a per capita basis.

Therefore it is important that "strong rights" be understood as basic rights *only*; for the ethics of integrity, the right to life and the right to health and physical integrity qualify. If we venture much beyond these, we come too close to weak anthropocentrism and possible conflicts with the principle of integrity and the second-order principles that follow upon it. It is clear that although sustainability is almost a buzzword today and few would speak against it, the conditions under which it might be attained do not have widespread acceptance; on the contrary, most find it hard to abandon their beliefs in the absolute power of the "technological fix," and the misplaced optimism of the "cornucopians," from Julian Simon to Wilfrid Beckerman. This is not the place for that debate, and the interested reader will find those arguments elsewhere.[69]

There is an apparent tension between the ethics of integrity, with its focus on holism, and individual rights. But the conflict is only apparent, at least at the basic, survival level that concerns us: noninterference with natural systems and their life-support functions is primary from our standpoint. For instance, the Index of Biotic Integrity (IBI), designed by James Karr, incorporates the Measure of Function Integrity (MFI) recently proposed by Orie Loucks.[70] That is the key to the solution of the problem. Ecological integrity (C) and individual biological integrity (c) are intimately connected, as we shall see, and it is primarily in terms of the former that the latter is valuable. From that standpoint only the right not to have one's physical integrity breached is a strong right, insofar as that right is closely connected to the ecological integrity that is our primary focus.

Throughout this work and in my earlier one as well, fairness and justice among humans have been emphasized. This emphasis can be supported first because, pragmatically, we must reduce our eco-footprint (see SOP 4), and all reductions automatically free additional sources and sinks (thus survival power) for the developing world and for oppressed minorities in the West. Second, to live "as in a buffer" emphasizes respect for systemic functions as well as for all the components of the systems whose functions are vitally needed by all life. In this sense "fairness and justice" that are (1) applicable to both humans and non-humans and (2) intended to support life, health, and natural capacities give rise to "rights," but only in this limited sense. The rights of individuals such as domesticated animals and pets can be defended, as they have been by many, on *other* grounds. From our point of view, the only requirement is that they remain compatible with the ethics of integrity. That is like saying that any civil, contractual, or legal right must be compatible with the right to life in order to remain meaningful.

Instead, it is time to turn to the true meaning of living in integrity. The last three SOPs (6, 7, and 8) will flesh out the meaning of that proposal and restate the argument that leads from the PI to my conclusion.

Reviewing the Argument: From the Principle of Integrity to the Ethics of Integrity

The argument I have presented for the value of integrity leads to the principle of integrity.[71] But having stated the principle, it is necessary to specify the meaning of the ethics of integrity that follow upon it. To this end, I have suggested so far five second-order principles; three more are proposed in this chapter, and all eight represent what I have termed the ethics of integrity. The first three second-order principles are intended to clarify the methodological and cognitive aspects of the ethics of integrity. SOP 1 requires the acceptance of complexity. Although *complexity* (as indeterminacy) refers to an *objective* state of natural systems, the *recognition* of that objective state demands a changed approach to science and to scientific knowledge. SOPs 2 and 3 serve to make this requirement explicit: the ethics of integrity demand a changed scientific paradigm and the switch to post-normal science, as well as the precautionary principle, to guide both individual and common actions and policy choices.

Because the final aim remains the protection and restoration of integrity (whenever possible), the next two SOPs entail accepting not only changes to our cognitive expectations and paradigms but also restraints on our activities, to ensure sustainability. SOP 4 requires changes to our "ecological footprint," as our present position is not only practically unsustainable on ecological grounds, but also morally unsound, even from the standpoint of accepted business practices. SOP 5 demands additional restraints, as many of the rights we take for granted are ecologically unsustainable and in conflict with justice and fairness.

Before turning to the last three second-order principles, it will be useful to specify the connection between all the SOPs and integrity.

The connection between (1) ecosystem and biological integrity as an ultimate value (based primarily on life and life support) leads to the articulation of the principle of integrity (PI), which (2) demands categorical respect for that ultimate value; and, in order to unpack and apply the principle, the ethics of integrity require (3) second-order principles that guide the application of the PI in practical terms. The argument that puts together these elements should be:

a. Respect for life in general and for individual integrity is primary (even in interhuman ethics).
b. But respect for individual life and persons demands that the necessary conditions for such life be accorded the same respect, because to do otherwise would represent an indirect attack of life, as in (a).
c. Actions that contravene SOPs 1 through 8 for the reasons outlined in the discussion and defense of those principles represent attacks on the integrity of individuals and wholes.
d. Therefore, all actions and policies that are in conflict with the norms set out in SOPs 1 through 8 represent direct or indirect attacks on the integrity of individuals and wholes and are morally wrong.

We can now proceed to present and discuss the last three second-order principles.

Second-Order Principle 6: Accepting the Limitations of Strict Zoning

SOP 6   It is necessary for humanity to learn to live as in a "buffer." Zoning restraints are necessary to impose limits on both the *quality* and the *quantity* of our activities. Two corollary principles follow: (a) we must respect and protect "core"/ wild areas;[72] (b) we must view all our activities as taking place within a "buffer" zone. *This is the essential meaning of the ethics of integrity.*

Both nature's services and biodiversity are absolutely vital to maintain life support and to ensure sustainability. Without self-management to replace the presumption of "ecosystem management" at least for a sizable proportion of landscapes, neither will be available to perform its functions. I have argued elsewhere that zoning is basic to the ethics of integrity.[73]

Thus, we must ascertain, according to the best possible information available from biology, conservation biology, and ecology, what areas we need to leave unmanipulated in order to ensure that the necessary processes may continue. The *kinds* of activities we may pursue will thus be restricted, as well as the *areas* where such activities may take place. The restrictions on "rights" to choose according to our preferences will therefore be equally necessary for the implementation of this essential principle. A recent case study on Costa Rica addresses the "Causes and Consequences of Biodiversity Loss."[74] Daniel Janzen says, "The cause of tropical biodiversity loss, by and large, is the very human behavior of liquidating natural capital to generate cash to finance human desires."[75]

Costa Rica is a good example, as three-quarters of its land "is destined to be agroscape (including urban zones), deliberately managed for quality in the production of conventional goods and services." In contrast, "about one quarter of the country is now conserved (or is to be conserved) for and through wildland biodiversity use."[76]

These are forward-looking policies, compared to most countries: Canada's *Red Book*'s policy (Summary of Liberal Policy) puts the goal of environmental policy at only 12 percent of all land, and makes no reference at all to marine areas. In comparison, 25 percent of all land is a great improvement, and comes a little closer to the recommendations of the *Wildlands Project.* Janzen recognizes that "conserved biodiverse wildlands have enormous potential for sustainable development."[77] From the standpoint of the ethics of integrity, it is *not* the "development" component that is basic, but nature's services, thus the sustainability of all life that such protected areas could engender.

Zoning restraints are meant to ensure life-support services for all living components of natural systems, including humans. The moral reason for these restraints lies in the respect for all life, including life-support systems. The practical reason lies in the deleterious consequences of the loss of individual functions and systems operations for which no substitutes are possible. Individuals and systems alike should be treated with respect, as there is a "continuum" between human and nonhuman life within nature. We can term SOP 6 the essence of sustainability and of the ethics of integrity: without accepting life as in a buffer zone, sustainability and respect for integrity are impossible. Respect for wildness for both its "services" and its component life is basic. Activities that intrude either quantitatively (spatially) or qualitatively (through inappropriate effects, even from afar) must therefore be restrained for both prudential and moral reasons.

Second-Order Principle 7: The Interface of Microintegrity and Macrointegrity, and Second-Order Principle 8: Accepting the Potency Thesis

SOP 7   We must respect the individual integrity of single organisms (of microintegrity) to be consistent in our respect for integrity and also to respect and protect individual functions and their contribution to the systemic whole.

SOP 8   Given the uncertainties embedded in SOPs 1, 2, and 3, the "Risk Thesis"[78] must be accepted for uncertainties referring to the near future. We must also accept the "Potency Thesis" for the protection of individuals and wholes in the long term.

These two principles will be discussed together, because they deal with closely related issues and in fact represent two sides of the same problem.

My work so far has considered ecological integrity, that is, the macro aspect of both structural and functional integrity in ecosystems. Integrity has been symbolized by *C* and defined in a way that centers on the optimum capacity of specific systems to continue their evolutionary paths, according to their time and location.[79] The emphasis on the *whole* rather than on individual components, it has been argued, is needed in order to combat the extreme individualism prevalent in our Western democratic societies. It is also necessary because the habitat is primary: no embryo can live except in the uterus; no life can arise and persist in an unsuitable environment.

But the presence of a holistic emphasis should not blind one to the intimate interconnection between individual and whole. To be sure, individual nonhuman components are necessary to the functioning of the whole structure in various degrees, whereas the humans' role is not as vital, as I argued earlier. Nevertheless, the importance of respecting the integrity in each component part was discussed in some detail in chapter 6, in regard to the genetic manipulation of plants and animals, although the emphasis remained on the consequences affecting the systemic function rather than the transgenic individuals involved.

Aside from this acknowledged difference in the relation between human individuals and their habitat and nonhuman components of the same natural habitat, the similarity is important, and the emphasis on microintegrity is a vital but neglected area of environmental ethics. In humans, as in animals and natural systems, we now often see something quite different from clear, deliberate, and visible harms being perpetrated. Even without the use of guns to kill wild birds or advanced technologies to destroy fish species, the physical integrity of all life may be at stake through subtle attacks. In each case, not only the environment, or the habitat, is imperiled but also the innermost being of each individual and species. The structural integrity of an individual human being is affected when her capacities, her potential, and her present and future development are under attack. To be sure, the same can be said about each single plant, insect, or other animal when anthropogenic stress is introduced into its habitat. But these harms are not all of the sort that can be seen as either present or imminent. The consequences may well happen sometime in the future. They may also curtail future capacities that are now only *potentially* present in the affected individual.

An example of this "harm" perpetrated on a potentiality might be the effect of certain toxic substances on the mental abilities, temperament, and attention span a boy would *normally* acquire as he grows. Another example may be found in the *naturally* evolving reproductive capabilities of a female infant. Both of these children have certain abilities *potentially*, as they are clearly present in their respective DNA.

The philosophical problems in defining this harm transcend the debate about Judith Jarvis Thomson's "Risk Thesis" discussed in chapter 3. The concluding argument in defense of that thesis addressed the problem of the harm's imprecision, in itself, and in circumscribing those who were potentially affected, or harmed, as a result of the "risk" imposed. Responding to these objections, we used the work of Anthony Ellis. The objections could be answered as (1) no matter who they might be, those eventually affected would be harmed, and (2) lack of specificity about a harm does not appear sufficient to warrant imposing unconsented and uncompensated risks on others. We also argued that it is arguable, even when both knowledge and compensation are present, that accepting harms remains immoral, particularly when they attack and diminish what we are as humans (see chapter 3).

The harms normally envisaged are primarily morbidity and fatality. The situation is far less obvious and more insidious when we turn our attention to potential harms (thus when we move beyond the risk thesis). The present thesis could be termed a "potency thesis" instead—a form of argument that has not fared well in philosophical debate, at least in the debate concerning abortion, the area where it is most familiar.[80] Recently, Don Marquis[81] proposed a "new" argument that abortion is almost always "seriously immoral." He bases his argument on the wrongness of killing in general. It is wrong to kill primarily because of the effect on the victim:

> The loss of one's life is one of the greatest losses one can suffer. The loss of one's life deprives one of all the *experiences, activities, projects* and enjoyments that would otherwise have constituted one's future.[82]

This argument accords with our intuitions that the loss of life is a grave injury, and that the younger the person to whom such loss applies, the worse the injury. In cases of disasters, "women and children first" is in line with our intuitive belief that it is far more cruel to snuff out a life that is just beginning, or to envisage the termination of a "future" that has just begun, than to stop a life that is almost played out. In rescuing people from fires or sinking ships, "children first," not "grandfathers first," represents the normal practice, and it appears to be morally right.

A similar argument is used by Thomas Murray in defense of fetal rights in the case of maternal/fetal conflicts.[83] Murray argues convincingly that "the timing of a harm is irrelevant," and that even "viability is irrelevant for nonfatal harms." Murray's argument does not address the abortion question at all, as he divides the unborn into two categories: fetuses "destined to be born" and those "who will not know extrauterine life."[84] I find the grounds for this division incoherent and thus insufficient to support the clear distinction Murray needs. Nevertheless, the rest of his argument is far more defensible. He offers an interesting example:

> Imagine two different cases. In the first, a man assaults a woman with the intention of inflicting grave harm on her fetus. He succeeds, causing permanent, irreparable—but not fatal—damage to the fetus's spinal cord, resulting in paralysis. In the second case, all the circumstances are identical, except that the man attacks an infant rather than a fetus, with the same result—permanent, irreparable paralysis; was the first act any less wrong than the second?
>
> In both cases, lifelong harm was done to humans who, whatever your beliefs about when personhood begins, would eventually cross that line and attain full moral status.[85]

This example leads Murray to conclude that "the timing of a harm is not morally relevant," and that a harm to a "not-yet-born-person . . . is as great a harm as if it were done later."[86] He maintains the same position in the case of viability, despite the fact that viability serves as a threshold in *Roe v. Wade*, when the "potentiality of human life," according to the Supreme Court, becomes closer to actuality.[87]

In addition, the existence of fetal therapies, fetal surgeries, and fetal rights points to the fact that there are good arguments for the protection of the *potential capacities* of individuals and therefore, I have argued, for the criminalization of future harms. These harms will only manifest themselves in the future, through the permanent curtailment of capacities that were only *possible*, or budding, at the time when the attack or injury occurred. In the example Murray presents, a blow affecting the spinal cord will not prevent the fetus from developing and being born, but it will prevent its capacity for self-originating movement in the future, when that capacity should have come to fruition.

The integrity argument and the value of ecological integrity are based on point *C*, or the point of optimum capacities.[88] This is a "potency" or "future" argument, at least in part. The other components of *C* are present, such as the system's ability to withstand stress now and to continue in its own evolutionary path. But the range of evolutionary paths available to the system, and its future capacity to resist anthropogenic stress, can only support "future" or "potency" arguments as much as the arguments cited in abortion or fetal rights issues did. A female infant cannot reproduce when she is in the womb and for a long time afterward. But regardless of whether she will ever choose to do so in the future, if her original capacity for reproduction is eliminated through some chemical exposure, she has suffered a grave harm, and the perpetrators of that harm should be subject to criminal prosecution. Further, the timing of that harm, before or after her birth, ought to be viewed as irrelevant in assessing culpability.[89]

Through these two applications of a "potentiality" or "future" argument against certain harms and attacks on individual integrity, I have argued that the defense of individual integrity (structural and functional, *C*, as I have termed it) exists already in philosophical debates, although these debates have not yet been extended to environmental issues, to my knowledge. In a move that could be based on a similar argument, the Ontario government has moved to criminalize truck safety violations, in the wake of a number of cases in which repeated infractions were dealt with as civil cases through fines and reprimands, without halting the carnage of innocent parties on the highways. One of the latest accidents killed two women in January 1997, as their car was hit by two runaway tires from a large rig with a history of fines and problems. With the support of public opinion, the Ontario Provincial Police now has the power to treat safety failures at the inspection site as criminal acts (similar to driving under the influence of alcohol) and take away an individual's license and right to operate the vehicle, *even if* no one has been harmed.[90] This is a clear instantiation of the risk thesis.

This practical application shows that future-oriented arguments can also be used for environmental issues, in two ways. First, a harm to individual integrity (and capacity) remains such even if it is not immediately visible or provable and even if it will affect the individual or her offspring only in the future. Second, from the standpoint of the perpetrators, the timing of the harm is irrelevant, and therefore it neither diminishes nor eliminates culpability (even if *mens rea*, or the deliberate intent to harm a particular individual, is absent). It could be argued in Murray's case that the attacker had no interest in harming a *specific*

individual. Therefore, even a future harm perpetrated on a *present* individual's potential capacity is as much a culpable act as if it had occurred
when the full extent of the harm would be disclosed and evident. Hence,
I have argued that the risk thesis ought to be accepted, and I have proposed an additional thesis, the potency thesis, to account for environmentally imposed harms with future effects.

It is easier to appreciate the import of the potency thesis when human
individuals are concerned, but the thesis is equally valid when we apply
it to individuals from other species whose (micro) integrity is under
attack. Not only should their individual capacities—hence their own unfolding future—be respected, but we also need to acknowledge the role
their individual function performs within the whole of which they are
a part. In other words, their individual integrity, or microintegrity (as
optimum individual capacity c) is valuable in and of itself; but it is also
valuable for the contribution of each undiminished individual to the
macrointegrity, or optimum capacity of the whole (C), within which it
dwells.

In this sense, and from the holistic perspective, nonhuman individuals
are "more" valuable, or perhaps additionally valuable, when compared
to human individuals, as they have a role and a function we do not
possess. For this reason, I have argued, when intrahuman considerations
are brought to bear on the holistic environmental position supported
by the principle of integrity, the principle of self-defense must be introduced. Further, the risk thesis and the potency thesis must *also* be
brought to bear to extend and enrich the meaning of self-defense, given
the scientific uncertainty and the slow development of the synergistic/
cumulative reality of environmental harms.

A Note on End-Points, Past and Future, in Relation to Ecological Integrity

In chapter 1 several critiques of the PI were challenged, such as the
introduction of moral and social values in line with post-normal science,
but without accepting the other components of the post-normal paradigm. Another critique, routinely brought forth against all deep ecology
and holistic positions, can now be addressed. Objectors argue that it is
incoherent to admit the objective existence of such a state as "integrity"
as an endpoint and goal of public policy, because of the mainstream
science disagreement about the precise sense of the concept.[91] What,
precisely, constitutes the structural inventory of the integrity we want to
restore and protect? What time frame should we consider, for instance,
for North America's natural systems? Should we aim for whatever existed

in pre-Colonial times, and use paleo-ecology to achieve our historical reconstruction?

But many argue that this approach threatens to implement a vision that owes more to Platonic forms than it does to the naturally evolving ecosystems we believe are worthy of respect. In a similar vein, not only is "retrovision" seemingly inappropriate, but even future oriented policy may be flawed, as it would require, paradoxically, an a priori decision about external input to reach our avowed goal of "natural" self-organization in a system.

The argument of the previous section offers an answer to these difficulties, both of which are often repeated as attacks on an ecologically supported holistic position in environmental ethics. According to the PI, what we are seeking to protect or reestablish is not a *specific* structural configuration (at least for areas defined as wild, core, or I_a), but *optimum functional capacity* for that specific location at that specific time. This optimum capacity *includes* the system's evolutionary history to the present, and it fully allows future evolutionary paths (undetermined by us), without any attempt to rank or select one eventual outcome over another.

To some extent this is like supporting the health and intellectual development of a fetus, not in order to "create" a genius or a model or an artist, but simply in order to allow it to eventually have the greatest possible number of options compatible with its own genetic makeup. A parallel case, if we think of an ongoing system, might be the adoption of a seven- or eight-year-old child, who has already had a short formative period in his life, during which certain experiences and a certain amount of learning have contributed to his present shape and capacities, tapped or untapped. The PI would support (and require) a stance mandating support, protection, and enhancement—without, however, any specific training or orientation toward one or another specific use—of the child's capacities.

An interesting parallel case in law can be found in the regulation governing the treatment of civilian concentration camp survivors and other onetime prisoners. Government officials, teachers, and other Dutch nationals were sent to occupy mainly professional posts in the Dutch East Indies (Indonesia). During the Second World War these officials were arrested by (then) Japanese victors and used for hard labor. Their families were divided according to gender and imprisoned in concentration camps.[92]

After the war, the survivors were granted pensions, for the most part, not because of "structural" losses, such as the loss of a limb or an organ, but because their camp experiences limited and "diminished" (official correspondence terminology) their native capacities to thrive and achieve in the world according to their own individual potential, *not* according to some specific configuration in the past or present to which they failed to conform. It is worth noting that these cases were not treated as cases of general "loss" or as deserving compensation for "pain and suffering," both of which would remain largely subjective and heuristic. The Dutch bureaucrats in charge of compensation, through discussion, medical examinations, and visits by psychologists and social workers, based their decision on *objective* conditions, described precisely as "diminished capacities."

To be sure, this is another point where the previous weak analogy between natural systems and individual human organisms breaks down. There comes a time in a fetus's development and in a child's life when respect for her "wild" or undirected and untrammeled capacities is an insufficient mark of care and respect. In contrast, some ecosystems, in sizes to be progressively agreed upon by interactive dialogue between conservation biology, ecology, and other disciplines, *must* be left to develop certain capacities or not, according to their evolutionary trajectories, and *not* according to our preferences, choices, or beliefs. In contrast, choices and beliefs about what is best for us, and perhaps for all life, can govern the treatment of areas of ecosystem health, within the limiting factors imposed categorically by the PI. These systems may be carefully used and manipulated in our interest, but the means used must never be such that they interfere with the free, evolutionary unfolding of the wild. Only in this way can we ensure that the "optimum capacities" of those areas will persist for their sake and our own.

Therefore, the objection that criticizes eco-holism, and especially the PI because of its inability to prescribe specific goals, is irrelevant to the position I defend. Not only is the objection inappropriately seeking a precision and specificity unavailable according to the post-normal scientific paradigm, but it does not address the real goal of the ethics of integrity—the respect and preservation, in certain areas of sufficient size, of undiminished optimum capacity for the natural system under consideration as well as for its component parts. Once again, as Hagen[93] argued, the presence of function ensures that appropriate structure will be maintained.

Conclusion

In this chapter I have pulled together all the strands examined in the previous eight chapters: the connection between human health and integrity; the difficulties in reaching environmentally just decisions even in Western democracies; the need to abandon anthropocentrism and turn to the ethics of integrity when assessing any human activity; the search for an intrahuman ethic compatible with the ethics of integrity; the role of integrity in local, national, and international law; and the role to be played by integrity in the problems confronted thus far, through the presentation and the discussion of the second-order principles that comprise the ethics of integrity.

A recent issue of *The Globe and Mail* (Canada's national newspaper) carried two stories that support the case I attempted to make first for the need for an ethic that *starts* with respect for natural systems and all that lives within them and, second, for an ethic that is global in its conception, implementation, and support. On March 17, 1997, Canadians discovered in their morning paper that the tobacco industry has been contributing millions to Agriculture Canada through the Canadian Tobacco Research Foundation: "The industry finances operations and the government pays researchers."[94] From 1985, "lines containing up to four-percent nicotine content have been selected in the high nicotine gene pool"; this research was carried out at a farm in Delhi in southwestern Ontario even as Health Canada was striving to curb smoking through fines, bans, and withholding permission to allow tobacco companies to support sports events. When confronted, "the chief Agriculture Canada scientist at Delhi says that nicotine levels must be maintained because that is good for business." It appears that even in a democratic country, where public policy is designed to protect citizens, economic interests at the local or national level continue to supersede moral considerations in defense of affected stakeholders. Hence, a *global* regulatory body based on laws supporting the position of the *Earth Charter*, and with it the ethics of integrity, appears to be far more desirable than the mandates and the regulatory limits of national democracies.

The second item from the *Globe and Mail* indicated that history seemed about to repeat itself. Playwright/activist Wole Soyinka warned the West that another ten activists were arrested in Nigeria on March 12, 1997. He argued that, after an "elaborate charade" purporting to be a trial, no doubt these ten will follow the fate of Ken Saro-Wiwa and the other eight murdered activists.[95] Canada, we were told, called for a Commonwealth Oil Embargo against Nigeria, but it is unlikely that Canada's limited influence will make a difference and that its plea will be heard. The multinational community stood by silently while General Sani Abacha deposed and jailed the elected president, Moshood Abiola, in 1994. They stood by without much protest while Ken Saro-Wiwa was murdered and, much earlier, they did not protest but continued business as usual while Ogoni land, rivers, and coasts were devastated and the protesters' health and lives were routinely destroyed by the operations of Royal Dutch Shell Oil. Once again the ethics of integrity would have mandated radical changes in the procedures necessary to permit the introduction of these large and hazardous technologies without information, without consent, and most of all without respect for the flora, fauna, and all life in the habitat the Ogoni shared. In this case, grave ecological and human rights abuses tended to go hand in hand; and the respect for national self-determination did not provide the necessary protection. Only a globally agreed upon adherence to a charter and an ethic that makes life-support systems primary could have prevented the series of horrors that has affected Nigeria for at least three decades. There are other examples. In all cases, end-of-pipe solutions cannot do justice to the complex environmental damage that we see the world over, particularly as this damage may be less obvious and perhaps less immediate in Western democracies—but it is clearly *not* prevented even by due process or by constitutions and laws that uphold human rights.

In sum, philosophers are seldom invited to the table by policymakers. But "integrity" (like sustainability) *is* already present in laws and regulations; it may not be highly visible or clearly understood in all its implications, but it *is* at the table already. And that is why this work was undertaken. I believe that understanding and respecting integrity and ensuring its strong global role are what is needed for real change. A less grim future is possible if we reemphasize and revitalize our commitment to the ecological commons, and learn to deemphasize the consumerist individualism that has contributed to this impasse.

Then we would accept that living with a vague understanding of integrity as something "out there," belonging to parks or areas we may never visit and irrelevant to our future or the future of all life, is wrong and totally insufficient. In contrast, we can learn to live with all others with whom we share our "commons" and our habitat on Earth, as "living in integrity" is, realistically, our only alternative to not living at all.

Notes

1. L. Westra, *An Environmental Proposal for Ethics: The Principle of Integrity* (Lanham, MD: Rowman & Littlefield, 1994).

2. Westra, *An Environmental Proposal for Ethics.*

3. Charles Little, *The Dying of the Trees: The Pandemic in America's Forests* (New York: Viking Press, 1995), p. 228.

4. Little, *The Dying of the Trees*, p. 229.

5. Little, *The Dying of the Trees*; see also D. Pimentel, C. Harvey, P. Resosudarmo, K. Sinclair, et al., "Environmental and Economic Costs of Soil Erosion and Conservation Benefits," *Science* 24 (February 1995): 1117–23.

6. Little, *The Dying of the Trees*, p. 229.

7. William Aiken, personal communication, June 1997.

8. Theo Colborn, Dianne Dumanoski, and John Peterson Myers, *Our Stolen Future* (New York: Dutton, 1996); see also M. Soulé, "Health Implications of Global Warming and the Onslaught of Alien Species," *Wild Earth* (Summer 1995): 56–61; and Westra, *An Environmental Proposal for Ethics.*

9. Klaus Meyer-Abich, 1993. *Revolution for Nature,* trans. M. Armstrong (Cambridge, England: White Horse Press, 1993).

10. K. Shrader-Frechette and E. D. McCoy, *Method in Ecology* (New York: Cambridge University Press, 1993), p. 8.

11. Shrader-Frechette and McCoy, *Method in Ecology,* p. 5.

12. Shrader-Frechette and McCoy, *Method in Ecology,* p. 1.

13. David Ehrenfeld, *The Arrogance of Humanism* (New York: Oxford University Press, 1978).

14. Shrader-Frechette and McCoy, *Method in Ecology,* p. 149; see also chapter 4.

15. Shrader-Frechette and McCoy, *Method in Ecology,* p. 149.

16. Shrader-Frechette and McCoy, *Method in Ecology,* p. 167.

17. Peter Taylor, "Environmental Capacity and the Limits of Predictive Science—The Precautionary Principle in Control of Hazardous Substances," *Joint International Symposium on Consequences of Hazardous Waste Disposals,* vol. 1 (1991): 29–38.

18. Taylor, "Environmental Capacity," p. 33.

19. Ernest Partridge, personal communication, June 1997.

20. S. Funtowicz and Jerome Ravetz, "Science for the Post-Normal Age," in *Perspectives on Ecological Integrity,* ed. L. Westra and J. Lemons (Dordrecht, The Netherlands: Kluwer, 1995), pp. 146–61.

21. Funtowicz and Ravetz, "Science for the Post-Normal Age," pp. 199–206.

22. Funtowicz and Ravetz, "Science for the Post-Normal Age," p. 200.

23. Funtowicz and Ravetz, "Science for the Post-Normal Age."

24. Funtowicz and Ravetz, "Science for the Post-Normal Age," p. 202.

25. Funtowicz and Ravetz, "Science for the Post-Normal Age," p. 204.

26. Funtowicz and Ravetz, "Science for the Post-Normal Age," p. 205; see also J. R. Ravetz, *Scientific Knowledge and Its Social Problems* (Oxford, England: Clarendon Press, 1971).

27. D. A. Brown, "The Role of Law in Sustainable Development and Environmental Protection Decision Making," in *Sustainable Development: Science, Ethics and Public Policy* (Dordrecht, The Netherlands: Kluwer, 1995), pp. 64–76.

28. K. Shrader-Frechette, "Hard Ecology, Soft Ecology, and Ecosystem Integrity," in *Perspectives on Ecological Integrity,* ed. L. Westra and John Lemons, pp. 125–45.

29. Kenneth Goodpaster, "Business Ethics and Stakeholder Analysis," *Business Ethics Quarterly* 1, 1 (January 1991).

30. W. Evan and E. Freeman, "A Stakeholder Theory of the Modern Corporation: Kantian Capitalism," in *Ethical Theory and Business,* 3d ed., ed. T. Beauchamp and N. Bowie (Englewood Cliffs, NJ: Prentice-Hall, 1988), pp. 97, 101–5; see also Goodpaster, "Business Ethics and Stakeholder Analysis."

31. Goodpaster, "Business Ethics and Stakeholder Analysis."

32. Brian Wynne and Sue Mayer, "How Science Fails the Environment," *New Scientist* 5 (June 1993): 33–35.

33. Shrader-Frechette, "Hard Ecology, Soft Ecology, and Ecosystem Integrity."

34. James R. Karr, "Ecological Integrity and Ecological Health Are Not the Same," in *Engineering within Ecological Constraints* (Washington, DC: National Academy Press, 1996); see also James R. Karr and Paul L. Angermeier, "Protecting Biotic Resources: Biological Integrity versus Biological Diversity as Policy Directives," *BioScience* (1994); James Kay, "A Non-Equilibrium Thermodynamic Framework for Discussing Ecosystem Integrity," *Environmental Management* 15, 4 (1992): 483–95; James J. Kay and E. Schneider, "The Challenge of the Ecosystem Approach," *Alternatives* 20, 3 (1994): 1–6, reprinted in *Perspectives on Ecological Integrity*, ed. L. Westra and J. Lemons, pp. 49–59; R. Ulanowicz, *Ecology, The Ascendent Perspective* (New York: Columbia University Press, in press); R. Noss, *Maintaining Ecological Integrity in Representative Reserve Networks*, A World Wildlife Fund Canada/World Wildlife Fund/United States Discussion Paper (January 1995); Reed F. Noss, "The Wildlands Project: Land Conservation Strategy," *Wild Earth*, special issue (1992): 10–25.

35. Westra, *An Environmental Proposal for Ethics*; see also Westra, "Ecosystem Integrity and Sustainability: The Foundational Value of the Wild," in *Perspectives on Ecological Integrity*, ed. L. Westra and J. Lemons.

36. A. Leopold, *A Sand County Almanac and Sketches Here and There* (New York: Oxford University Press, 1949).

37. Joel N. Hagen, *An Entangled Bank: The Origins of Ecosystem Ecology* (New Brunswick, NJ: Rutgers University Press, 1992), especially chapter 8, "Evolutionary Heresies," pp. 146–63.

38. Hagen, *An Entangled Bank*.

39. Frank B. Golley, *A History of the Ecosystem Concept in Ecology* (New Haven: Yale University Press, 1993).

40. Hagen, *An Entangled Bank*, especially chapter 8; see also Leopold, *A Sand County Alamanac*.

41. Westra, *An Environmental Proposal for Ethics*, chapter 1, pp. 1–7.

42. Hagen, *An Entangled Bank*.

43. K. Shrader-Frechette, "Sustainability and Environmental Ethics," in *The Notion of Sustainability*, ed. Gunnar Skirbekk (Oslo, Norway: Scandinavian University Press, 1994), pp. 57–78.

44. Shrader-Frechette, "Sustainability and Environmental Ethics," p. 58.

45. Jorgen Randers, "The Quest for a Just Society, A Global Perspective," in *The Notion of Sustainability*, pp. 17–27, especially p. 12.

46. Randers, "The Quest for a Just Society."

47. Gretchen Daily, ed. introduction to *Nature's Services* (Washington, DC: Island Press, 1997), pp. 3–4.

48. Daily, introduction to *Nature's Services*, p. 5; see also Paul Ehrlich and H. Mooney, "Extinction, Substitution and Ecosystem Services," *Bioscience* 32 (1983): 248–54.

49. W. E. Rees and M. Wackernagel, *Our Ecological Footprint* (Gabriola Island, BC: New Society, 1996).

50. Thomas Garrett, *Business Ethics* (Englewood Cliffs, NJ: Prentice-Hall, 1966), pp. 88–91.

51. K. Shrader-Frechette, *Risk and Rationality* (Berkeley: University of California Press, 1991), see chapter 10.

52. Thomas Donaldson, "Moral Minimums for Multinations," in *Ethical Issues in Business*, ed. T. Donaldson and P. Werhane (Englewood Cliffs, NJ: Prentice-Hall, 1993), pp. 58–75; see also Thomas Donaldson, *The Ethics of International Business* (Oxford, England: Oxford University Press, 1989).

53. Manuel Velasquez, *Business Ethics Concepts and Cases* (Englewood Cliffs, NJ: Prentice-Hall, 1991), p. 380; see also Richard De George, *Business Ethics*, 4th ed. (Englewood Cliffs, NJ: Prentice-Hall, 1995), pp. 292–98.

54. Velasquez, *Business Ethics Concepts and Cases*, p. 380.

55. Robert E. McGinn, "Technology, Demography, and the Anachronism of Traditional Rights," *Journal of Applied Philosophy* 11, 1 (1994): 57–70.

56. Paul Ehrlich and Anne Ehrlich, *Betrayal of Science and Reason* (Washington, DC: Island Press, 1997), p. 15.

57. Ehrlich and Ehrlich, *Betrayal of Science and Reason*, p. 16.

58. McGinn, "Technology, Demography, and the Anachronism of Traditional Rights," p. 58.

59. McGinn, "Technology, Demography, and the Anachronism of Traditional Rights," p. 58.

60. Irene Baskin, *The Work of Nature* (Washington, DC: Island Press, 1997); see also Daily, introduction to *Nature's Services*.

61. Samuel C. Florman, "Technology and the Tragic View," in *Technology and The Future*, 7th ed. (New York: St. Martin's Press, 1997), pp. 93–103.

62. Baskin, *The Work of Nature*; see also Daily, introduction to *Nature's Services*.

63. Shrader-Frechette, "Sustainability and Environmental Ethics," pp. 57–78.

64. Shrader-Frechette, "Sustainability and Environmental Ethics," pp. 57–78.

65. Shrader-Frechette, "Sustainability and Environmental Ethics," p. 69.

66. Shrader-Frechette, "Sustainability and Environmental Ethics." Shrader-Frechette does not simply contrast "anthropocentric" with "biocentric" ethics. She states outright that hierarchical holism is "unavoidably anthropocentric rather than purely biocentric" (p. 69) instead. She also suggests that one second-order principle might be to give priority to strong human rights (such as the right to bodily security) over duties to any other environmental or biocentric goal, and to give priority to environmental or biocentric goals over weak human rights (such as the right to property). Although in this article Shrader-Frechette terms her "hierarchical holism" an *"integrated"* position, "strong rights" or "basic rights" are open to a number of well-defended interpretations, some of which are inappropriate from the point of view of integrity. For instance, Jack Donnelly, in *Universal Human Rights in Theory and Practice*, cites many possible interpretations of these notions, ranging from that of Fouad Ajami (1978) to the International Convention on Civil and Political Rights, nonderogable rights, to the position of Henry Shue (1980) (J. Donnelly, Cornell University Press, 1989, pp. 37–40). Even without failing prey to relativism, many of these formulations support such basic concepts as "liberty," for instance; but I have argued at some length why in today's societies, "liberty" may not be always viewed as a nonderogable right from the standpoint of the ethics of integrity.

67. Ehrlich and Ehrlich, *Betrayal of Science and Reason*, pp. 65–89.

68. Robert Goodland, "South Africa: Environmental Sustainability Needs Empowerment of Women," in *The Faces of Environmental Racism: The Global Equity Issues*, ed. L. Westra and P. Wenz (Lanham, MD: Rowman & Littlefield, 1995); see also Westra and Wenz, *The Faces of Environmental Racism*, pp. 207–26.

69. Ernest Partridge, "Holes in the Cornucopia," in *The Business of Consumption—Environmental Ethics and the Global Economy*, ed. L. Westra and P. Werhane (Lanham, MD: Rowman & Littlefield, in press).

70. Orie Loucks, "Forest Wildland Integrity in the Eastern U.S.A.: Measuring Paradise Lost," presented at the Global Integrity Meeting, Corona, Italy (June 23, 1997).

71. Westra, *An Environmental Proposal for Ethics*, chapter 3.

72. Noss, "The Wildlands Project: Land Conservation Strategy"; see also Reed F. Noss and A. Y. Cooperrider, *Saving Nature's Legacy* (Washington, DC: Island Press, 1994).

73. Westra, *An Environmental Proposal for Ethics*, chapter 6.

74. Daniel Janzen, "Causes and Consequences of Biodiversity Loss: Capital Liquidation of Natural Biodiversity Resource Development in Costa Rica," in *Biodiversity and Human Health*, ed. F. Grifo and J. Rosenthal (Washington, DC: Island Press, 1997), pp. 302–11.

75. Janzen, "Causes and Consequences of Biodiversity Loss," p. 302.

76. Janzen, "Causes and Consequences of Biodiversity Loss," p. 304.

77. Janzen, "Causes and Consequences of Biodiversity Loss," p. 304.

78. J. J. Thomson, *The Realm of Rights* (Cambridge, MA: Harvard University Press, 1990).

79. Westra, *An Environmental Proposal for Ethics*, chapter 2.

80. J. J. Thomson, "A Defense of Abortion," in *Biomedical Ethics*, 4th ed., ed. T. Mappes and D. DeGrazia (New York: McGraw-Hill, 1996), pp. 445–51; see also Mary Anne Warren, "On the Moral and Legal Status of Abortion," in *Biomedical Ethics*, ed. T. Mappes and D. DeGrazia, pp. 434–40.

81. Don Marquis, "Why Abortion is Immoral," in *Biomedical Ethics*, ed. T. Mappes and D. DeGrazia, pp. 441–44.

82. Marquis, "Why Abortion is Immoral," p. 441.

83. Thomas Murray, "Moral Obligations to the Not-Yet Born: The Fetus as a Patient," in *Biomedical Ethics*, ed. T. Mappes and D. DeGrazia, pp. 464–72.

84. Murray, Moral Obligations to the Not-Yet Born," p. 465.

85. Murray, Moral Obligations to the Not-Yet Born," p. 466.

86. Murray, Moral Obligations to the Not-Yet Born," p. 466.

87. Murray, Moral Obligations to the Not-Yet Born," p. 467.

88. Westra, *An Environmental Proposal for Ethics*, chapter 2.

89. Murray, Moral Obligations to the Not-Yet Born."

90. *The Globe and Mail* (Toronto) (January 3, 1997), p. A3.

91. Hagen, *An Entangled Bank*; see also Shrader-Frechette, "Hard Ecology, Soft Ecology, and Ecosystem Integrity."

92. Dick van Engelenbur, *Jongeskamp Baros 6*, Tjimahi 1994–45 (Amersfoort, The Netherlands: Kwiek BV, 1989).

93. Hagen, *An Entangled Bank*.

94. *The Globe and Mail* (Toronto) (March 1997).

95. *The Globe and Mail* (March 1997).

10

A Design for a Global Ethic

Design is the first signal of human intention.[1]

It is both frightening and exhilarating: the multiple threats and crises that confront us and the gloomy worldwide situation we have detailed through the previous chapters all appear to suggest insurmountable problems. When individual survival and species survival are at stake, as well as the survival of all life on the planet, we need to change our present "design" for living, move beyond the guilty role we have played so far, and awaken a kernel of hope and even excitement for the opportunity that lies before us.

Although our past and even our present activities have been essentially an attack on life, we can still redesign our living, so that our legacy to the world is not the elimination of all future generations. William McDonough is right: our intentions are declared and embodied in our design. He offers an example of a misguided design:

> Today we need to reexamine the way we use GNP and GDP as records of our prosperity, because they only record our activity, not our legacy. Prince William Sound, for example, showed up as a prosperous place after the Exxon Valdez disaster. The region was doing extremely well economically because there were so many people trying to clean up. Is this how we measure prosperity? Where is this design leading us? We should not be just measuring our activity, we should be measuring our legacy. We should be developing ways to measure prosperity according to the efficacy of our legacy, and we should redesign with this in mind.[2]

But it is not only the respect for our "legacy" that urgently requires that we redesign our activities; it is also respect for individuals within our species and beyond. Respect for nature as a whole as a prima facie principle cannot be separated from respect for all its component parts and processes, present and future. The principle of integrity refers at the same time to macro- and microintegrity: in order to respect a whole, its parts and their functions must be respected as well, at least insofar as these functions may affect the present and future processes within the whole. In this sense, the microintegrity of the members of the human species must be respected for the species as a whole to survive and flourish.[3]

The new "design" I have proposed in this work demands respect for the whole and for the future in a way that is different from the approach used by other environmental ethics theories, and far more demanding. Respect for the microintegrity of individuals goes beyond respect for present and future persons; it is, like respect for integrity itself (in its systemic sense), respect for the potential, that is, the untapped capacities of both individuals and whole systems. There is a wide gap between outlawing, or proscribing morally, all visible, demonstrable harms to present individuals (as is done now) and the elimination of risks and harms, as proposed by the ethics of integrity. For the latter, we must start from the notion of a "nature" of humankind, comprising the basic capacities that one may expect to find in such a being, normally (or for the most part, excluding defects, deviations from the norm, or the effects of disease).

This is a controversial position. "Deviations" and "variations" are here intended simply as descriptive of certain states of affairs, without any attempt to rank these abilities or their lack from a moral point of view. Nevertheless, we must be prepared to describe some of these states of affairs as deviations from normality, thus implying the existence of a broad standard of the "normal," rather than calling all variations "normally different" or simply representing equally normal states. For instance, this approach may apply to reproductive capacities.

The problem is that in our enlightened "civilization," we believe in the ideal of equality, and we strive to accommodate and respect differences. But if any and all differences are deemed "normal," then we lose the ground for both moral and legal redress, in the case of imposed changes. For instance, if we claim that all infertile persons are "normal but different," we cannot also claim that those who have lost their capacity to reproduce have lost a normal function they possessed and now require compensation for that loss. The same argument could apply to those who, because of exposure to toxins and chemicals, might have lost the full use of their immune system, or those whose intelligence, disposition, or gender-related characteristics have been altered through low-dose exposure to those chemicals. When so affected, people no longer exhibit the normal capacities and functions of their species and gender. Moreover, even if the alteration that may occur is viewed by some as a positive change,[4] the fact that there is no open information or discussion about the change, but that it is imposed without consent, renders it unacceptable in principle. In addition, the changes to which we are exposed are often irreversible for the individual affected and for their progeny.

The reality of these changes and mutations that our political system cannot control—even in democratic countries, as we have seen in chapters 3 and 8—clearly indicates the need for a radically new design, one I have termed "living in integrity." Our present designs are implemented by our present institutions, and they are intended to affect at best one area of life at a time with limited concern for the consequences that ensue as they may affect life or human health. For instance, transnational fisheries debates take into consideration fish stocks, sport fishing associations, and most of all the fishing industry in the countries affected. The effects of climate change, pollution, large and small amounts of chemicals in oceans, and the industrial complex that produces all of these are all routinely ignored, as complex reality is reduced to component parts that are viewed as more manageable. Of course, management based on simple reductions is most often an ecological disaster.

Design, intent, and approach are therefore flawed and need to be revised: solutions cannot be found if the Earth is fragmented in our science and our policies. For a parallel problem, we can consider Larry Harris's work, *The Fragmented Forest*. He explains why simply establishing "wild" areas over the globe as nature reserves (mostly forests) is not sufficient to to provide necessary ecosystem services, ultimately it is not even sufficient to preserve the very forests it is designed to protect. Kenton Miller points out the reasons for this failure:

> Existing reserves have been selected according to a number of criteria including the desire to protect nature, scenery and watersheds to promote cultural values and recreational opportunities. The actual requirements of individual species, populations and communities have seldom been known, nor has the available information always been employed in site selection and planning for nature's reserves.[5]

This is the wrong approach, because (1) the concept of a reserve is viewed as intrinsically inimical to human welfare, which often leads those outside the reserve to "forage" for their needs, particularly in existing developing countries; (2) "most existing protected areas are small and are at considerable distance from one another"; (3) most such areas are surrounded by encroaching human projects that are seldom compatible with the aims and the needs of the wild areas.[6]

Several steps are required immediately to rectify the impotence of present-day designs in this field and others (related to environment and health, primarily) to accomplish their goals. As McDonough puts it, "If you recognize the tragic consequences of bad design and mindlessly continue to do what you are doing, then you are negligent."[7] The argument of this work as a whole has been a two-pronged one: the negligence of which McDonough speaks is, I maintain, both moral and legal. It is no longer sufficient (although it remains necessary) to preach from the pulpit and to decry academically today's moral failures. We are witnessing a grievous attack on all life, and a particularly brutal one directed at the disempowered, minorities, and the destitute worldwide.

It is not enough to agree that they whoever they are (greedy corporations, corrupt governments, consumerist Westerners) are merely "bad." Despite the difficulties of criminalizing these offenses (see chapter 8), we can no longer tolerate the harms perpetrated, and laws must be designed to enforce zero tolerance. If piecemeal designs will not serve to sustain life and respect micro- and macrointegrity through appropriate policies, then a radically new design and direction is needed. Our new laws and regulations must be aggressively holistic, so as to include protection for both biotic and abiotic components of natural systems. The strong individualism that prevails now, and the distaste for government regulations that reigns in North America, must be subject to ethical evaluation, as some individual rights are not protected at all, whereas others are accorded more protection that is defensible from the moral point of view.

Ethicists are already part of the decision-making team for life-and-death problems in hospitals. The environmental problems discussed in this work are also life-and-death problems, and they affect all life. One could also argue that the presence of modern liberalism, exalting and defending all "freedoms" to do and to be, uncritically, without moral evaluation of all choices, is a pervasive symptom of a malady endemic to democratic nations: the lack of a conception of the "good" (see chapter 7). The usual references to the public interest most often intend consumer preferences, not a philosophically defensible ideal.

A shift is urgently required, and I believe it is still possible: it requires a move from the emphasis on rights (as any and all choices) to obligations, as Onora O'Neill has recently proposed.[8] Our first obligation might be to come up with an appropriate, intelligent design, one that looks at the whole rather than simply at competing parts. Although this sounds easy, the change of mind-set and the implementation of such a shift represent monumental tasks. Our survival and that of all life depends on whether we are equal to that task.

The moral requirement for such a shift has been traced in this work, as our aim is to define a global ethic. The move from an environmental ethic to an intrahuman ethic requires emphasis on the close ties between human life and environmental respect as a starting point. This approach is implicit in biocentric holism, but it needed to be rendered explicit throughout this work.

In chapter 2, the links between integrity and present human health and between integrity and the future were defended. In chapter 3, the ability of existing national institutions to deal with human rights violations was questioned. If we (and life in general) are exposed to grave risks of harm in the present and the future—risks that are beyond the control of present democratic institutions—then we must support mechanisms that might be better suited to that task. Chapter 4 argued that our affluent lifestyle (in the Northwest) is inimical to the goals of integrity, as provisionally sketched in chapter 2. Chapters 5 and 6 provided case studies as specific examples of this conflict between developed and technologically advanced lifestyles and the necessity to respect and restore "nature's services." Chapter 7 argued for virtue ethics in support of the ethics of integrity, primarily through the work of Plato, Aristotle, and Kant. With chapter 8, we moved from moral imperatives to public policy. Through a detailed analysis of some of today's laws and regulations, we found that only the new *Earth Charter* could be supported by the ethics of integrity and offered some hope for improvement in our environmental crisis.

Finally, the ethics of integrity was the topic of chapter 9, where personal morality and public policy were shown to be jointly fostered by the eight second-order principles proposed to represent the required global ethic. What remains to be done is to acknowledge the failures of present democratic states and their institutions to either curtail the spread of environmental problems or prevent new disasters from coming to pass.

The question then remains: if the nations of the Northwest have failed for the reasons discussed, despite the sustained presence of democratic institutions, then what? What controls could erect a barrier to hazards, assaults, and human rights violations through environmental means? Even if the ethics of integrity were accepted, the problems of implementation and enforcement would require at least another lengthy volume, one that might best be written by political scientists or a team of philosophers of law and political scientists.

The problem of implementation is surely the most difficult one. How are we to reconcile the cosmopolitanism implicit in a global ethic with individual commitments to ethnic, group, or national ideals? Fortunately, although global ethics are often viewed as a fairly new development in philosophical discourse, arguments in support of such ethics can be found from Stoic antiquity (and even earlier) to Kant himself, although ecological life-support systems are never named as the reason or focus for such ethics. For instance, the conflict between "citizen" and

cosmopolitan human being is well discussed (although not resolved) by
the Stoic Cicero, in *De Officiis*.[9]

Eric Brown terms Cicero's position one of "limited cosmopolitanism"
in contrast to the early Stoics' strict cosmopolitanism.[10] "Limited Cosmopolitanism" may be closer to our present need: we tend to believe
that we owe our children, families, and maybe fellow citizens more than
other distant citizens of the cosmos. But the reality of our kinship to the
whole human race—and from our point of view to the whole community
of life—demands cosmopolitanism understood as kinship to all living
things.

Neither the Stoics nor Kant were concerned with ecology; their concern was with peaceful social coexistence and universal morality in
human interaction. Kant's words, however, are somewhat prophetic, as
his conditions for peace include the "cosmopolitan law of world citizenship." In *Perpetual Peace*, he says:

> Since the narrower or wider community of the peoples of the earth has
> developed so far that a violation of rights in one place is felt throughout the
> world, the idea of a law of world citizenship is no high-flown or exaggerated
> notion. It is a supplement to the unwritten code of the civil and interna-
> tional law, indispensable for the maintenance of the public human rights
> and hence also of perpetual peace.[11]

The "public human rights" could refer equally to the right to respect
for individual life and integrity, as we argued in chapters 3 and 7. It is
evident from the environmental standpoint that a "violation of rights in
one place is felt throughout the world," and much of this work has
argued this point and supported the argument with scientific research.
It is worth emphasizing: for Kant, the realization of a world community
in which respect for the infinite value of life and for the natural mental
and physical capacities of human beings could be termed "both a practical idea and a moral task for human beings" (as Cheryl Hughes argues,
speaking of peace)[12] can also be viewed as a moral imperative.

Kant's *Perpetual Peace* also refers to "three phases of public law,
namely, civil law, the law of nations, and the law of world citizenship."[13]
It seems clear that he views the latter as the culmination of all other
phases. In the "Second Supplement," "Secret Article for Perpetual
Peace," Kant also adds some reasons that help connect "world citizenship" with the universal morality he intends to support. The introduction of philosophers in the implementation and perhaps even the
formulations of these laws may be one reason Kant believes that universality and rational morality may be found beyond nationally bound laws.
He appears to view philosophers as both beyond corruption ("by nature") and peculiarly apt to give moral advice to rulers. Kant says:

But kings or king like peoples which rule themselves under laws of equality should not suffer the class of philosophers to disappear or to be silent, but should let them speak openly. This is indispensable to the business of government.[14]

The work of philosophers is viewed as the only possible antidote to that of politicians, who lack moral theories and do not even possess "the practical science they boost of." In contrast, these politicians' practices only support their "private advantage," to which they willingly "sacrifice the nation, and possibly, the whole world."[15] Without holding Kant's optimistic view of philosophers in general, this work has been advancing a plea for the inclusion of philosophers in public policy decisions.

There is yet another aspect of Kant's political philosophy that is suggestive in relation to the ethics of integrity. Kant's "Idea for a Universal History from a Cosmopolitan Point of View," advances nine "theses,"[16] most of which argue for a teleological unfolding of human capacities through history and for the need for a universal, cosmopolitan "constitution." Kant's goal is to see mankind develop and implement an institutionalized system of international laws, as the result of the constantly improving state of morality and rationality for our species. In the language of integrity, this might suggest yet another C, as the unimpeded development of species capacities, evolving through time in ways we could not now anticipate or specify.

This goal is not environmental, so it might best be reserved for a future project on social/political applications of integrity. In this sense, these "species capacities" must be related to environmental conditions before they might fit well within the ethics of integrity. But, even as they stand in Kant, this is another "capacity" or "potency" argument. It provides another strong reason in support of the natural unfolding of these "capacities," and against any interference with their unfolding.

Finally, we need to turn briefly to another grave difficulty, one as serious as the implementation problem I have alluded to. Another particularly thorny problem is the unresolved tension present in the ethics of integrity between the emphasis on the basic right to reproductive capacities of "normal" individuals and the equally basic obligation to maintain core reserves in all landscapes and to modify human activity to render it compatible with life in a buffer zone. I have postponed a discussion of population issues, because I wanted to ensure that all the various aspects of the ethics of integrity were clearly set out, before attempting an answer.

The only possible and coherent answer, it seems to me, must run parallel to the answer proposed in my earlier work (*The Principle of Integrity*), in regard to predation.[17] I have argued that only if our personal/species survival is at stake may we take measures based on "self-defense" (and "self-preservation") rather than the ethics of integrity. This means not only that killing a carrot or a fish or—if it were the only nourishment available—even a bird or mammal to survive is permissible from the moral point of view but also that killing viruses or bacteria is permissible, on the same grounds. Overpopulation worldwide may threaten some of the requirements of the second-order principles outlined and discussed in the previous chapter. The answer is that we may support our own survival, in a way proportional to our needs, not necessarily our preferences.[18] The arguments against overconsumption are relevant there as well. Changing to a diet that is primarily vegetarian is an important first step, as it would eliminate the need for grazing lands and the inefficient use of grain protein, as we saw in chapter 2. Limitations on property and mobility rights would be another way to save land for appropriate agriculture to support growing populations, as would the elimination of all hazardous industries. Multiple-use, ecologically sound designs may need to be found to accommodate the basic needs of all humans, not just the preferences of the affluent few.

I can only hint at the form such new "designs" and solutions might take, and I emphasize that advocating birth control practices, compatible with respect for life *and* for individual choices, does not conflict with the relevant second-order principles dealing with individual (micro-) integrity. It is one thing for me to say that I will attempt to limit my family to one or two children, or even elect to have none, and quite another to acquiesce to the industrial practices that take that ability and that choice away from me without my knowledge or consent. It is also one thing to be informed and aware of my obligation to do my share in limiting population growth and quite another to insist on my "rights" to activities that will conflict with that moral commitment and resort eventually to practices contrary to respect for life.

Despite the acknowledged exponential population growth and its effects,[19] the practice of the ethics of integrity will promote fairness and justice globally. Our approach demands that those who live in affluent northwestern countries "step back" in their consumption habits (hence in their number as well) so that others in developing countries may increase theirs. The practical steps this might require, as well as the difficult details about the whole population question, need a far more detailed account than I can provide here. The proposed ethics of integrity represent only a first step, an effort to begin a dialogue with philosophers and scientists. The dialogue must be open in many different directions, if living in integrity is to become more than a philosophical wish and if we are to turn that vision into a more promising, saner, and more just reality.

Notes

1. William A. McDonough, "A Boat for Thoreau" in *The Business of Consumption: Environmental Ethics and the Global Economy,* ed. L. Westra and P. Werhane (Lanham, MD: Rowman & Littlefield, in press).

2. For a discussion of Aristotle on the relation between individuals and wholes, see L. Westra, *An Environmental Proposal for Ethics: The Principle of Integrity* (Lanham, MD: Rowman & Littlefield, 1994), especially chapter 4. In that work, as well as in the present volume, the expression "whole" is intended to include species and communities, biotic and abiotic components of an ecosystem. The term "whole" is used here and in reference to all future generations in a somewhat different sense.

3. I am indebted to James Sterba for a discussion of this point. He explained that some may view a feminization of males leading to "more nurturing behavior," for instance, as a positive development. However, the fact that the activities leading to these alterations are not part of an openly discussed and agreed public policy makes the imposition of such changes morally and legally wrong. It is one thing to desire and openly implement, for instance, a less aggressive behavior for males through social constraints; it is quite another to ensure this through hormonal/endocrinal alterations, without disclosure or debate.

4. Kenton Miller, foreword to *Restoring the Fragmented Forest,* by Larry R. Harris (Chicago: University of Chicago Press, 1984), p. xii.

5. Miller, foreword to *Restoring the Fragmented Forest. p. xiii.*

6. McDonough, *"A Boat for Thoreau."*

7. Onora O'Neill, *"Environmental Values, Anthropocentrism, Speciesism,"* *Environmental Values* 6, 2 (1997): 127–42.

8. Cicero, *De Officiis.*

9. Cicero, *De Officiis.*

10. Immanuel Kant, *Perpetual Peace,* ed. Lewis White Beck (Indianapolis: Bobbs-Merrill, 1957), p. 23.

11. Cheryl Hughes, "Human Rights, State Sovereignty, and World Community," paper presented at the North American Society for Social Philosophy, Queen's University, Kingston, Ont., Canada, July 19, 1997.

12. Kant, *Perpetual Peace,* p. 29.

13. Kant, *Perpetual Peace,* p. 34.

14. Kant, *Perpetual Peace,* Appendix I, "On the Opposition between Morality and Politics with Respect to Perpetual Peace," p. 39.

15. Immanuel Kant, "Idea for a Universal History from a Cosmopolitan Point of View," in *On History,* ed. Lewis White Beck (Indianapolis: Bobbs-Merrill, 1963), pp. 11–26.

16. Westra, *An Environmental Proposal for Ethics,* especially chapter 6.

17. James Sterba has recently argued that a "principle of proportionality" as well as a "principle of "self-preservation" could be used to modify the principle of integrity. I acknowledge that argument here, although mine is somewhat different. Thomas Aquinas had both a principle of "self-defense" and a "principle

of proportionality," used to modify "natural law," and I learned from those arguments.

19. Paul Ehrlich and Anne Ehrlich, *The Population Explosion* (New York: Simon and Schuster, 1990); see also R. Orenstein and Paul Ehrlich, *New World, New Mind* (New York: Doubleday, 1989), especially chapters 7 and 10.

Index

About the Author

Laura Westra received the Ph.D. in philosophy from the University of Toronto. Currently she is associate professor of philosophy at the University of Windsor. She is a founding member of the International Society for Environmental Ethics (ISEE) and, at present, is ISEE secretary. Westra is author of two books, *An Environmental Proposal for Ethics: The Principle of Integrity* (Rowman and Littlefield, 1994) and *Freedom in Plotinus* (Mellon, 1990) and coeditor of *Ethical and Scientific Perspectives on Integrity* (Kluwer, 1995), *Roots of Ecology in Ancient Greek Thought* (University Press of North Texas, 1996), *Faces of Environmental Racism: Confronting Issues of Global Justice* (Rowman and Littlefield, 1995), *The Greeks and the Environment* (Rowman and Littlefield, 1997), and *Technology and Values* (Rowman and Littlefield, 1997). She also has published numerous journal articles and chapters in books, most on environmental ethics and ancient, Hellenistic, and Medieval philosophy.